Memories of Tyne Tees Television

Geoff Phillips

 Geoff Phillips 1998

Published by G P Electronic Services
87 Willowtree Avenue, Durham City, DH1 1DZ.
First published 1998

ISBN 0 9522480 6 9

Front cover design by Geoff Phillips and Bill Lyon-Shaw.
Main text, interior design, typesetting,
and graphics by Geoff Phillips.
Sketches by David Petrie and Christine Phillips.

Printed by: Blamire Printers, Ferryhill, Co Durham

Front Cover photographs, left to right:

Tom Coyne, Mike Neville, Adrian Cairns,
Valerie Dennis, James Lloyd
George Romaine, Jack Haig, Larry Mason,
Shirley Wilson
Sally Morton, George Taylor, Bill Steel,
David Hamilton, Chris Langford.

Back cover photographs:
Sir Jimmy Savile on his 1960 TTT show 'Young at Heart'

An outside broadcast with Sally Morton. George Adams
is on camera

Acknowledgments:

I would like to thank the following people for their contributions and help towards this book:
June Barry, Alfred Black, Ms E M Brannigan, Margaret Brown, Herbie Butchert, Adrian and Laura Cairns, Doug and Marj
Collender, Tom and Patricia Coyne, Alan Davison, John Davison, Maxwell Deas, Heather Ging, Chris and Richard Guinea,
David Hamilton, Bob Herrick, Norma Hope, Philip Jones OBE, Rosa Kennedy, Tony Kysh, Jim Lloyd, Bill, Anne and Wand
Lyon-Shaw, Des Martin, Larry Mason, Bill Maynard, David McBeth, Ken McKenzie, Anna Moore, Malcolm Morris, Sally
Morton, Mike Neville MBE, Larry Parker, John Peart, David Petrie, Christine Phillips, Bernard Preston, John Reay, George
Romaine, Tony Sandford, Sir Jimmy Savile, Sylvia Scarll, Ben Stanger, Bill Steel, Ken Stephinson, Jane Summers, Gavin
Taylor, George Taylor, Howard Thompson, Frank Wappat, Christine Williams, Claire Westwater, Shirley Wilson,
Andrea Wonfor.
Photographers: N Davison, Bob Herrick, John Learwood, Tom Oxley, Ian Westwater, Geoff Phillips
In particular, I would like to thank Tyne Tees' ex-Head of Cameras Ian Westwater who has acted as my mentor throughout th
preparation of this book. I met Ian just by chance when I contacted the Macmillan Nurses Fund to purchase some audio tape
of a local musician which Ian had produced to raise funds. (Ian raised over £12,000 for the Fund.)
I would like to thank Tyne Tees Television for giving permission to write this book and allowing me to visit the studios to
search through the company's archives and interview the staff.
A special thank you goes to my wife June for checking the text and correcting my spelling and grammar.

Foreword by Mr Alfred Black - one of the founders of Tyne Tees Television

At five o'clock on 15 January 1959 when the red light signalled 'ON AIR', the North East of England had its own commerci
television station... TYNE TEES TELEVISION. From the outset, the station was a success due in no small measure to th
unwavering loyalty of the viewers who then had what they referred to as 'our own station'. The success was due in a larg
measure to the experience, expertise and enthusiasm of the staff who had been recruited during the previous twelve months.
would be invidious to pick out any one person who contributed to the success of the station ..they were all TTTV and the Head
of all the departments did everything they could to ensure the smooth running of the programmes. To the uninitiated, a TV stati
is rather like a giant jig-saw puzzle with pieces everywhere, but when the 'ON AIR' button is pressed, all the departments fall in
line and the puzzle and the programme are completed. It should be remembered that when the station started there were no tape
programmes, every programme went out live; no Take 2 in those days. If there were any mistakes, they were there on the scree
for everyone to see, but these were few and far between.

My brother George and I had a very happy five years at Tyne Tees and made many friends, in fact the studio was like one bi
happy family and functioned as such, which helped towards the success of the Station. I wish you well with your book and a
sure that it is a worthy contribution towards the understanding of Tyne Tees Television.

Yours Alfred Black

P.S. On a personal note, my late brother George and I were the third generation of the Black family in showbusiness in the North
East. Our grandfather George Black opened the first cinema in the North-East in Sunderland. It was located at the end of th
bridge over the River Wear. Our father George Black the Second (of London Palladium fame) with his two brothers Alfred an
Edward, successfully ran a chain of cinemas in and around Sunderland and Newcastle, so for George and me, having been bor
in Roker, it was like coming home, and it was a pleasure returning to where we started.

Introduction

I was born in Byker, Newcastle upon Tyne at 516 Shields Road. My father worked as a costing clerk at C A Parsons just across the road from our house. He had a part-time evening job as leader of a small dance-band and played Hawaiian guitar. With the income from the band I suppose we must have had a little more money than other people in our street as we were the first to own a television set. Unless you had a Rediffusion TV which received its signal by cable, the only television station you could receive in the North-East in the mid 1950's was BBC. I remember that the programmes were not all that entertaining for young lads, however, one high spot of the week was Saturday teatime and 'The Lone Ranger'. Every Saturday there would be about six or seven kids from our street packed into our living room to watch the 'cowboy'. I was ordered to bed at 8 o'clock so I didn't see many other programmes. I remember 'What's My Line' was quite good fun and there was the odd variety programme but I'd rather go to bed than watch 'The Brains Trust' or 'Animal, Vegetable, Mineral?' Our TV set was a Vidor with a 12 inch screen. Its case was highly polished wood and just below the screen was a drop-down hinged panel which revealed the controls. As well as volume and brightness, there were the 'horizontal hold' and 'vertical hold' controls. You needed these because once in a while, for no particular reason, the picture would start to roll up or down. There wasn't a channel change control; it would have been a waste of time anyway.

A few years later we moved to Forest Hall, a suburb of Newcastle and my dad decided to buy a new telly. Well, it wasn't new but it had a new kind of switch on it which was quite hard to turn and it clicked loudly as you rotated it. It was the channel change switch. I remember the evening my dad brought the TV home. My mam was as excited as I was. I think my dad was playing in the band that evening as it was only mam and I who watched 'Wagon Train'. We thought it was great. And then there were the adverts which were as entertaining as the programmes. We watched right through till closedown; we even watched the Epilogue. This was a new era in television: programmes we wanted to watch, not programmes they wanted us to watch. Every weekday morning in the schoolyard the conversation was always about what had been on TTT the night before. When I got home from school, the TV was switched on ready for the 'Three Rivers Fantasy' music followed by the jingle where the anchor changed to TTT. More often than not it was Adrian Cairns' face which appeared, to welcome you to the station and then there were programmes like 'The Adventures of Robin Hood', 'Abbott and Costello Show', 'Sir Lancelot', and on a Friday, 'The Mickey Mouse Club'.

We subscribed to The Viewer which was TTT's very own programme listings magazine. Even as a young lad I could see that this was a much better printing quality paper than the Radio Times or the Evening Chronicle. The photographs were clearer and the paper was better quality. I kept scrap books of the programme schedules and photographs of the stars (I still have them). It was my scrap books which gave me the idea to write a book about the early years of Tyne Tees Television.

I contacted Tyne Tees Public Relations Office at City Road and told them about my idea. They said a book had been produced in the late 1970's which was called 'Tyne Tees Television: The First 20 Years', however, it was a corporate book by the Company for the Company and since then no one had considered producing another. They looked at the draft pages I had produced and said,
'We shall have to consult the Group Directors at Yorkshire Television on this one.' A few weeks later I was told I could go ahead with the book and work in the public relations office from time to time and carry out whatever research was needed. Working at City Road was a memorable experience for me. In the original buildings at City Road is a maze of corridors and staircases where the uninitiated can soon lose their way. On the first two visits I was shown the way from the staff entrance to the Public Relations Office but after that I had to face the challenge of the Tyne Tees labyrinth. Up two flights of stairs, keep right (or is it left) past the CAR dept. (I never found out what that stood for), through the door with the square window (in true TV Play School tradition) and 'Voila' you are in the Public Relations Office. It's part of a Public Relations Officer's job to watch television while they are working, consequently there are TV sets everywhere, all tuned to Tyne Tees of course. The sound volumes are kept fairly low until an interesting item prompts a jab at the remote control. A small crowd gathered around our set one Monday afternoon when Tyne Tees' ex-Chief Announcer Bill Steel appeared in 'Coronation Street'. Lunch in Tyne Tees' canteen offered an opportunity to spot the occasional personality. One day, Sports Presenter Ian Payne was seen dining with some of the production staff and on another occasion Luke Casey was spotted. One Thursday lunchtime, Nick Owen was seen on the next table to ours. He was dining with Production staff before rehearsals for the 'Football Show' began.

In the Public Relations Office, they have every copy of 'The Viewer' going back to when transmission started on Thursday 15 January, 1959. 498 editions in total; (the TV Times took over in 1968). These have been an invaluable source of facts and figures about the programmes, the personalities, and even the way of life in the late 50's, early 60's. I have enclosed many sample pages from the early 'Viewers' as I consider them to be a fascinating record of the time. Even the advertisements may trigger memories.

Contacting the original Tyne Tees personalities proved to be a challenging task. Some people had moved away from the North-East to pursue their careers. Many were retired which made it even more difficult to track them down. Sadly, some of the early stars like Jack Haig had passed away. Once I did make contact, I was greeted with tremendous enthusiasm for my project, and a sincere affection for Tyne Tees Television. 'It was like one big happy family,' said one staff member. Meeting the personalities and production staff of the early years of the station was the most enjoyable part of the project. I hope that reading this book gives you as much pleasure as I gained by compiling it and I hope it brings back, MEMORIES OF TYNE TEES TELEVISION.

The Early Years

Commercial television (or independent television as it was known) was first introduced into the UK in the London region in 1955. The North-East of England had to wait until 1957 before there was even hope of a commercial station of its own. In November 1957 the ITA had narrowed down the number of applicants for the new franchise, to three plus ABC. It was the more local group headed by Sir Richard Pease and Claude Darling that found most favour with the ITA, and on 12 December 1957, a formal offer of contract for the new franchise was made. Early in the next year, the news broke that a new commercial television station would be set up which may have the name 'North-East Television'. (The name: 'Three Rivers Television' was also proposed.)

A board of directors was set up under the chairmanship of Sir Richard Pease who was a local industrialist and JP. Claude Darling, a senior partner in a North-East firm of solicitors became Vice-Chairman. Two Sunderland born brothers, George and Alfred Black, who were sons of the famous impresario George Black, joined the Board of Directors of the new station. George Black senior owned many cinemas in the North-East one being the Black's Regal in Byker. Sydney Box a film producer, and E G Fairburn a North-East industrialist, also joined the Board. There was substantial

press backing for the station by the Daily News who nominat Lord Layton and Peter Cadbury for the Board. Bill Lyo Shaw, a former Senior Producer for BBC Light Entertainme was appointed Controller of Programmes. Mr Lyon-Sha assisted in the creation of ITV in 1955 and became Executi Producer at ATV. Some time later he was 'head-hunted' by t Bernstein Brothers to join Granada Television. He opted join Tyne Tees, however, as he had assisted the Black Brothe in the application for the North-East ITV franchise. Anthor Jelly, who was Sales Director of Scottish Television, w appointed Managing Director. The company opened its fir Newcastle office at Bradburn House in Northumberland Stre and on 3 January 1958 the Directors of the company held Board meeting there. 300,000 ordinary shares were issued four shillings each and £300,000 of loan stock was raise Investment in the company proved to be a profitable ventu with shares increasing 28 times in the first few years of tradin

On 2 May 1958 the date of commencement of transmissio was declared to be 15 January 1959. The original plan was start transmissions in time for Christmas 1958, but buildi work in the studios could not be completed in time. Soon aft the date of transmission was announced, the advertising ra card was issued by the company's Sales Director, Peter Pai

Left to right are Anthony Jelly - Managing Director, Alfred and George Black - joint Programme Directors arriving a Television Centre, City Road, Newcastle upon Tyne on 26 Nov 1958 for the first board meeting to be held there.

om the company's London office at No1 Great Cumberland
ace. A top rate (8pm to 10:15pm) Sunday minute was to
st £240 and a 15 second lunchtime spot would be £25. Local
vertisers could buy a five second 'flash' advertisement for
.

October 1958, it was announced that the old name of 'North-
st Television' was to be dropped in favour of
yne Tees Television'.

TYNE TEES

TELEVISION
CHANNEL 8

Don't be late for Channel 8

eorge and Alfred Black took on the roles of joint Programme
rectors and promised that many of the programmes would
ature talent from the region. The Whitley Seaside Chronicle
oted the Black Brothers as saying, 'There is a wealth of
lent in this area and we shall find that talent.' They were
ed to the razzmatazz of the entertainment world and did an
cellent promotion job for the new company. Tony Martell
as engaged as the station's 'talent scout' and auditioned
ousands of performers for Tyne Tees 'At the Golden Disc'
lent show. Dennis Ringrowe scored a 'hat trick' when he
came Head of Music and conducted the orchestra on the
ening night of Tyne Tees. He had been in charge of the
chestra on the opening nights of ITV in London in 1955 and
Birmingham a year later. Dennis had started his musical
reer in 1947 as a singer in the George Mitchell Choir.

alter Williamson was appointed Northern Sales Manager
Tyne Tees. He was an impressive looking man with a
ndlebar moustache and had served in the RAF during the
cond World War. He had worked at ATV before joining
TT. Maxwell Deas joined the company as Public Relations
fficer. He later became Head of Religious Broadcasting and
as a well respected and much-liked member of the staff
City Road. 'Lew' Lewenhak, who was a journalist,
aded the team of Producers and was responsible for
ogrammes such as 'North-East Roundabout' and
potlight'. He used to wear a cloth cap and a 'muffler'
d it was alleged that he was a member of the
ommunist Party. Lew's friend Leslie Barrett joined
yne Tees as Features Editor and was with the station
r many years. Raymond Joss, son of a Glasgow
resbyterian Minister, had worked for eight years in
e Foreign Office before he joined ATV in 1955 as a
ansmission Controller. He was appointed Head of
resentation at TTT and his staff included the four
nouncers, Adrian Cairns, Tom Coyne, Sally Morton

and James Lloyd. Later, Raymond became Head of Outside
Broadcasts. Dennis Packham became Chief Engineer and John
Gibson was appointed Head of Sound. Head of Lighting was
Charlie Scott and George Adams was appointed Head of
Cameras. John Dinsdale was appointed Head of Design. He
had been the stage designer at the Library Theatre Manchester
before joining ATV where he designed many of the programme
sets including 'Emergency Ward 10' a popular 'soap' in the
late 50's early 60's. John was responsible for the design of
most of the sets for Tyne Tees programmes.

Terry Wynn joined Tyne Tees as News Editor. He had been in
newspapers all his working life and had written for papers
such as the Blyth News and the Shields Evening News. Brian
Harrison was recruited as Sports Editor. Brian had worked
as a news journalist in the North-East and before joining TTT
had specialised in sports reporting. George Taylor, a respected
reporter for the News Chronicle, became the station's Sports
Presenter. Gordon F Laing, who was an experienced Fleet
Street journalist became the Editor of Tyne Tees' programme
listings magazine called 'The Viewer'. The company's Press
Officer was Alan Brown.

**ports Presenter George Taylor (left) goes through
e script with Brian Harrison (Sports Editor) before
e very first transmission of 'Sports Desk' on TTT.**

The Publicity Campaign

Tyne Tees Television was aware of the great importance of market research. Surveys were carried out to estimate the number of possible viewers in the reception area. With the assistance of a firm of advertising consultants - Erwin, Wasey, Ruthrauff, and Ryan, Tyne Tees Television planned a publicity campaign of a magnitude that had never been carried out by any other television company in the UK.

A series of stunning publicity posters were designed which appeared on advertising hoardings throughout the region. Similar advertising banners appeared in over twenty newspapers in the North-East area having a combined readership of over two and a half million. Viewers were urged not to leave it too late before having their sets converted to receive ITV, and the sales phrase, 'Don't be late for Channel 8' soon became a familiar slogan to North-Easterners.

Television dealers were contacted and advised of the technical details of the new station and kept up to date with developments. The dealers were supplied with advertising material which was often personalised with the dealer's name. A team of ten marketing representatives were despatched to visit the dealers to ensure they were receiving the information and point-of-sale literature they needed.

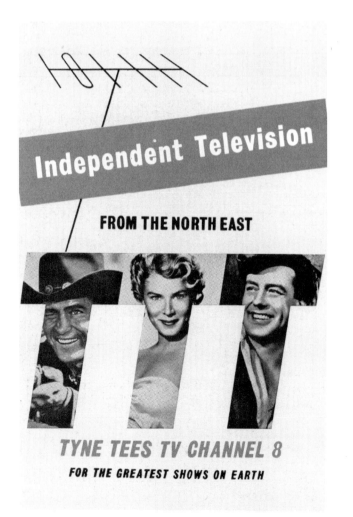

At a press conference addressed by Mr Peter Cadbury and Mr George Black, two of the new company's directors, Mr Cadbury said that 80 per cent of the North-East's programmes would be networked from existing ITV companies such as Associated Rediffusion, ABC, and Associated Television. The remaining 20 per cent would originate from within the North-East area, and it was hoped that some programmes from TTT would be networked outward to other companies.

Mr Cadbury, a one-time test pilot and a barrister who gave up the law in 1954 to become chairman and managing director of Keith Prowse, said the company would pay particular attention to originating new programmes for young people and children. Two well-known authors keen to write for children's TV were Eric Ambler and Emlyn Williams. Other local items announced by Mr Cadbury and Mr Black were a teenage programme about careers, another in which 'the angry young men' of the North-East could question those in authority, a lunchtime variety show, and a North-Country serial in dialect.

Many 'interest' programmes would have the guidance of Professor E. J. R. Eaglesham, Professor of Education at Durham University. Professor Eaglesham, who was voted onto Tyne Tees Board of Directors, had put forward ideas for a 'University of the Air'. (Did this idea lead to the Open University as we know it today?)

A booklet was produced for TTT which described how the company had promoted the station and the lead-up to the first day's transmission. It had an unusual avant-garde design of front cover which did not have any wording, but a sketch of the studios surrounded by an artistic representation of houses in the North-East. The booklet was published on the opening day, Thursday 15 January, 1959.

The Independent Television Authority started low power transmissions from the Burnhope transmitter to coincide with the start of the Press campaign. Full power transmissions were scheduled to begin on December 15th, 1958, however, during the autumn, Tyne Tees asked the ITA for permission to run full power transmissions continuously from 9 am until 1pm on all days except Sundays. Throughout each daily test transmission, at 15 minute intervals, the test card was replaced by an 11 minute live transmission giving details of forthcoming programmes and again exhorting the public to get ready for opening night. The transmissions featured the voices of the staff announcers and the recorded station signature tune 'The Three Rivers Fantasy'.

In 11 of the most important towns - Darlington, Durham, Middlesbrough, Newcastle, North Shields, South Shields, Stockton, Sunderland, Wallsend, Hartlepool and Whitley Bay, Tyne Tees carried out intensive advertising campaigns with literature, travelling displays, and their outside broadcast van the first to belong to the North-East. The displays, six feet in height, were established strategically in all the principal stores in each town. They consisted of three panels bearing pictures and information and incorporating a TV screen linked directly with the OB van. People were able to view live transmissions of other people walking about the streets of their own town, a feature which caused intense interest.

Promotional displays were used in shop windows which sometimes incorporated a concealed Vidicon TV camera linked to the TV receiver. Passers-by looking at the display would suddenly see themselves on the actual screen! This innovation resulted in the display being one of the most effective eye-catchers in the whole campaign.

The Studios

The site for the studios was to be on City Road, Newcastle upon Tyne. Two disused furniture warehouses separated by a wooden shed were purchased by the company and converted to television studios and offices. The architect in charge of the project was Edward Lawson and the contractors were Cussins. The site for the studios was partly chosen because of its close proximity to the telephone switching centre in Carliol Square. Television signals had to be relayed by land-line from the studios to the switching centre. If the length of the land-line had been greater than one mile, it would have added enormous costs to the day to day running of the station because many of the programmes were networked from other ITV stations throughout the country.

The photograph above shows the Central Control Room at Television Centre. The man on the right is the Transmission Controller and to his left is his assistant. On the left is part of the engineering section which monitored the picture quality. The photographs below show the warehouses before and during conversion.

8

e picture opposite shows the part
the old warehouse which was to
studio 1. The whole building was
ipped down to the basic shell
fore the structure was redesigned
ecifically to serve television's
mands. Offices, a modern, up-to-
te canteen, switchboards, porter's
lge and, most important of all,
idios and control rooms were
nstructed. A large, high bay
rved the scenery builders and
rage needs.

idio One boasted a floor space of
300 square feet. It had three
arconi mk. III camera channels
ing 4 1/2" I.O. Tubes, Vinten
nes and dollies **. The vision
ntrollers there could mix, cut, and
per three cameras to five other
irces. Studio Two had a floor
ea of 2,600 square feet.

sound facilities, the studios had 36 microphone inlets, a
und control console which handled 12 microphones and 4
gh level sources, film, disc and tape. There was an echo
idio fold-back and audience public address system. Lighting
nsisted of floods, spots, etc., on telescopic hoists.

ie Central Control Room (CCR) was equipped with the latest
iparatus, and provided station synchronisation and driving
ilses to the studios, controlled pictures and sound, enabled
eview and monitoring, and controlled the Presentation Suite.
ie Suite used what was the latest in broadcast quality Vidicon
meras manufactured by Peto Scott.

Presentation mixing facilities to combine announcements, news
and commercials with any other picture sources, came from
the CCR which also controlled the presentation camera. The
engineering control desk in the CCR enabled the quality and
levels of the outgoing transmission to be checked and
controlled, before being fed to the network.

There was a fully equipped telecine studio with four EMI
Vidicon chains for showing 16 mm and 35 mm films. There
were two RCA 36 capacity slide projectors and an additional
Vidicon was available for showing the station clock,
identification and captions.

Two Ampex vision / sound tape recording machines were
installed but editing of the tape had
to be done by hand with a
chinagraph pencil and a razor blade.

In total, the cost of equipping the
studios reached a staggering
£250,000.

**The picture opposite shows studio
One during the commissioning
period in 1958 before transmission
started.**

** A 'dolly' is a type of trolley on
which a camera is mounted.

GUIDE TO YOUR STATION
From derelict warehouses to this!

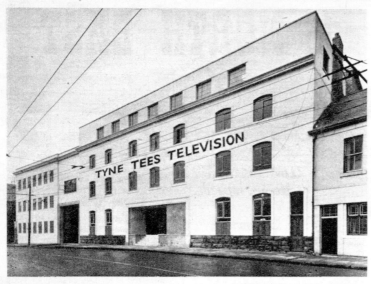

FROM derelict warehouses to one of the finest TV studios in the country in less than six months—that is the story of the new TV centre in City Road, Newcastle.

Two warehouses divided by a wooden shed were stripped to a shell to leave 400,000 sq. ft. of space for the building.

NOT AN INCH OF THAT SPACE HAS BEEN WASTED. TTT chiefs, led by Director **George Black** and Programme Controller **Bill Lyon-Shaw**, knew exactly what was wanted and proceeded to make their dreams of the ideal TV studio a concrete fact.

" Planned economy " is the result. Everything is streamlined to side-step hitches.

Programmes will reach your fireside from three studios—big shows from No. 1, smaller shows and advertising magazines from 2 and news and interviews from 3.

In the middle of the group of studios and control-rooms is the Master Control—centre of the web —including Ampex equipment, which records both sound and vision and can be played back almost instantaneously.

NO OTHER STUDIO IN THE

Played leading part
A man who has played a leading part in creating the new TV centre is Tyne Tees managing director Anthony Jelly. Aged 37, Mr. Jelly has had extensive television experience in Scotland and London. He is married, with two children, and lives at Humshaugh, near Hexham.

COUNTRY HAS HAD THE ADVANTAGE OF BEGINNING WITH THIS EQUIPMENT.

Looking like a Hammond electric organ, the huge lighting control unit acts as nerve centre for 102 different circuits.

A mains electricity sub-station ensures that power cuts do not affect the studio.

No effort has been spared to make the TTT Television Centre a studio of which the North-East can be justly proud.

SCENE DOCK AND STORE

PROPERTY STORE

MAINTENANCE

Scenery dock has direct access to the studios and is built to house even the biggest scenery. Bordered by carpenters', engineers' and electricians' rooms.

In the middle of the building in Master Control sits the Transmission Controller. It is his responsibility alone to see that what is happening on the studio floor goes out 100 per cent perfect to the viewer at home.

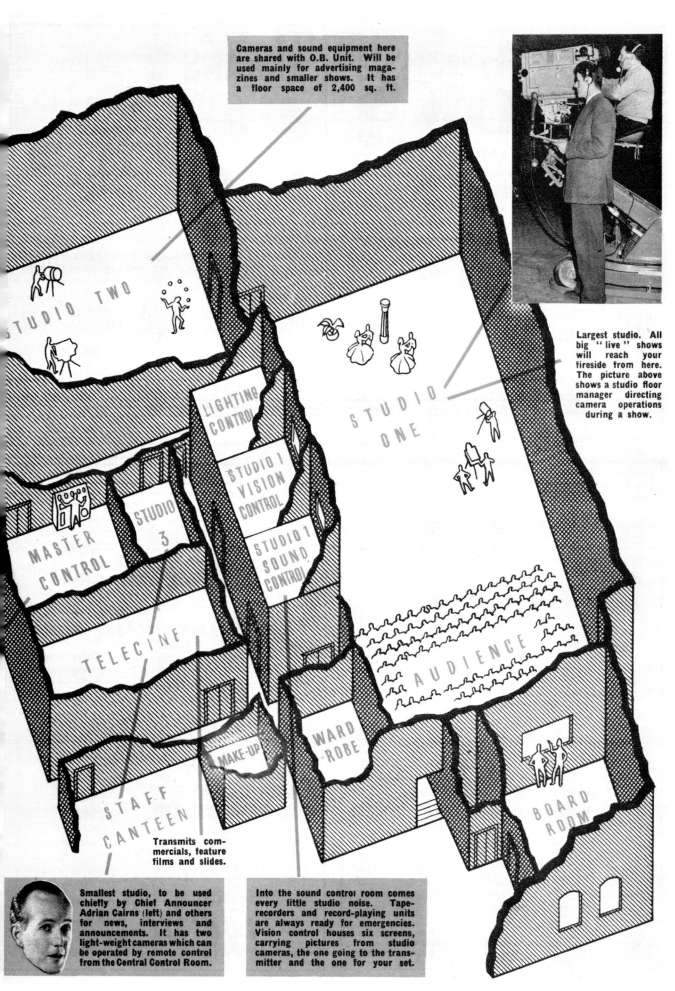

Cameras and sound equipment here are shared with O.B. Unit. Will be used mainly for advertising magazines and smaller shows. It has a floor space of 2,400 sq. ft.

Largest studio. All big "live" shows will reach your fireside from here. The picture above shows a studio floor manager directing camera operations during a show.

STUDIO TWO

STUDIO ONE

LIGHTING CONTROL

STUDIO 1 VISION CONTROL

STUDIO 1 SOUND CONTROL

MASTER CONTROL

STUDIO 3

TELECINE

AUDIENCE

MAKE-UP

WARD-ROBE

STAFF CANTEEN

BOARD ROOM

Transmits commercials, feature films and slides.

Smallest studio, to be used chiefly by Chief Announcer Adrian Cairns (left) and others for news, interviews and announcements. It has two light-weight cameras which can be operated by remote control from the Central Control Room.

Into the sound control room comes every little studio noise. Tape-recorders and record-playing units are always ready for emergencies. Vision control houses six screens, carrying pictures from studio cameras, the one going to the transmitter and the one for your set.

The Technical Aspects

In the North-East of England the BBC transmitted their programmes from Pontop Pike on channel 5 which was about 65MHz, a frequency just below the VHF stereo radio band. Most TV owners used a dipole aerial with one reflector (in layman's terms: this was an H-shaped aerial which was about 7 feet long.)

The ITA built a new transmitter at Burnhope, southwest of Chester-le-Street and this would cover an area from Alnwick to Northallerton and west to Middleton-in-Teesdale. They were to transmit on 189.75MHz at an enormous power of 100kW. The much higher frequency meant that an additional aerial was required to obtain the best picture. The aerial was called a Yagi array and consisted of a folded dipole (which looked like an elongated chain link) a reflector and a number of directors which were single rods. The rods were about two feet long. The aerials became status symbols as you were saying to your neighbours, 'We have a TV that can receive

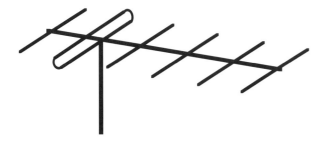

The map above shows the area of coverage of the Burnho▨ transmitter. During early transmission tests a Land-Ro▨ with television reception equipment drove around the regi▨ covering five thousand square miles monitoring the quality ▨ reception.

ITV.' Some people became TV snobs and remained faithful to the BBC. They would delight in telling their friends, 'We have decided not to receive ITV.' To receive the new station you needed a TV set that could tune to channel 8, which was the old 405 line black and white transmission on 189.75 MHz, not button No 8 on your set. TV's didn't have buttons but a large switch which clicked noisily as you rotated it. The contacts on the switch got dirty after a while and you had to rotate the switch backwards and forwards until the picture settled down. You then had to fine tune the station with a second knob. To view the picture during the day you had to draw the curtains as the cathode-ray tubes were not very bright in those days. The biggest fear a TV owner had was their tube 'going'. This was a very costly repair job. It was almost like a 'death' in the family if the telly broke down and it was a fate worse than death if it happened at Christmas. I heard a story about one viewer (who was a TV repair man) who brought a second TV home during the Christmas holidays, just in case.

You could enjoy worry-free viewing by taking out insurance against such a catastrophe.

First Day's Transmission

Tyne Tees Television started broadcasting from their City Road studios on Thursday 15 January 1959. Throughout that day last minute preparations were underway ready for the opening ceremony which was scheduled to be transmitted at 5 pm. The Duke of Northumberland was to open the station and he was to be introduced by the Chairman of Tyne Tees Television, Sir Richard A Pease. Sir Richard, in his opening speech, boasted,

'We are the eighth child of the ITV family, and although we are not as big as some of the other members, we are young and lusty, and we are going to make our voice heard.'

In Studio One, rehearsals were in progress for 'The Big Show' which was to be screened at 7pm. At midday, a telephone call from London threw the studio into a panic. The star of the Big Show, Dickie Henderson was ill and could not appear. George and Alfred Black had to make a last-minute search for a stand-in and by 5:30pm, they had managed to sign up the comedian Jimmy James to take over. There were to be two local singers in 'The Big Show'; George Romaine, an ex-electrician from Shildon, and Rikki Price from Sunderland who had been a shipyard worker.

The first voice to be heard on the opening night was that of Chief Announcer Adrian Cairns. Adrian recalled his memories of the first day.

'As we went on air precisely at 5 pm, I made the initial announcement: 'This is Tyne Tees Television, Channel Eight.' I may have added, 'Serving the North East of England,' and then went on to introduce His Grace the Duke of Northumberland. Sir Richard Pease made a formal introduction before viewers were taken on a roving camera tour of the new Studios.

The first programme, 'The Adventures of Robin Hood' starring Richard Greene, was the first of a long series of the same. Allowing for the equal fascination in the area of the first television commercials, it was followed by a ten-minute Popeye cartoon and the first North-East News. Meanwhile, behind the scenes in that first hour, I was meeting the Prime Minister, Harold Macmillan, and being taken aside by his PPS. (Parliamentary Private Secretary) to check on my intended

The voice of Adrian Cairns was the first to be heard on the new television channel.

questions. Needless to say, Bill Lyon-Shaw who was directing the interview had already told me to avoid anything 'political', which when you come to think of it is not easy when you spend as long as eight minutes talking to a Prime Minister. It left me little scope beyond asking things like whether he enjoyed the garden at No 10 and whether he took cabinet papers to bed like Winston Churchill before him, although I've just made that up and doubt whether I would have been allowed anything so intimate in 1959! In the event, Macmillan was marvellous, probably recognizing my special difficulty on this opening occasion (not to mention my nervous condition), and I only had to ask four or five questions. For the rest he ad-libbed with professional ease about his love for the North-East and the local foodstuffs enjoyed by Dorothy and himself. I was gratefully relieved. It is interesting to note from the News Chronicle front page picture of the next day that I had been placed on a lower seat than the PM, indicating the subservient position expected of a mere interviewer in those days (although it didn't happen with Hugh Gaitskell whom I interviewed shortly afterwards for 'balance'). Today, politicians and journalists mostly sit across a table at equal level and address each other by their first names!

That was in the smaller Studio Two, and now I had half-an-hour to change from a suit to a dinner-jacket before moving into an excited Studio One preparing for THE BIG SHOW at

The Big Show

A videotape of 'The Big Show' s... exists in Tyne Tees' massive libr... at City Road. 'The Big Show' I... been transferred from the origi... two inch wide Ampex tape to ... modern day professional B... format. One aspect which is rea... outstanding is the high standard... the musical accompaniment. Af... Jimmy James' spot, which featu... the 'Lions in the cardboard b... routine, the Dennis Ringro... Orchestra was heard to strike ...

seven o'clock. Up in the 'control box' where Bill Lyon-Shaw had also changed studios, there was a panic going on. Jimmy James, a comedian who was then very popular in the North-East, was to be a 'surprise' opening act, with just a few minutes to go before we were live on air, he hadn't turned up. I say 'surprise' for I note that he is not mentioned in the Viewer's first day programmes line-up. Indeed, as the News Chronicle reported the next day, he had been stuck in a traffic jam on his way from Sunderland, but in those days before cell-phones no-one knew that. The Black Brothers were pacing up and down in the entrance lobby, and Bill instructed me to alter my introductory spiel to announce Terry O'Neill as the compere. It was seven o'clock and we were on air. The show started with a song and dance number, 'There's No Business Like Show Business' featuring the Beryl Kaye Dancers with vocal refrain by The Raindrops, a top harmony group of the time. George Romaine, Chris Langford, Ethna Campbell and Rikki Price also gave brief vocal contributions and as the overture came to the coda, I started my announcement: 'Here he is, our very own and very talented... I was about to say Terry O'Neill, who indeed was waiting to make his entrance on the studio set to my left, when a frantic floor-manager (who unlike myself in vision, had head-cans) gesticulated towards the studio main door on the right - I turned and saw the Black Brothers push in a somewhat flustered Jimmy James - and you can hear on the tape of the show, how I pause, almost mouthing 'T..' and changing it into a 'J.' for 'Jimmy James!' Terry walked towards the camera and had to swerve away as the camera panned over to Jimmy who started his routine noticeably out of breath.'

The author would like to thank Adrian Cairns for recalling his memories of the first day's transmission.

with music from Bizet's Carmen and local girl Eileen Brenn... (who worked as a tracer in Wallsend) sang the famous a... 'Habanera'.

Next on camera was the BBC personality, Jack Payne wh... after admitting it was his first appearance on Independe... Television, interviewed Linden Travers, sister of the actor E... Travers. It was her first appearance on television as she h... given up showbusiness some ten years earlier. George Romai... and Rikki Price sang the song 'Witchcraft' followed by... comedy sketch by the 'One O'Clock Show' hosts Terry O'Ne... and Austin Steele.

Both Studios One and Two were in operation simultaneous... for 'The Big Show' and dancers Beryl Kaye and Malcolm Cl... performed a modern dance routine to the music 'Begin t... Beguine'. The dancers moved from one studio to the next... the camera tracked in reverse on what must have been t... longest tracking shot possible in the Tyne Tees studios at t... time.

The commercial break included adverts for Luxol Paint (o... coat covers any colour) and Summer County margarine wi... the memorable tune and the image of the white barred-g... leading to a field in summer.

Bill Maynard opened the second half with his 'Folks With Jok... routine where members of the audience were invited to t... their favourite gag. The first joke-teller was Felix McC... from Stockton-on-Tees. Bill then introduced Bella Armstror... a theatrical artistes' lodging house landlady. She ticked hi... off for that and said that she took in boarders not lodge... After telling her joke, she was presented with a prize to he... her with the boarders' washing - a bar of soap (closely follow... by a brand new washing machine wheeled on by Ch... Langford).

One of the mothers interviewed by Tom Coyne in the preview of 'The Boys Request' was Mrs Dunbar who had two sons stationed in Cyprus. Thirty years later, Tyne Tees produced the 30th Birthday Show which featured nostalgic clips from many of their early programmes including the 'Boys Request' spot on the 'Big Show'. Thirty years later Tom Coyne was seen to interview the same Mrs Dunbar.

...very nervous Sally Morton then introduced Tom Coyne who ...oke with members of the audience and in particular, he ...atted with mothers of sons who were stationed abroad with ...armed forces. Following the interviews, to the mothers' ...azement, film of their sons appeared on a big screen in the ...dio with personalised messages to the 'folks back home'. ...was all a bit too much for one mother who broke down in ...rs.) This feature was the introduction to the regular TTT ...ogramme called 'The Boys Request' introduced by Sheila ...thews. In 'The Big Show', Sheila sang 'A Lovely Way to ...end an Evening' followed by 'Today will be a Lovely Day' ...companied by the Raindrops. The singer on the left in the ...otograph above is Vince Hill who became a solo singer and ...d a No2 hit in 1967 with the song 'Edelweiss'. The girl ...ger of the Raindrops is Jackie Lee who was married to Len ...adle, the tall blond man, who was leader of the group. The ...rth member is John Worth who wrote most of the hit songs ...Adam Faith and Eden Kane.

...e of the adverts in the second commercial break was for ...lls Sausages. The glamorous vocalist Jill Day opened the ...rd section of the show with a medley of the songs - 'Love ...n be a Moment's Magic', 'There Goes my Lover', and 'When ...ur Lover Has Gone'. The final section of the show was a ...medy sketch by Bill Travers and his wife Virginia McKenna. ...l Travers held a place in North-Easterners' hearts at the ...ne as he had played the leading role in the film 'Geordie' ...ich was about the Highland Games. He gave several plugs ...his current film which was 'The Bridal Path'.

...nong the networked programmes screened by TTT later that ...ening were, 'Double Your Money', 'Wagon Train', and 'I ...ve Lucy', all of which proved to command massive viewing

figures. The complete first day's programme schedule is shown overleaf.

By the end of the first week's transmission, the Neilson Audience Research reported an audience of 37% of all homes in the reception area. It was the highest viewing figure achieved by an ITV station in its opening week.

POPEYE

HUGHIE GREEN

DESI ARNAZ

FIRST DAYS

RICHARD GREENE

5.0 STATION OPENING PROGRAMME

OPENING CEREMONY
by
THE DUKE OF NORTHUMBERLAND, J.P.
who will be introduced by
SIR RICHARD A. PEASE, Bart, D.L., J.P.,
Chairman of TYNE TEES TELEVISION LTD.
Viewers will then be shown round the new studios to meet the people who will be bringing them the Independent Television programmes

5.15 THE ADVENTURES OF ROBIN HOOD
presents
THE COMING OF ROBIN HOOD
Robin Hood .... Richard Greene
Sheriff of Nottingham .... Alan Wheatley
Sir Richard .... Ian Hunter
Robin of Locksley arrives home after several years of fighting in the Holy Land with King Richard and finds his estate has been seized

5.40 POPEYE
Laugh at the crazy adventures of Popeye

5.55 NEWS
News of the minute from the ITN newsroom

6.5 NORTH-EAST NEWS
Local news coverage at its brightest and best

6.15 THE PRIME MINISTER
The Rt. Hon. Harold Macmillan, M.P., greets the people of the North-East in a live broadcast from the Tyne Tees TV Centre
Interviewer : ADRIAN CAIRNS
Produced by BILL LYON-SHAW

6.25 STRANGE EXPERIENCES
SAFE AND SOUND
Your storyteller—Peter Williams

6.30 HIGHWAY PATROL
Starring
BRODERICK CRAWFORD
as Highway Patrol Chief Dan Mathews

7.0 THE BIG SHOW
(SEE PANEL ON THE RIGHT)

8.0 DOUBLE YOUR MONEY
starring
HUGHIE GREEN
Questions, prizes, laughs and the
£1,000 Treasure Trail
Organist ROBIN RICHMOND
Questions edited by JOHN HEYMAN
Produced for Hughie Green by ERIC J. CROAL
An Associated-Rediffusion Network Presentation

8.30 THIS WEEK
ITV's special news magazine introduced by
LUDOVIC KENNEDY
Exclusive news flashes, features and interviews from all over the world
An Associated-Rediffusion Network Production

9.0 WAGON TRAIN
starring
WARD BOND and **ROBERT HORTON**
An exciting adventure in the first of this hour-long Western series
Guest star : **RICARDO MONTALBAN**

10.0 NEWS
ITN brings you the latest news from all over the world

10.15 MURDER BAG
with
RAYMOND FRANCIS
as Supt. Lockhart in
LOCKHART FINDS A FLAW
From the story by Glyn Davies
A team of country-housebreakers plan a robbery, but murder intervenes . . .
An Associated-Rediffusion Network Production

10.45 SPORTS DESK
Introduced by
GEORGE TAYLOR
You will be introduced to the Tyne Tees Sports Desk team who will be appearing in

24 THE VIEWER

Stars of the Big Show

JILL DAY

BILL MAYNARD

BILL TRAVERS

LUDOVIC KENNEDY

ROBERT HORTON

PROGRAMMES

7.0 George and Alfred Black present

THE BIG SHOW

introducing
STAR ARTISTES FROM THE WORLD OF SHOW BUSINESS
including

DICKIE HENDERSON
Direct from his successful season in Las Vegas and New York

JILL DAY
Television's most glamorous star

BILL MAYNARD
introducing FOLKS-WITH-JOKES

TERRY O'NEILL
and the

ONE O'CLOCK SHOW ARTISTES
Dancers
BERYL KAYE and **MALCOLM CLARE**
Choreography by BERYL KAYE
Singers
RIKKI PRICE
GEORGE ROMAINE
CHRISTINE LANGFORD
presenting the Forces' show
THE BOYS REQUEST
with
SHEILA MATHEWS
THE RAINDROPS

DICKIE HENDERSON

Produced by BILL LYON-SHAW

GUEST APPEARANCE OF
JACK PAYNE
who will introduce
AT THE GOLDEN DISC

ALSO

GUEST APPEARANCE OF
THE NORTH-EAST'S OWN FILM STAR
BILL TRAVERS
and his sister
LINDEN TRAVERS
the actress

The Malcolm Goddard Dancers
The Consett Citizens' Choir
Felling Male Voice Choir
Choreography by MALCOLM GODDARD
Settings by JOHN DINSDALE
A BLACK BROTHERS PRESENTATION FOR TYNE TEES TV LTD.

BRODERICK CRAWFORD

future programmes. Other interesting items will include an excerpt of the **Sunderland v. Preston** F.A. Cup final of 1937 and the **Newcastle United v. Manchester City** final of 1955
Edited by BRIAN HARRISON
Produced by RAYMOND JOSS

10.55 I LOVE LUCY

starring
LUCILLE BALL
and
DESI ARNAZ
in
THE BLACK EYE
Lucy and Ricky argue about who is to read a

mystery book, and a hilarious scene is the result

11.25 MEET GEORGE AND ALFRED BLACK

Tyne Tees TV's Directors of Programmes who will give viewers a preview of some of the shows to be seen from the North-East's new station and introduce

THE EPILOGUE

given by
THE BISHOP OF DURHAM
THE RT. REV. MAURICE HARLAND

CHOIRS
The Consett Citizens' Choir
(*Conductor* W. WESTGARTH)
The Felling Male Voice Choir
(*Conductor* N. WILLIAMS)
The Low Fell Ladies' Choir
(*Conductor* MOLLIE PEACOCK)
The Newcastle Ladies' Choir
(*Conductor* C. TINDALL)
The North Seaton Colliery Brass Band
(*Conductor* H. LAYCOCK)
Massed choirs under the direction of
DENNIS RINGROWE

Close down

SHEILA MATHEWS   TERRY O'NEILL

Bill Lyon-Shaw

Bill Lyon-Shaw was no stranger to the entertainment world when he was appointed Tyne-Tees' first Programme Controller in 1958. After the Second World War, many of the revues that Bill had been involved with had been blitzed and he had nothing to return to.

Bill met a dancer he had employed in his pre-war revues who told him that George and Alfred Black were taking out their late father's magnificent show from the Opera House in Blackpool and they were looking for a touring manager and stage director. He met George and Alfred and was engaged on the spot to take out that wonderful show around the top theatres.

Later Bill joined Jack Payne as his Director of Productions to produce revues, plays, and summer shows throughout the country. Bill got his first taste of television when the BBC did their first ever outside broadcast from a theatre when they covered the pantomime 'Cinderella' starring Jean Kent and Derek Roy from the Regal Theatre, Edmonton. Later the BBC asked if they could do an outside broadcast of the Derek Roy Summer Show which Bill was producing at Bournemouth for Jack Payne. It was not practical to do that but Bill said that he would re-create the show in the BBC's studios. The show was transmitted from the Alexandra Palace studio A and it was a huge hit attracting the highest viewing figures the BBC had ever had for such a show at that time. That was the turning point for Bill as far as television was concerned as he was offered a job with the BBC as senior producer for the magnificent salary of £1025 per year. It was £1000 reduction in salary but Bill thought Television was going to be the medium of the future and he was proved right. He was Senior Producer with the BBC until 1955 when he was appointed Executive Producer with ATV when Independent Television first started up. Bill produced many shows for ATV, the most prestigious being 'Sunday Night at the London Palladium' which commanded record viewing figures and the popular 'Saturday Spectacular' mostly written by Eric Sykes. When Tyne Tees Television was in the planning stages, Bill was actually 'on loan' from ATV to help George and Alfred Black to apply for the franchise. Later he accepted the offer of a permanent position at TTT as Programme Controller.

Now retired from television, at the age of 85, Bill is still very active, and has an interest in an antiques and fine arts business in Stow on the Wold where he lives with his wife Anne. He told me that the secret of his longevity was to do 'everything' but not in excess. I met Bill at his home and he recalled the early years at City Road.

'George and Alfred Black had been producing 'Saturday Night Spectaculars' for ATV, which were directed by Peter Glover. They rang me up one day to say they'd been asked to join the Board of Directors of a company which had been formed by Sir Richard Pease and Mr Claude Darling, to apply for the ITV franchise for the North-East of England. I was asked to help to put together the application for the franchise which I was very happy to do. Several months later I was invited to go along to their office in Half Moon Street as they had something to tell me. The moment I walked through the door, the Champagne corks started to 'pop' and they announced that they

**Bill Lyon-Shaw at TTT's Northumberland Street offic
'Bradburn House', during the planning stages of TT**

had been awarded the ITV franchise and were going to laun Tyne Tees Television. They said that they were going to a Lew Grade and Val Parnell for my help for a few months help establish the new station. I said, 'fine' and began by visiti Newcastle several times to look for a suitable location for t studios. After a few months, the Blacks asked if I would jo the station permanently and become the first Programs Controller - I agreed. We didn't even talk money funni enough, but I knew what the going rate was as I had be advised on proposed salary levels.

We had to appoint a General Manager, preferably someo who knew about sales. Tony Jelly, who was Head of Sales Scottish ITV, and previously was No2 Sales Director at AT applied for the job and the Board were impressed. They decid to offer him the job there and then, but being a very astu businessman, he said he would only take the job if it carri the title 'Managing Director'. I was the only person not agreement, but the whole Board decided to offer him t position of Managing Director. Mr Jelly accepted t appointment and Peter Paine became Head of Sales and a excellent Head of Sales he was.

During the early part of 1958, George Black and I visit many workingmen's clubs and cinemas to see what the peop of the North-East liked. I found that they didn't like 'sm but they liked good local humour. In the cinemas, they shriek with laughter at the 'blood and guts' horror films. They ju didn't take them seriously. They liked 'down to earth' stu they liked a little music, but nothing too highbrow.

I had some difficulty in trying to persuade production peop in London to come with me to Tyne Tees as most thought th the North-East was a pretty grim place.

ey've got tigers and bears up there,' said one of the staff
hen I asked him to come to Newcastle. We arranged 100%
ortgages for many of the production people to buy bungalows
a new estate in Gosforth.

emember the first day the staff assembled in the North-
st; we all met in the evening at the Egypt Cottage pub next
the studios. I knew the production staff were probably
ing to try to get me drunk that night, so I thought I'd better
y safe. In London, the weakest drink you can buy is brown
, so when they asked me what I wanted to drink, I asked for
t.

Newcastle Brown Ale alright?' they asked.

ne!' I replied, not realising it was the strongest beer in the
b. By about 8:30 I passed out. They had to take me home
d put me to bed. That's the only time I've ever passed out
th drink. I've been really 'happy' plenty of times, but had
ver passed out until I drank Newcastle Brown Ale.

e opening night on 15 January 1959 was hectic. The Duke
Northumberland was to open the station, I had 'The Big
ow' at seven o'clock, and I was also producing the interview
th the Prime Minister, all in the same night. I was also
sponsible for the smooth running of the station - I was rather
sy. The then, Prime Minister, Harold Macmillan was in my
fice and he put me at my ease rather than the other way
und. He was extremely amusing and was cracking gags, so
aid to him,

xcuse me sir, but when you've finished your term of office,
ould you join us as scriptwriter because we need writers of
medy material?'

asked him to sign the visitors book. He said,
o you want my temporary address or my real address?'
is temporary address of course being 10 Downing Street.

celebrate the opening night, we had cases of Champagne in
ur offices. George and Alfred Black had a case each and I
d a case, but it was going very
uickly because artistes and
gnitaries were coming in all the
ne throughout the day. I ran out
Champagne just before the 'Big
ow' so I asked Jack Payne if he
ould like to go to the Egypt Cottage
xt door for a drink. When we went
, the place was packed as it was
e break between the run-through
d transmission. All the drink had
en sold; bottles of beer,
erything. So I asked Jim the
ndlord if he had anything at all.

**ill Lyon-Shaw (far right)
njoying a drink after a live
resentation of 'Your Kind of
lusic'. Next to Bill is George
lack, then Hattie Jacques, Eric
ykes and Aud Penrose. Seated
Rawicz of Rawicz and
andauer, and on the far left is
rthur Wilkinson.**

He remembered he had some bottles of Champagne in the cellar
so I asked him to bring one up so we could have a look at it.
Jack Payne said he would pay and asked Jim the price. Jim
told us that he would have to charge what was on the stock
sheet - five shillings. We had been paying well over a pound
for the Champagne in the studios so I asked him how many
bottles he had in his cellar. Jim thought he had about 24 so I
quickly said,
'Right! They are mine, now!'
The Champagne must have been on his stock list when he
took over the pub. It could have been 20 years old. He would
never have sold Champagne before Tyne Tees opened. In the
Egypt Cottage on that opening night, the takings at the bar
were more than for the whole of the month before. I remember
Jim used to wear a shirt without a collar and his wife Jessie,
who had a wart on her nose, used to wear a black dress with
cigarette ash all down the front from the fag always dangling
from her lips. When the breweries found out how much they
were taking at the Egypt Cottage, they told Jim and Jessie to
smarten themselves up. Jim was told to wear a collar and tie
and Jessie bought a lurex dress which was worse than the
black one with the stains, but they were warm friendly people.
One of the managers of Scottish and Newcastle Breweries
came to see me and asked for my opinion on how they could
improve the Egypt Cottage pub. The room upstairs was used
by Tyne Tees artistes for rehearsals and I thought it might be
a good idea to convert it into a bar. I think one of the staff of
the Brewery must have been to Spain for his holidays as they
built a Spanish bar upstairs. I could think of nothing more
out of character than a Spanish bar on City Road, unless it
was an Egypt Cottage bar in Spain.

The Bishop of Durham was presenting the Epilogue on the
opening night and we asked him to come to the studios at
about 10 o'clock so we could brief him. He was to do the
Epilogue for five minutes at about 11:30pm. He arrived at

THE TYNE TEES ITV PROGRAMME JOURNAL

DEC 18 TO 24 5ᴰ

'THE VIEWER

No. 101 © The Daily News Ltd., 1960

Petrushka

TTT'S GREAT BALLET SUCCESS RETURNS BY POPULAR DEMAND SEE PAGES 4-5

FULL DETAILS OF CHRISTMAS EVE PROGRAMMES

The front cover of 'The Viewer' in December 1960 sho_
the Tyne Tees Television production of the ballet 'Petrushk_
with Keith Beckett (centre) as Petrushka, Malcol_
Goddard (bottom left) as the Charlatan, and Patri_
Kirshner (top right) as the Ballerina.

seven o'clock and Sergeant Wonfor, our commissionaire, marched into my office and said,
'Sir, the Bishop of Durham is here. Will you see him?'
I was just going into the gallery to direct 'The Big Show', George Black said he couldn't entertain him either as he wanted to be with me in the gallery, so Alfred Black took him into his office and offered him some Champagne. After the show finished, I went into Alfred's office and the Bishop was still enjoying his Champagne. When he went on air at 11:30 he was, shall we say, 'very happy and relaxed'. He was supposed to do five minutes but he extended the time somewhat. He blessed the studio, he blessed the staff, and he even blessed the studio cat. We had a 'studio cat', which had come into the studios one day when we were first setting up the studios and we let it stay for good luck. It walked onto the set, and the Bishop blessed it. The choirs were waiting to sing the Hallelujah Chorus; they'd been standing for two hours under the lights and by then some of the choir members were collapsing with the heat, but the Epilogue went on and on.

At first we had a large resident studio orchestra but when the Musicians' Union doubled the rates I didn't have the budget to keep the large orchestra so we had to cut it down to a quartet and sometimes augment it to an eight piece when it was necessary. We tried to introduce good music gradually via the locally produced shows. Dennis Ringrowe and the boys of the band were excellent musicians and would feature a jazz number on the 'One O'Clock Show' from time to time, and even the odd operatic aria.

Once the station became established, I think the programm_
that gave me the most satisfaction was 'Your Kind of Musi_
The idea of the programme was to introduce popular classi_
music to the viewers. We helped to establish the Northe_
Sinfonia Orchestra, and we brought classical music, ope_
and ballet to the North-East. One of my great loves was t_
ballet, but when we came to Newcastle they all said,
'Ballet! whey they are all Jessies prancing around in their uni_
suits. They won't watch them, man!'
So I thought we are going to have to teach the viewers. T_
BBC had the edict, 'To educate, inform and entertain.'
My aim was 'To entertain, inform, and through entertainme_
and information, educate.' When I first came to Newcast_
and they had ballet at the theatre, there was an empty hou_
Tyne Tees helped to popularise ballet and several years late_
a production came to the theatre, tickets were sold out wee_
before the performance. At Tyne Tees we produced a seri_
called 'Stories from the Ballet' introduced by the famous Ant_
Dolin. We brought well known dancing families into the stud_
effectively showing that they were not all effeminate weakling_
We had the dancer John Gilpin training with Newcastle Unit_
football team and he wore them out. He was more of an athle_
than they were. We were educating the viewers, but withou_
being obvious. My No1, Peter Glover directed most of t_
'Your Kind of Music' programmes and was often responsib_
for the choreography. A great asset to the station was Kei_
Beckett who joined us as Trainee Producer/Director. Kei_
had been a Premier Dancer with the National Ballet Compa_
and the Royal Ballet Company. Keith adapted the Russi_
ballet 'Petrushka' for television and we presented the televisi_
version from the City Road studios on Monday 28 Marc_
1960. John Dinsdale, Head of Design, produced a wonderf_
set of a Russian 18th century marketplace, and Arth_
Wilkinson conducted the orchestra. It was a great succe_
and technically beautiful.

Arthur Wilkinson was a great and gifted musician who w_
responsible for writing, arranging and conducting the mus_
for 'Your Kind of Music' as well as for many other production_
He orchestrated some of the music for 'Bonanza' and ma_
other American 'soaps' as they found it cheaper to use a Briti_
writer than to orchestrate the music in the States. Arthur di_
suddenly from a heart attack when he was only 44. He ha_
been working 18 hours a day, getting up at five o'clock, worki_
on the 'Bonanza' music until nine, then he'd have breakfa_
and take the dog for a walk. He'd work on the scores for Ty_
Tees, then he'd be working on a score for the Royal Ball_
Company. No wonder he had a heart attack; he was worki_
18 hour days, seven days a week.

Edmund Purdom and Adrienne Corri star in another " Sword of Freedom " adventure at 6.30

0 REQUEST TIME
introduced by
NORMA EVANS
starring
THE BARRY SISTERS
DAVID MACBETH
SHIRLEY WILSON
with
THE **DENNIS RINGROWE ORCHESTRA**
(Conducted by **Billy Hutchinson**)

night's requests include *Hernando's Hide-*
ay, Way Down Yonder In New Orleans
d Misty

Tonight's guests :
The Five Smith Brothers
and
TTT's Discovery
LARRY MASON
Singing *Tenement Symphony*
Produced by PHILIP JONES
A Tyne Tees Production

30 DOUBLE YOUR MONEY
starring
HUGHIE GREEN
e comedy master of the quiz with another
ogramme of questions, laughter and big
ney prizes
An Associated-Rediffusion Production

0 THE ARTHUR HAYNES SHOW
starring
ARTHUR HAYNES
AILEEN COCHRANE
with
NICHOLAS PARSONS   KEN MORRIS
JACK PARNELL and his ORCHESTRA
An ATV Production

30 WAGON TRAIN
starring
NOAH BEERY Jr.
WARD BOND   ROBERT HORTON
in
THE JONAS MURDOCK STORY
CAST INCLUDES :

dams	**Ward Bond**
lint McCullough	**Robert Horton**
onas Murdock	**Noah Beery Jr.**
hief Red Hawk	**Joe Bassett**

he people of the wagon train, desperate for
od, are enraged by the refusal of Indian
hief Red Hawk to allow them to kill a few
er. Then Major Adams catches Jonas
urdock snaring rabbits . . .

(See Page 7)

9.25 NEWS
World events from ITN

9.35 PROBATION OFFICER
with
JOHN PAUL   DAVID DAVIES
EMRYS JONES
and
BETTY McDOWALL
CAST INCLUDES :

Mr. Ross	**Eric Dodson**
Judge	**Raymond Rollett**
Molly Stacey	**Betty McDowall**
Arthur Stacey	**Emrys Jones**
Jim Blake	**David Davies**
Philip Main	**John Paul**

Produced by ANTONY KEAREY
An ATV Production

10.30 PETRUSHKA
Adapted for television by KEITH BECKETT
Original choreography by MICHAEL FOKINE
Music by IGOR STRAVINSKY
Original decor by ALEXANDER BENOIS

Petrushka is the creation of the world's greatest choreographer and is considered to be
ballet at its most perfect. It is a simple story
of the shrove-tide fair, where an old charlatan
presents his animated dolls to the crowd, and
the tragedy that results when he brings the
dolls to life

CAST :

Petrushka	**Keith Beckett**
The Ballerina	**Patricia Kirshner**
The Blackamoor	**Rodney MacDonald**
The Charlatan	**Malcolm Goddard**
The Devil	**John Massey**

Designed by JOHN DINSDALE
Produced by PETER GLOVER
A Tyne Tees Production

11.0 NEWS
Late night news

11.2 DOUGLAS FAIRBANKS PRESENTS
A LIKELY STORY
CAST INCLUDES :

Phyllis	**Betty McDowall**
David	**William Franklyn**
Susan	**Nicola Braithwaite**
Miss Applegate	**Mary Jones**

David and Phyllis Butler call their eight-year-
old daughter " Miss Mitty " because in the
secret world of her imagination she is so many
different people, never just Susan Butler. They
are very worried, though, for she seems in-
capable of distinguishing between truth and
falsehood, and when she comes home with a
story about a man who jumped out of the
hedge with a pair of scissors and tried to snip
off her pigtails, they don't know whether she
is telling the truth or not. . . .

THE EPILOGUE
Close down

In 1962, one of our film cameramen, Jim Hodkinson, won an award as Television News Cameraman of the Year. Alfred Black, Tony Jelly and I went to the presentation ceremony at the Savoy Hotel in London to see Jim receive his award which was for a superb newsreel sequence of a factory fire in Newcastle. Among the guests of honour at the ceremony was Hugh Gaitskell who was leader of the opposition at that time. The photo opposite shows me on the left and then Tony Jelly, Hugh Gaitskell, Alfred Black, and Jim with his wife Mireille. It was a lovely evening and after the ceremony, I caught the 11:30 sleeper train back to Newcastle. I was chatting to the steward on the train and he said,
'It's a shame about Gaitskell.'
I said, 'What do you mean?'
'Well he's dead.'

I said, 'He can't be dead, I just left him an hour or so ago.'
We turned the radio on for the 12 o'clock news and it was true, Hugh Gaitskell had died that same night at 10 pm. I could hardly believe it. He was a charming and clever man.

We had a good board of Directors at Tyne Tees. There was one gentleman whom we appointed; a Brigadier. After a few weeks, when he had settled in, we asked him if he had any suggestions to make to improve the station. He quickly replied, 'Yes! get rid of those damned commercials.'
The Finance Director had to take him to one side and explain to him how we received our income in Independent Television. The Brigadier lasted a few months and then resigned.

In the first few years of Tyne Tees, we had a problem getting the right people to run the staff canteen. We had outside caterers at first but we started getting a lot of complaints about the quality of the food. It was always a difficult job for the caterers as they never knew how many people they were going to have to cater for. One day there could be all the members of the Consett Citizen Choir wanting lunch, and the next day, there may have on been a handful of people. I decided to take on the responsibili of the canteen myself and advertised for a Chef. An Austri chef applied for the job. His CV was very impressive inde with a Royal coat of arms on the front. He had prepared fo for Barons, Earls and Dukes, and was not asking for enormous salary, so I thought I'd give him a try. At first was brilliant but after a few weeks we started getting ev more complaints than before. He sometimes didn't turn up work until 11 o'clock. Things got really out of hand and made a few enquiries about him. It turned out that the m was an alcoholic and had been thrown out of just about eve hotel in the North-East. I asked my secretary Nan Coats

The surprise guest on 'The Birthday Show', not listed in 'The Viewer', was Shirley Bassey.

d him to my office. I had warned him about his conduct
fore, and when he came to my office I think he knew what
s coming. When I told him he was fired, he was furious
l suddenly produced a meat-cleaver from under his apron
l he went for me. I ran out of my office with this maniac
asing me down the corridor brandishing the meat-cleaver. I
ought my days were over, but I was rescued by Sergeant
onfor. A few weeks later I took on Connie Richardson as
nteen Manageress and she stayed with us for many years.
e had an animal spot on the 'One O'Clock Show' quite
gularly and it was presented by Edgar Robinson. His most
emorable act was with his performing dogs, and one day my
ughter Wanda came up to see me. (She had a job getting
st my secretary, Nan Coats who used to insist that Wanda
de an appointment whenever she wanted to see me.)
nyway, Wanda had fallen in love with one of Edgar's dogs
nich was a wire-haired terrier pup. Edgar was giving it away
d Wanda pleaded with me to keep the puppy. I wasn't
ing to get any peace until I agreed. So for years after that
e had that wire-haired terrier around the house until 18 years
er it killed itself - it went barmy and started to eat nails.

hen the station was one year old we planned a special variety
oduction called the 'Birthday Show'. We had a terrific line-
of stars for the programme but just after 'The Viewer'
agazine had gone to press, Shirley Bassey's manager rang
e to say that he'd heard we were doing a special show and as
irley was available that night would we like her to appear
in our show. I said 'yes' very quickly and Shirley was our
surprise guest on the 'Birthday Show'. We planned a special
entrance for her where she'd come into camera shot on a sleigh
pulled by four male dancers. When it came to the rehearsal I
was called onto the studio floor because there was a problem.
Shirley couldn't make the entrance we'd planned and when I
asked why she said,
'There's no way I can step onto the sleigh in this dress. The
dress cost me £10,000, wardrobe have had to sew me into it,
and I can hardly walk never mind step onto a sleigh.'
I just had to change the introduction so that the camera tracked
to where she was standing. It worked fine and the rehearsals
continued without a hitch. Later that afternoon, during
rehearsals, my secretary Nan Coats came into the gallery and
said,
'I want to speak to you.'
'Not now,' I said.
'It's very important, please come outside.'
We went into the corridor and she told me that my mother had
died. I asked my No1, Peter Glover to take over while I went
home to arrange family contacts. I returned to the studio at
about 6:30 just as the rehearsals were finishing and I said to
Nan that on no account should anyone know about my mother's
death as I didn't want sympathy or any depression in the studios.
I did tell George and Alfred Black as George had known my
mother very well and he took the news very badly as did Nan
Coats who often sat with my mother at the nursing home. We
did the show which was a great success and when I returned

'yne Tees' staff and artistes of the 'Birthday Show' January 1960

to my office, I found Nan flat out on the settee foaming at the mouth. She had taken too many pills to calm her nerves and also had drunk several large whiskeys. We had to rush her to hospital and get her 'pumped out'.

I'd arranged a party at Michaels' nightclub that evening for the cast of the 'Birthday Show' and I thought it would be best to still go ahead with it and not tell anyone about my mother. We had the Lord Mayor and Alderman McKeigh as our guests. I'd also invited Sarah Churchill who was appearing in a play at the Theatre Royal at the time. Alderman McKeigh was a great admirer of Sarah's father Winston Churchill and he was very 'Churchillian' in his manner, politics and way of speaking. I arranged for Sarah to sit next to the Alderman and he was chatting away to her in his Churchill-like voice saying,

'My dear, - I would like, - to say, - how much, - I admire your father....'

After a while, Sarah turned to me and said,

'Is he taking the mickey out of my old man?'

When we returned home, I broke down and I was able to grieve for my mother. That was a night that I will never, ever forget - success and tragedy all in one day. What a day!

I was with Tyne Tees for five years and was stressed out and heading for a breakdown but didn't realise it at the time. We didn't use the word 'stress' in those days; it was called over-work. I decided to get out of the 'rat-race' and retired to our cottage on the banks of the River Beaulieu in the little village of Beaulieu. The local pub was the Montague Arms and when I visited the pub one night I found that I knew the manager from when he was at the Palace Hotel in Buxton. He said that the Montague Arms was closing down at the end of the week as the pub was really run down and there was no money to refurbish it. To cut a long story short, I took over control of the pub by buying shares in the limited company which owned it. It gave me something to do because after eight weeks of retirement with nothing to occupy my mind, I was frustrated. I had a great time building that hotel up and went on to buy other hotels and restaurants. My wife and I now live in Stow on the Wold so as to be near to our daughter, Jennifer Mould, who runs a racehorse stud farm. I am involved with an antiques business here in the village.'

Bill Lyon-Shaw in 1998

Wanda Lyon-Shaw

'I joined the Make-up Department at Tyne Tees when I wa 16 years old. The Head of Make-up, Heather Jackson wa a very professional lady and did her job 'to the letter' of th rulebook. I remember being rushed off my feet most of th time with queues of artistes waiting to be made-up. On day there was a cosmetics rep waiting to see Heather. made him up along with all the others not realising he wasn an artiste. George Romaine used to walk into ou department dragging his toupee along the floor on the en of a lead as if it was a little dog. He used to ask us to clea and style it. He hated that toupee.'

Wanda still works from time to time as a Senior Make-u Artist for major International film companies.

Bill recalled a story from his early touring days.

'Before the war I produced and presented shows such a 'Sweet and Lovely', 'Hip Hip Hooray' and 'Forty Winks 'Bonjour Paris' was the big one, and we were playing at top theatre in Cardiff. Anne and I had just been marrie and I asked the stage manager to get me the best digs i Cardiff. As the Governor, if anybody was ill, I stepped in One of the singers was ill and so I was singing for the firs week. (I was a trained singer, by the way.) It was a Monda night and all the complimentary ticket holders were in, which usually included landladies from the boarding houses wher the cast were staying. We did the show and later that evening I asked our landlady if she had enjoyed the performance She folded her arms and started to lecture me.

'We only have top of the bills here you know. I heard yo sing tonight and I've heard better singing in the pit-hea baths. I'm sorry but you'll have to go.'

I quickly replied, 'But I'm the Governor; it's my show. I an the Producer and the Presenter.'

'I don't care,' she said, 'we only have top of the bills here We had Donald Peers last week. I'm sorry but you'll have to leave.'

Next day Anne and I had to move into a hotel. Such is fame.'

Tyne Tees 'Firsts'

From the very beginning, Tyne Tees Television was setting new broadcasting standards and pioneering television production methods. It was the first station to employ Ampex video recording equipment from the beginning, rather than the inferior tele-recording system where a movie film of a television picture was made to 'time-shift' a programme's transmission. TTT was the first company to use a mobile videotape facility capable of recording whilst on the move. The machine was the size of a Wurlitzer organ and took so much power that a generator housed in a separate trailer had to be towed by the outside broadcast van. Today, equivalent broadcast-standard equipment may be carried on a person's shoulder.

It is said that Tyne Tees were the first television company to demonstrate to the public in the North-East, a closed circuit colour television system, in 1962. The demonstration was using the American colour standard which was denoted as NTSC. It was an inferior system (in terms of colour integrity) to PAL which was eventually adopted by Britain. Tyne Tees cameramen nicknamed the American NTSC system 'Never Twice the Same Colour '.

TTT was the first company to transmit a church service from a prison, when one of the outside broadcast units televised the Sunday service in the chapel of Durham Prison. David Petrie, one of the station's original cameramen, remembers that the whole experience was very frightening as he was pointing his camera at some notorious criminals. Some of the prisoners had given permission to be filmed, and others hadn't, consequently it turned his job into a nightmare. As he panned the camera, he had to stop before he reached inmate xxx as they hadn't given permission, and so on.

TTT was the first company to use a mobile video recording system. Reg Jones (inside the van) adjusts the machine while Brian Ranger (sound) chats up Monica - later to become his wife.

7.0 SPOTLIGHT ON NATO

On the eve of the Atlantic Congress in London, Tyne Tees turns its searching spotlight on NATO and gives representatives of the British Press the chance to question leading NATO personalities, including **General Norstad, M. Spaak, Senator Kefauver and M. Reynaud** Chairman **LORD BOOTHBY**
Produced by H. K. LEWENHAK
This is Tyne Tees Television's first Outside Broadcast—see Page 5 for the full story

Tyne Tees' first ever Outside Broadcast was screened on Thursday 4 June, 1959.

Tyne Tees gave Sir Jimmy Savile his first ever television series when 'Young at Heart' was first screened on Wednesday, 4 May, 1960.

Tyne Tees produced 'Say it in Russian' which was the first language programme an ITV company had produced.

In 1968 Frank Entwhistle, of the features department, invited Prince Philip to appear live on Tyne Tees' new discussion programme 'Face The Press'. The Company achieved a remarkable 'scoop' when the Prince agreed, and it was the first time a Royal had been interviewed on a live, unscripted television discussion programme.

In December 1997 Margaret Fay was appointed Managing Director and General Manager of Tyne Tees Television and became the station's first female MD.

Tyne Tees was the first television company to conduct a live, unscripted interview of a Royal, when Prince Philip agreed to 'Face The Press' in 1968.

The Tyne Tees 'Family'

Many of the staff and personalities I have spoken with during the research for this book have referred to the special bond between people at Tyne Tees especially in the early years. 'I have always thought of the station as one big family,' said one of the Programme Directors who started his career at TTT in the early 60's. 'Not always a happy family,' he added. 'We've had our ups and downs, but in general, you can usually rely on your colleagues to help out when problems loom.'

In the first few years of the company, the average age of the staff was about 25 and although some of the production staff had worked for the BBC and companies such as Rediffusion, many people were very new to television and relied on each other for support when the TV production process ran into problems. A culture evolved which was to be one of the major strengths of the company. Within the 'family' at Tyne Tees were many families. The most notable brothers in Tyne Tees were of course the station's founding fathers George and Alfred Black who hailed from Sunderland. Jack Haig, better known as Wacky Jacky, joined the company in 1959 along with his sister Peggy who married 'One O'Clock Show' host, Terry O'Neill. The station's first commissionaire was Sergeant Fred Wonfor. His son Geoff joined Tyne Tees in the early 60's and Geoff's career grew at City Road during a time when Tyne Tees developed a name for producing top quality pop music programmes such as 'Geordie Scene' and 'The Tube'. Much later, after leaving Tyne Tees, Geoff was commissioned to produce the 'Beatles Anthology' being the definitive television documentary of the famous 'pop' group. Geoff married a researcher called Andrea whose career developed at an equally impressive rate culminating in her current position as a Managing Director of Granada Productions within the Granada Media Group. It is thought that Fred Wonfor is the oldest surviving original employee of Tyne Tees Television.

The Wardrobe Department at TTT was headed by Irma May whose husband was Andy May, a TTT sound maintenance engineer. Some time later their daughter Anne May joined TTT and worked with her mother in the Wardrobe Department. Many people remember Irma having protruding front teeth,

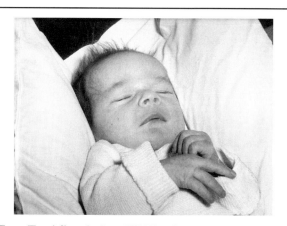

Tyne Tees' first baby. Jill Herrick, daughter of Stills Photographer Bob Herrick, was born on 23 March 1959 and was the first child of a TTT employee to be born after the station started transmitting. This picture and the announcement were included in the local TTT news.

always having a cigarette in her mouth, and complaining that everyone was overweight.

David Croft, the producer of many of the light entertainment shows at Tyne Tees, was married to Ann who appeared with Kenneth Horne on TTT's advertising magazine 'Trader Horne'. Ann was an actress and in the early 60's she was understudy to Barbara Kelly in the play 'Anniversary Waltz' which was playing at the Theatre Royal in Newcastle. When Barbara Kelly fell ill, Ann stepped in to act her part.

Some people today may disagree, but to young and enthusiastic people, a television studio must have been a glamorous place to work. In an era when the main core of television programming was light entertainment, music, singing and dancing, it is not surprising that many romances blossomed at Tyne Tees. Cameraman Ian Westwater met and courted Claire Caldwell who was Philip Jones' PA (she PA'd TTT's opening show). Claire remembers working with Russ Conway on Granada TV's 'At Your Request'. Russ, a popular pianist in the late fifties / early sixties, had written a new melody but could not think of a title. Claire suggested 'Side-saddle' and the record became a number one hit early in 1959. Much later Claire was a newsreader on Metro Radio and even presented Bill Steel's show one day when Bill was delayed in traffic. Ian and Claire married and are now living in Gosforth. Another cameraman, Arthur Best married Maureen Hudson who was also a production assistant in 1959. They are now both retired and live in Morpeth. The third member of Camera Crew A was David Petrie who also married a PA called Lynne Kirkup.

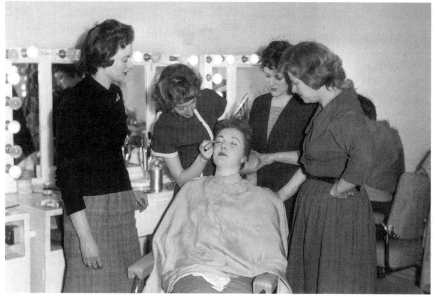

Tyne Tees make-up department c1960. Left to right: Aileen Condon, Heather Jackson, Jackie Harris, Yvonne Coppard. The artiste being made-up is Chris Langford.

meraman Lewis Williams married Production Assistant ristine Fuller. Christine went on to become Producer of ny of Tyne Tees quiz shows such as 'Cross Wits' and ainletters'. Jack Archer, who became Head of Lighting rried Monica who worked in Sales.

n Brown, Assistant House Manager married Elsie, a itchboard Operator. Bob Baitman of the Transmission ntrol department married Margaret Thwaites of the Script partment in September 1959. John Loukes started his duties TTT in the Property Department but was promoted to a dio manager later in 1959 when he married 'Happy-Go-cky's Kate Beckley.

ll Slark was the studios' Master Carpenter. His two sons d daughter all worked at Tyne Tees. Bill Slark junior was a ember of the studio floor staff and Vic started his career as a ll Boy. Bill's daughter Violet was a receptionist.

nes Hughes had been a theatre lighting technician when e married Bob Hughes who was floor manager on the very st edition of the local news on TTT. John Reay, now a ogramme director, remembers a time when he was working a film vaults boy and he sneaked into Studio One to see the ne O'Clock Show'. Bob Hughes, very good at his job as oor Manager, but a stickler for Studio discipline, saw him nging around and turfed him out of the studio. Bob's wife nes was one of the company's first Vision Mixers.

e and Heather Ging were writers and theatre artistes who ote scripts for many of Tyne Tees' productions. Heather joyed a varied career at Tyne Tees, starting as a PA, and er became Head of Arts. At one time her secretary was an Knighting whose sister was Sally Morton, the first woman nouncer on Tyne Tees.

ad of the make-up department was Heather Jackson seen in e photograph on the opposite page, applying eye shadow to nris Langford. Chris, Heather and Yvonne Coppard (on the ght of the photograph) shared a flat in the early years of TT before Chris married Jim Goldby from the sound partment, and Heather hitched up with Jim Nurse who was les Director. Bill Lyon-Shaw's daughter Wanda joined the ake-up department when she was only 16. Several years ter she married one of TTT's announcers Jon Kelley. drienne Harper joined the make-up department in 1960. She

The Egypt Cottage pub next door was in constant competition with the Rose and Crown (on the opposite side of City Road) for the custom of Tyne Tees staff. The Egypt Cottage took its unusual name from the fact that grain shipped in from Egypt was often stored in warehouses nearby. When Tyne Tees first started, it was said that Scottish and Newcastle Breweries offered to sell the Egypt Cottage to the station for £8000, an offer they declined.

married cameraman Chris Palmer who later left Tyne Tees to produce the long running ITV classic, 'Wish You Were Here'.

Tyne Tees staff canteen was a place where you could obtain good advice on any subject under the sun. Say you were installing central heating and you wanted to know where to buy the cheapest boiler, or say you'd had a car crash and you needed some legal advice; you could usually get advice from a fellow member of staff. If you went to the canteen and asked around, you would eventually find someone who had experience of that subject. You could come out of the canteen with thousands of pounds worth of good solid advice, all for free.

It was said that the station was fuelled on copious quantities of nicotine and alcohol. Nearly everyone smoked, and if you passed your cigarette packet around the canteen table, by the time the packet came back, you were lucky if there was one or two left. But then a few minutes after you'd finished your cigarette, someone else's packet would be coming around. People recalled smoking habits of 50 a day. Most television productions ended with the final scene taking place in Studio 5, which was the nickname for either the Egypt Cottage pub next door, or the Rose and Crown across the road from the studios. The patter in the pub was always about television; how things had gone that day, how techniques could be improved, and excited chat about the new programmes which were coming up. Throughout the years, the staff's allegiances switched between the two pubs several times depending upon the condition of the beer, or the landlord's attitude to television company employees. When the pubs closed, many of Tyne Tees' staff moved on to a nightclub such as Billy Botto's in Byker where the partying continued until the early hours.

he 'late' Rose and Crown known by many Tyne Tees nployees as Studio 5.

The ITV Revelation

To hundreds of thousands of viewers in the North-East who had been used to the BBC's low entertainment value programmes, Tyne Tees Television was a revelation. Many of the programmes were networked from the other ITV companies around the country. Programmes such as 'Wagon Train', 'Sunday Night at the London Palladium', and 'Take Your Pick' commanded huge viewing audiences.

ABC, a subsidiary of Associated British Pictures, operated

studios in Manchester, Birmingham and London and transmitted programmes on weekends. Their most memorable programmes were 'Candid Camera', 'Opportunity Knocks', 'Thank your Lucky Stars', 'Armchair Theatre' and 'The Avengers'.

Associated Rediffusion was the first company to operate an ITV franchise. They were based in London and transmitted on weekdays. Their Wembley Studios produced some classic ITV programmes including 'Double Your Money', 'Take Your Pick', 'Ready Steady Go', and 'No Hiding Place'. In 1968 the company merged with ABC to form Thames Television.

Granada's main studios were located in Manchester and company is one of the few major ITV companies to retain original name. Transmissions started on 3 May 1956. Th produced 'Bootsie and Snudge', many of the 'Plays of the We and 'Television Playhouse' dramas but their 'flagsh programme was of course 'Coronation Street'. In 19 Granada Media Group purchased Tyne Tees Television alo with its partner, Yorkshire Television.

Associated Television produced programmes from the Wo Green Empire, the Hackney Empire, and later the Elstree Stu Centre in Borehamwood. They had a London franchise weekends and started transmissions there on 24 Septeml 1955. The next year they won a contract to cover the Midlan on weekdays. Transmissions started there on 17 Februa 1956. Their most memorable programmes were, 'Sunday Nig at the London Palladium', 'Emergency Ward 10', and the qu show 'Dotto'.

ATV was reconstituted as Central Independent Television 1981 when the IBA's franchise conditions were changed.

Before each TTT transmission there was a musical overture called the 'Three Rivers Fantasy' (written by Arthur Wilkinson which was a medley of Tyneside songs such as Blaydon Races and Water of Tyne. Part of the medley was a jingle which was based on the Sailor's Hornpipe. An anchor gradually transformed into the Tyne Tees logo in synchronisation with the jingle. To an impressionable 13 year-old this was nothing short of magic. Tyne Tees staff nicknamed the animated logo 'The Polo Mint'. *(Images transferred from Tyne Tees Television's archives by Multicord Video, Dunston.)*

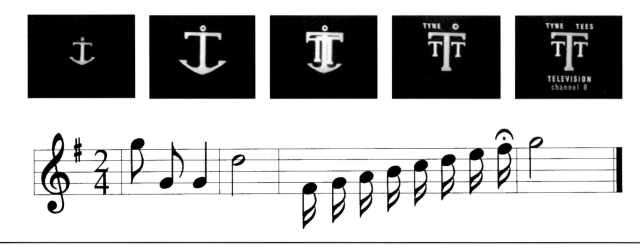

e Networked Programmes

V's 'Dotto', introduced by Shaw Taylor, was based on the
ldren's magazine game where you join up the dots to make
icture. The contestants had to guess the name of the
sonality whose face was made up by a series of dots. A
rectly answered question was rewarded by some of the dots
ng joined up. There were no fancy computers in those days
the dots had to be joined up by hand. The dot picture was
wn onto a frosted glass screen by an artist who stood behind.
u could sometimes see the artist's hand as he worked away.
he contestant guessed correctly early in the round, there
s pandemonium as the artist had to quickly complete the
ole face in seconds flat while the quiz master padded. I
nember that sometimes the face was still being completed
en the camera panned over to confirm that the contestant's
ess was correct. As a child, I constructed a miniature Dotto
me where I used greaseproof paper on a piece of picture
me glass as the dotto screen. I would lightly trace a face in
ncil on the paper and then draw in a series of dots in ink.
om the front of the screen you could see the ink dots but not
pencil lines. I would then connect the dots in ink as my
usin David, who was sat in front of the glass, correctly
swered some questions from my quiz book.

nother quiz show with an interesting piece of razzmatazz
s 'For Love or Money'. The prize money for each question
s displayed on the screen   with a stroke separating the
llings and pence.
   22/2   When the question was posed, the stroke moved
om left to right and back again. When the contestant
swered, the stroke froze. A correctly answered question
uld therefore win 2d minimum or 222s (£11.10) maximum.

British-made hour-long film series with a haunting whistled
eme tune was 'Ghost Squad' which was first screened on
TT at 8:30pm on Saturday 9 September 1961. Shortly after
e war, Scotland Yard, worried by rising crime figures,
stituted the famous Ghost Squad which comprised specially
ined officers out of uniform. Their job was to keep an
tra close watch on criminal activities throughout the country
d often actually, to masquerade as criminals themselves.
-Detective Inspector Gosling, once in charge of the Squad,
ote a book about his work and it formed the basis of 'Ghost
quad'. In charge of the 'Ghost Squad' in the series was Sir
ndrew Wilson, who expanded the organisation to an
ternational level. He was a tough and experienced police
ficer who picked and trained all members of his highly
pable team. Sir Andrew was played by a real-life knight-
r Donald Wolfit.
an still whistle the theme tune after 37 years. (The power of
levision on a young mind!)

The famous movie director Alfred Hitchcock gave his name
to a murder mystery series which was first transmitted on TTT
at 10:30pm on 22 September, 1961. The stories , which always
had a twist in the tail, were introduced and concluded by the
man himself. The memorable theme tune was entitled 'Funeral
March of a Marionette' ** and was actually from a ballet by
Alexander Gounod. The programme's logo was a caricature
of the Master of Suspense.

Probably the most popular networked programme of all time
is 'Coronation Street' which was (and still is) produced at
Granada's Manchester studios. The first episode of the 'Street'
was transmitted by Granada on 9 December, 1960 but the
programme did not form part of Tyne Tees' schedule until
Wednesday, 25 January 1961 The programme first went out
on Wednesdays and Fridays from 6:55pm till 7:30pm. but
later in the year it moved to Mondays and Wednesdays.

Many North-Easterners thought that all ITV programmes were
made at Tyne Tees and autograph hunters would wait at the
foot of the City Road studios' steps waiting to see Ward Bond
from 'Wagon Train', Clint Walker from 'Cheyenne', or any of
the many other Hollywood stars who appeared in ITV's film
presentations.

** This theme and many more from early TV programmes are
featured on a series of CD's called 'Televisions Greatest Hits'.

Another great favourite was 'Bonanza'. I remember being fascinated by the map which was shown bursting into flames during the opening credits. I used to try and trace the map with a fountain pen onto the TV screen. It was useless as the map was only on screen for two seconds. My mother used to say, 'What are all these dirty marks on the TV screen?' I wrote to Tyne Tees to ask if they could send me a copy of the map and they wrote back saying,
'Sorry, the map is copyright.'

Two years ago, during a holiday in California and Nevada, we visited the Ponderosa Ranch, now a tourist attraction in a village called Incline located on the north shore of Lake Tahoe which straddles the border between the two states. The ranch-house there is where some of the filming for the series actually took place (indoors and outdoors.) When we walked into the souvenir shop, I couldn't believe it. There it was for only one dollar! - the map of the Ponderosa. It was a childhood dream come true 35 years later.
Reproduction of the map is by kind permission of the Ponderosa Ranch theme park.

The schedule shown opposite epitomises a superb Saturday evening's viewing on Tyne Tees in 1961. 'Candid Camera's most famous stunt was where Jonathan Routh pushed his broken-down car into a repair shop where the mechanics were bamboozled by the fact that it did not have an engine. Thirty-six years later Bob Monkhouse is still presenting peak-viewing time TV shows. As a schoolboy, my pronunciation of the programme title 'Cheyenne' caused a few laughs in my auntie's house when I read her copy of the Viewer out loud. Lonnie Donnegan's appearance in 'Saturday Spectacular' recalls memories of my efforts to construct a string bass with a tea chest and broom handle. Morecambe and Wise make a guest appearance soon before their own BBC show took off. Ruby Murray also appeared in 'Saturday Spectacular'. Her song 'Softly Softly' had been a No1 hit six years earlier in 1955.
'77 Sunset Strip' was my favourite networked programme. It was first transmitted on Saturday 25 June, 1960. The main characters were Jeff Spencer (Roger Smith), and Stuart Bailey (Efram Zimbalist, Jr.) as the Private Eyes, and Kookie (Edward Byrnes) the 'jive-talking' car park attendant of Dino's Restaurant next door. As a budding musician, I loved the incidental music and used to practice my drumming technique on my knees when the show was playing, much to the annoyance of my parents. I kept a scrap book of cuttings from 'The Viewer' about 'Sunset Strip' and to complete the set of episodes, I made an appointment to go to 'The Viewer' offices

in Forth Lane, Newcastle to look through their archives. remember the woman who saw me was rather puzzled abo my over-enthusiasm for the programme. I was so obsess with 'Sunset Strip' that I constructed a cardboard model of t exterior set of the famous detective agency's premises a Dino's Restaurant. In 1998 I made a pilgrimage to 8524 Sun Boulevard in Hollywood, Los Angeles which is where sor of the outdoor scenes for '77 Sunset Strip' were filmed. T original buildings have gone and the site is now occupied by cinema, however, a plaque on the pavement confirms th Warner Brothers filmed scenes of the programme at that sp from 1958 to 1964.

Max Bygraves' programme 'Roamin' Holiday' featured fil of Max on holiday, roaming around the town of Alassio on t Italian Riviera. Occasionally he would meet residents w could sing and he'd invite them to appear on his show. A ni year-old Italian girl called Piccola Pupa appeared many tim singing and entertaining during the second half of Max's sho which was staged as a cabaret in the Cafe Roma.
There were many weird and wonderful products advertised 'The Viewer'. The advertisement for a sunray lamp show opposite seems to describe the device as a panacea for all ill

●●●

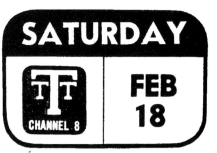

15   CANDID CAMERA
starring
BOB MONKHOUSE
who introduces
JONATHAN ROUTH
and the *Candid Camera*
elevision's "Hidden Eye" catches you in
se-up as you face some of life's unexpected
problems
BILL BRAMWELL supplies the music
Devised by ALLEN FUNT
Ideas by JOHN WHITNEY *and*
ARTHUR DAVIDSON
Additional material by DENIS GOODWIN
Directed by RONNIE TAYLOR
An ABC Production

45   CHEYENNE
starring
CLINT WALKER
in
THE LONG ROPE
CAST:

eyenne	**Clint Walker**
go Parma	**Peter Whitney**
th Graham	**Merry Anders**
ed Baker	**Donald May**
ed Moriarity	**Alan Baxter**
Warren	**James Hurst**
nny Kent	**Frank Albertson**
Maybe	**Dehl Berti**
ry Pierce	**Mary Alan Hokanson**
eyenne as a boy	**Dick Bellis**
ndy Pierce	**Craig Marshall**
yette Pierce	**Cherrill Lynn**
nister	**Forrest Taylor**

eyenne Bodie returns to the town where
was raised and finds himself settling an
bitter score with the powerful, ruthless
go Parma. Trouble really begins when
eyenne decides to run for sheriff against
rma—and wins!

40   SATURDAY SPECTACULAR
This week
LONNIE DONNEGAN
introduces
RUBY MURRAY
MORECAMBE AND WISE
MIKI AND GRIFF
MALCOLM GODDARD DANCERS
ACK PARNELL and his ORCHESTRA
Dance Direction by MALCOLM GODDARD
Designer PHILIP HICKIE
Produced by DICKY LEEMAN
An ATV Production

30   NEWS

35   77 SUNSET STRIP
starring
ROGER SMITH
EDWARD BYRNES
in
THE JUKE BOX CAPER
CAST:

ff Spencer	**Roger Smith**
okie	**Edward Byrnes**
zanne	**Jacqueline Beer**
arylyn King	**Patricia Donahue**
n Gale	**Ted De Corsia**
Temple	**Anthony George**
Gilmore	**Keith Byron**
nda Atkins	**Lisa Davis**
ike Andre	**Michael Harris**
eet Johnson	**Oliver McGowan**
nnie Mayes	**Suzanne Edward**

ff Spencer poses as a singer in order to
mask the master mind of a clever blackmail
g. But when Jeff and Kookie begin to probe
ey find themselves close to death
Directed by IDA LUPINO
Produced by HOWIE HORWITZ
Executive producer: WILLIAM T. ORR
Produced under the personal supervision of
JACK L. WARNER

9.30   ROAMIN' HOLIDAY
starring
MAX BYGRAVES
with
ERIC ROGERS and his ORCHESTRA
Written by MAX BYGRAVES *and* PETER DULAY
Photographed by WARWICK ASHTON
Directed by DICKY LEEMAN
Produced by BILL WARD
A Blossom TV Production
An ATV Presentation

10.0   THEATRE 70
presents
ANSWERED PRAYERS
by FREDERIC RAPHAEL
From a story by TRUMAN CAPOTE
starring
NIGEL STOCK
MARGOT VAN DER BURGH
and
MARGARET TYZACK
CAST:

Jimmy	**Nigel Stock**
Gwenda	**Margot Van Der Burgh**
Porter	**George Dare**
Operator	**Peggy Evans**
Mrs. Breasley	**Doris Hare**
Roger	**Terence Brook**
The woman	**Margaret Tyzack**

Jimmy is a parasite who has never found it
difficult to graft his way through life, until a
mysterious voice comes to warn him that his
course is just about run
Produced by ANTONY KEAREY
An ATV Production
(See Page 7)

11.0   ARTHUR HAYNES ENTERTAINS
A few minutes of fun with one of the best-
loved television personalities
An ATV Presentation

11.10   WHIPLASH
starring
PETER GRAVES as Christopher Cobb
in
DIVIDE AND CONQUER
CAST:

Chris Cobb	**Peter Graves**
Dan Ledward	**Anthony Wickert**
Sir John Wickett	**Harry Dearth**
Cowan	**Colin Croft**
Fry	**Owen Weingott**
Bryant	**Kirk Fabian**
Witton	**Lionel Long**
Everett	**Bruck Wheeler**
Billy-Jo	**Henry Murdoch**
Tom	**Simon Cain**
Nellie	**Patricia Connolly**
Briggs	**George Wallace, Jr.**

Chris Cobb is commissioned by the Government to escort Land Commissioner Sir John
Wickett on an expedition into the outback
to search for a pass through a dividing mountain range that would open up the pastoral
land beyond for development and settlement.
But, unknown to them, this pass is already
in use by a vicious mob of killers and cattle
thieves led by a man called Fry

11.40 (approx) THE EPILOGUE
Canon O. N. Gwilliam, Rector and Rural
Dean of Houghton-le-Spring, Co. Durham

Close down

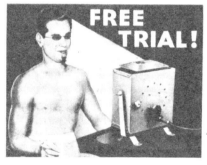

A memorable Sunday night's viewing on Tyne Tees Television in 1960.
To fulfil the franchise conditions, the 'God-Slot' started at 6:15pm.

On this night in January, Brucie introduced Cliff and the Shads. On 'Beat the Clock' the contestants were nearly always asked if they could come back next week. The finale featured the famous revolving stage and the theme tune that everyone 50ish or older can hum whilst shuffling sideways and waving.

'Maverick' was on at 10 (as my old pappy used to say).

6.5 NEWS
ITN brings you the latest news

6.15 SUNDAY BREAK
The Sunday Club for Teenagers
with
**THE REV. KENNETH SLACK
KENNY BAKER**
Club's music by
THE ROY MARSH QUINTET
with young people from the British Isles ; a window on their world and their approach to religion and living
Directed by EDDIE KEBBELL
An ABC Production

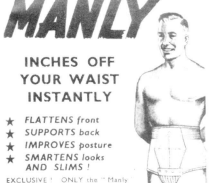

●●●●●●●●●●●●●●●●●●●●●●●●●

7.0 ABOUT RELIGION
THE QUESTION OF UNITY
A discussion on the divisions that exist between the Christian Churches, and the hopes for reunion with one another, with :
The Rev. Kenneth Woollcombe, Anglican Chaplain of St. John's College, Oxford
The Rev. Donald Soper, Methodist Minister of Kingsway Hall, London
and **The Rev. Edward Taylor,** of the Catholic Missionary Society
Chairman : **Norman Fisher**
Produced by MICHAEL REDINGTON
An ATV Production

7.25 NEWS
ITN brings world news to you

7.30 CANNONBALL
starring
PAUL BIRCH as Mike
WILLIAM CAMPBELL as Jerry
in
ROADEO
Jerry has a difficult time persuading Mike to enter the annual trucking roadeo—a test of driving skills and the mastery of safety rules and regulations. Mike has twice been a winner of the competition and he wants Jerry to be this year's victor

8.0 VAL PARNELL'S SUNDAY NIGHT AT THE LONDON PALLADIUM
Direct from the world's most famous variety theatre
starring
CLIFF RICHARD
and the Shadows
THE PLATTERS
with full supporting company
**The London Palladium Girls and Boys
Cyril Ornadel and the Palladium Orchestra
BRUCE FORSYTH**
comperes this sparkling show and introduces
BEAT THE CLOCK
the ever-popular game in which the audience takes part
(Presented by arrangement with Goodson and Todman and CBS)
THE JACKPOT PRIZE—£500
(unless won Jan 10)
Dance direction by LIONEL BLAIR
Designed by ANTHONY WALLER
Executive producer : VAL PARNELL
Produced by ALBERT LOCKE
An ATV Production
(See Page 19)

9.0 NEWS
Keep up to date with **ITN**

9.7 ARMCHAIR THEATRE
presents
MISFIRE
by LESTER POWELL
starring
**ADRIENNE CORRI ROBERT SHAW
JOHN BENTLEY**
CAST IN ORDER OF APPEARANCE :
Police Sergeant .... **Colin Douglas**
Helen Renfrew .... **Adrienne Corri**
Mark Renfrew .... **Robert Shaw**
Stephen Craig .... **John Bentley**
Clergyman .... **Anthony Woodruff**
Miss Pembroke .... **Mary Wimbush**
Designed by TOM SPAULDING
Directed by GUY VERNEY
Producer SYDNEY NEWMAN
Helen Renfrew is alone in her house on Salisbury Plain when the police warn her that a murderer is at large. Later a man tries to force her door . . .
An ABC Production
(See Page 11)

SUNDAY

TT CHANNEL 8 JAN 17

10.7 MAVERICK
starring
JACK KELLY
in
THE BURNING SKY
Danger is Bret Maverick's business . . . business is good ! He is a man alone, roan free as an unbranded calf. Another exci hour of action-crammed stories of the Wes frontier

11.0 MANTOVANI
MUSICAL JOURNEY
Relax and listen to the music of the Manto strings

THE EPILOGUE
by the **Rev. Thomas G. Aikman,** Tri Presbyterian Church, Newcastle-upon-T
Close down

3 MID-WEEK ROUNDABOUT

magazine that takes you round about North-East and casts a lively eye on the ts of the week

Interviewers:
TOM COYNE
ALERIE PITTS   JACK CLARKE

Edited by LESLIE BARRETT
Designed by JOHN DINSDALE
Produced by AUD PENROSE

A Tyne Tees Production

30 YOUNG AT HEART

teenage programme with mum-and-dad eal

Compere : JIMMY SAVILE

featuring
LERIE MASTERS   RAY COUSSINS
THE HILLCRESTERS
THE VISIONAIRES

uest Stars : THE ENGLAND SISTERS

Settings by BILL McPHERSON
Produced by MALCOLM MORRIS

A Tyne Tees Production

0 RAWHIDE

starring
IC FLEMING   CLINT EASTWOOD

in
INCIDENT AT RED RIVER STATION

with
Guest star JAMES DUNN

CAST :
Favor .... Eric Fleming
wdy Yates .... Clint Eastwood
Flood .... James Dunn
kin .... Robert F. Simon
u Paris .... Stanley Clements
e Nolan .... Sheb Wooley
shbone .... Paul Brinegar
shy .... Jim Murdock
Quince .... Steve Raines
Scarlet .... Rocky Shahan

Written by CHARLES LARSON
Directed by GENE FOWLER JNR.
Produced by CHARLES MARQUIS WARREN

and Rowdy come across a dedicated ysician attempting to fight ignorance and r of smallpox along the frontier. They are rrified to learn that the doctor is being vented from giving vaccinations by a man o has taken it upon himself to fight the ease with his own ignorant methods

(See Pages 8-9)

55 THE LOVE OF MIKE

starring
MICHAEL MEDWIN

with
BRIAN WILDE
CARMEL McSHARRY
GEORGE RODERICK

Settings designed by BERNARD GOODWIN
Edited by RAY HELM
Directed by BILL HITCHCOCK

An Associated-Rediffusion Production

25 SPOT THE TUNE

with
JACKIE RAE and
MARION RYAN

n ear for " pop " music n win challengers cash rizes in this gay musical uiz. And someone may ve a chance for the ckpot, which increases y £100 weekly until on. If not won on May 5th the jackpot will and at £200

Music by
PETER KNIGHT and his ORCHESTRA

Designed by DAN SNYDER
Directed by WILFRED FIELDING
Produced by MARK WHITE

A Granada Production

8.55 FOUR JUST MEN

starring
DAN DAILEY
HONOR BLACKMAN

in
THE GRANDMOTHER

CAST :
Tim Collier .... **Dan Dailey**
Nicole .... **Honor Blackman**
Madame de Seiberd .... **Marie Ney**
Colonel de Seiberd .... **Fred Kitchen**
Guy de Seiberd .... **Trader Faulkner**
Madeleine de Seiberd .... **Joanna Dunham**
Raoul .... **John Van Eyssen**
Waiter .... **John Dearth**
Manservant .... **Arthur Gomez**

Screenplay by MARC BRANDEL
Directed by DON CHAFFEY
Produced by JUD KINBERG
A Hannah Fisher Production for Sapphire Films Ltd.

A scandal, involving the supply of faulty ammunition to a French battalion fighting in Algiers, is investigated by American journalist Tim Collier. Collier discovers that if all the facts are brought to light the reputation of one of the most honoured families in France will be ruined, and for this reason the proud and aristocratic matriarch of the family is determined to prevent him revealing the truth

9.25 NEWS

ITN's spotlight on world news

9.35 SPORTS DESK

introduced and edited by
GEORGE TAYLOR
of the *News Chronicle*

Tyne Tees Television brings you the latest news, views and personalities from North-East sport

Directed by DON GOLLAN
A Tyne Tees Production

9.50 OVER THE COUNTER

A five-minute Advertising Magazine featuring
DAVID REES

Script by LISLE WILLIS
Produced by DON GOLLAN

A Tyne Tees Production

9.55 SEAT IN THE STALLS

presents
BURMA VICTORY

The story of the epic achievement of the 14th Army from 1942 to the surrender of the Japanese at Rangoon. The film includes the arrival of Admiral Louis Mountbatten to take over the S.E.A.C. Command and the landing of 10,000 of Wingate's Chindits in a jungle clearing.

Directed by CAPTAIN ROY BOULTING
Produced by the British Army Film and Photography Unit
(See Page 7)

11.20 NEWS

THE EPILOGUE
by the REV. MALCOLM A. BEATON, Geneva Road Baptist Church, Darlington

Close down

The Adverts

By today's standards the advertisements then were probably very poor and corny, but were such a novelty for many people in the North-East, that they remained riveted to their seats during the commercial break. The first advertisement to be screened on TTT was for Welch's Toffee. The daughter of Mr Welch is Denise who plays Natalie in Coronation Street.

Remember the beatnik dog who wore dark glasses whilst playing the drums and pleading to his owner to 'Open the can man'.

A brand of cigarettes called Herbert Tareyton were often advertised in The Viewer. An image of the advert has been deliberately omitted because of the advertising restrictions for cigarettes these days, but the ads always featured a photograph of a scantily clothed young woman and the caption, "Today's girl prefers a man who smokes Herbert Tareyton cigarettes with the rich Kentucky flavour. Only 4/- (20p) for 20.'

A young lad looks out of the window and watches his mother walk down the front path. She opens the gate, closes it behind her and makes her way to the shops. The lad is thinking to himself all the time he watches her, 'Don't forget the fruit gums, mum.' On the following adverts text typed in *italics* is an invitation to sing the words... preferably alone in a locked room, in case your family think you've gone barmy.

What's blue and has four bums?
'Bum, bum, bum, bum, Esso Blue.'
Esso sign means happy motoring, call at the Esso sign.
Murray Mints, Murray Mints, the too good to hurry mint.
Raelbrook Toplin; the shirts you don't iron.
John Collier, John Collier, the window to watch.

A mother sends her young son to buy some Plumrose chopp ham with pork. After a long walk to the shops, reciting name of the product all the way, he holds up the money to shopkeeper and asks for, 'Humrose plopped pam with cha (Or something like that.)

You'll look a little lovelier each day, with wonderful p Camay. Sung by Matt Monroe.
Keep going well, keep going Shell. Sung by Michael Hollid

Can you remember when paper tissues were interleaved in box so you didn't have to fumble for a tissue like you have now? As you picked one, the next was ready automatically *Soft, strong, pops-up too, Kleenex Tissues are made for yo*

Opal Fruits made to make your mouth water.
Fresh with the tang of citrus. Four refreshing fruit flavou
Orange, lemon, strawberry, lime. Opal Fruits made to ma your mouth water
.

Cherry B, Cherry B, Cherry B.... It's Cherry B for me.

Folks invented some strange uses for vacuum cleaners in those days but "drying your hair?"

Name the product - answers on page 137.
(Extra points if you can sing the jingle.)

1. *Make the day, make the day.....*
2. *A little dab'll do ya...*
3. *You'll wonder where the yellow went.....*
4. *Don't just say brown ....*
5. *All around the house......*
6. *Do yourself a favour, have a ***, chocolate bar with the fruit surprise.*
7. *Bridge that gap......*
8. *A million housewives every day, pick up a tin of beans and say.....*
9. *You're never alone with a .....*

SPOT ADVERTISEMENT RATES

Segment	15 seconds	30 seconds	45 seconds	60 seconds
MONDAY to FRIDAY	£	£	£	£
Lunchtime	25	40	50	55
Up to 5.00	20	35	45	50
5.00 to 6.00	50	75	95	110
6.00 to 7.00	60	90	110	130
7.00 to 7.30	80	120	145	170
Mon. to Thur. 7-30 to 10-35	90	140	170	200
Friday 7-30 to 10-35	100	155	190	220
10.35 to 11.00	55	80	100	115
11.00 to Close	25	40	50	55
SATURDAY				
Up to 4.40	20	35	45	50
4.40 to 6.00	40	60	75	85
6.00 to 7.00	45	70	85	100
7.00 to 11.00	80	120	145	170
11.00 to 11.30	55	85	105	120
11.30 to Close	20	35	45	50
SUNDAY				
Up to 2.30	20	35	45	50
2.30 to 3.15	30	45	55	65
3.15 to 5.00	65	100	125	145
5.00 to 6.15	70	105	130	150
6.25 to 7.35	60	90	110	130
7.35 to 10.45	120	180	220	260
10.45 to 11.15	60	90	110	130
11.15 to Close	20	35	45	50

Shepherds of Gateshead, the
biggest and the best store.
Shepherds of Gateshead,
have what you're looking for, there's
so much to see and the
car-park is free, come
shopping at Shepherds with the
whole family.

In the 1960's Tyne Tees launched a major marketing campaign to sell advertising time. It was called 'Through Plan' and many marketing techniques were devised and promotional material distributed. Among the promotional material was a poster called 'Sweet Sixteen' which showed the 16 people who were involved with the campaign; 15 men and one woman. There were photographs of all 16 people and accompanying the photo of each man was his full name and job title, and a resume giving his age, marital status, qualifications and career history. Accompanying the woman's photograph was simply, Judith, 34-26-37. It was a profound statement of the culture of the time and would certainly cause an uproar if such a thing was done today.

How much did it cost to advertise on Tyne Tees in 1959? The table opposite gives the rates of charges in September 1959. £100 for 15 seconds of prime time may not seem very much until you compare it with the average wage then of £12 a week.

The Ad Mags

The Advertising Magazines purported to be programmes but were simply out-and-out selling. Tyne Tees wasn't the first station to produce Ad Mags but seemed to produce more than any other company. Programmes such as 'Ned's Shed' and 'Mary Goes to Market' appeared regularly on TTT. They usually had a loose story line running through them which linked one product to the next. There was always a Production Assistant timing each mention of a product to the second. This was essential as many of the advertising agents who had commissioned the ad would time the items when they were transmitted and if someone had paid for ten seconds and only got nine, there was big trouble.

When TTT first started transmissions there were three Ad Mags. 'Information Desk' went out on a Sunday at 4:40pm, 'Ned's Shed' was screened on Mondays at 6:40pm and 'Come Shopping with Daphne Padell' was transmitted on Tuesdays at 6:45pm.

**6.45 COME SHOPPING WITH
DAPHNE PADELL**
An Advertising Magazine
Join **DAPHNE PADELL** and **BARRIE GOSNEY**, and see the latest ideas in food, fashion and furnishings
Script by DAPHNE PADELL
Designed by MALCOLM DAWSON
Produced by LEONARD WHITE
A Tyne Tees Production

Floor Manager John Loukes relaying the Director instructions to Daphne Padell and Barrie Gosney durir rehearsals of 'Come Shopping'. Arthur Best is on camer

36

6.40 NED'S SHED

CAST:

Ned .... **Lisle Willis**
Knocker Brown .... **Dan Douglas**
Wife .... **Maud Foster**

Ned and his next door neighbour, Knocker,
introduce a new style of advertising magazine

Produced by DAVID CROFT

A Tyne Tees TV Advertising Magazine

Lisle Willis was one of the writers and presenters on Ned's Shed. Lisle later became a producer/director at TTT and was noted for his production of 'Say it in Russian' which was the first of its kind on ITV.

avid Petrie, who was Trainee Cameraman when Tyne Tees rst started transmitting, remembers the ad mags vividly and calls some of his memories.

he advertising magazines, very fashionable at the time, were minute programmes which endorsed about 12 products. hey moved at breakneck speed. I was responsible for moving e main camera dolly about the studio, and the senior meraman produced a pile of cards which contained a list of l the scripted shots, including price captions and close-ups products. We began a basic rehearsal, with the production sistant calling times and shot numbers over the headphones. vo minutes elapsed and proceedings ground to a halt at about ot 27. The cameraman, Chris Palmer, turned to me, looked the stationary dolly and said 'We should have moved position ur times in that section and it gets faster later.' The camera e lights were going on and off every four seconds and a rrent of instructions was coming from the control room. I member being thoroughly confused and scared.

ne of the first ad-mags Tyne Tees produced was called 'Ned's hed' which was supposedly set on an allotment in East orthumberland with Ned talking to his neighbour Knocker rown about garden tools, slug pellets and all sorts of do-it-ourself products. The script was very superficial and corny ecause they had to invent ways of introducing new products. or example, Ned would accidentally trip over a wheelbarrow hich prompted him to say, 'Oh this is my new wheelbarrow. o you like it? You can buy one just like this at Shepherds of ateshead.' It was appalling and there was only a very limited ange of products you could advertise in this way. On the last oisode of 'Ned's Shed' it was arranged for the shed to catch re, much to the delight of the Production staff.

dvertising costs were relatively large, even in those days, nd the clients kept a strict eye on the presentation of their ares and the time they were paying for. The clients' epresentatives were asked to sit in a viewing room while the rogramme was being rehearsed, and all communication from em had to be through a member of the Sales Department. ou would be two minutes into the rehearsal and the 'phone rom the viewing room to the control gallery would ng................. 'The necklace is too far to the left of frame.' fter a correction you would start again, and one minute later ey would say, 'Stop! The Daz packet is reflecting the light,' r 'the last reference to a particular product lasted only 29 econds instead of 30. This would continue for the next two ours until the show was finally recorded.

4.25 TRADER HORNE

An Advertising Magazine
featuring
KENNETH HORNE
with
ANN CROFT   STALLIBRASS
(*By permission of Graham Tennant*)
Script by KENNETH HORNE
Designed by JOHN DINSDALE
Produced by GEORGE ADAMS
A Tyne Tees Production

Ann Croft is David Croft's wife. Elaine Wells took over from Ann in May 1960.

10.45 MARY GOES TO MARKET

An Advertising Magazine
Introduced by
MARY MALCOLM
and
MICHAEL RATHBORNE
Designed by JOHN DINSDALE
Produced by MALCOLM MORRIS
A Tyne Tees Production

Mary Malcolm was one of the BBC's continuity announcers when television transmissions resumed after the Second World War. She was the grand-daughter of actress Lily Langtry.

6.45 HI THERE!

with
**CAROL AUSTIN   MAUREEN BECK
GILLIAN GALE
PETER LAYTON   DENNIS KIRKLAND**
Designed by BILL MCPHERSON
Produced by MALCOLM MORRIS
A Tyne Tees Production

'Hi There', was an ad-mag specifically aimed at teenagers and featured holidays, careers, clothes, cosmetics, confectionery, record players, and many other products that would be of interest to young people. Dennis Kirkland worked in Tyne Tees' property store but much later left Tyne Tees to make a name for himself as Producer of the Benny Hill Show.

The Announcers

The announcers at Tyne Tees Television gave the station its identity and guided the viewers through the wonderful new experience of Commercial Television. In those days the announcers were 'in vision' and were always immaculately dressed and groomed as if they had been invited to the Lord Mayor's Ball. They were as excited as the viewers at being involved with the birth of ITV in the North-East and their voices were filled with enthusiasm about the programmes they were introducing. The original team of four comprised Chief Announcer - Adrian Cairns, South Shields-born former radio personality Tom Coyne, 26 year-old actor James Lloyd, and Tyne Tees' first woman announcer, Sally Morton.

They became stars overnight and soon were in big demand by local business people to make public appearances in connection with company promotions.

Valerie Pitts (left) and Valerie Dennis discussing the next programme item.

In the early 1960's announcers, Jon Kelley, Valerie Dennis, David Hamilton, Valerie Pitts, and Mike Neville became familiar faces to North-East viewers.

Unknown to the viewers, one of the announcer's duties was to 'fill in' if a programme under-ran. This could happen without warning and one announcer described his job as long perio of boredom interspersed with moments of terror. 'It was very lonely job at times,' recalled Tom Coyne. ' One Christm Day, I agreed to do the afternoon duty. Most of the programm were either networked, on film or videotape, consequently the

MICHAEL NEVILLE

VALERIE DENNIS

TOM COYNE

JON KELLEY

ADRIAN CAIRNS

TWO GUINEAS will be paid to the writer of the best letter published in this feature every week. All letters published will win two free tickets to a Tyne Tees show. Address is: " In Your View," " The Viewer," Television Centre, City Road, Newcastle upon Tyne, 1.

THE 'GENIAL' ANNOUNCERS

★ **TWO-GUINEA LETTER** ★

SINCE 1957, I have been a regular visitor to the Nort East, spending about four or five months every yea there. When I get back to South Wales I find myse wishing for a glimpse of TTT's genial and friend announcers, Adrian Cairns, Valerie Dennis, Tom Coyn Jon Kelley and Michael Neville. May I say Thank yo to TTT for giving me such a warm, homely feeling ? T first time I ever saw TV was after an operation Sunderland Eye Infirmary, where I had my sight restore after years of blindness. Good luck to you all.—(M HUGH MORGAN, Pontypridd, South Wales.

38

ren't many people on duty. I think there was me, a VT/film [op]erator, and a security man. To cheer myself up, I thought [I'd] put on an act as if there was a party going on. I bounced [bal]loons, threw streamers, and talked to imaginary guests off [cam]era. I would say something like, 'We're having a great [par]ty here at Tyne Tees. I hope you are at home. I say Bing, [sto]p fooling around with Valerie over there.'

[So]me of the viewers were actually taken in. I received a lovely [let]ter from an old age pensioner who lived alone. She said [wh]at a marvellous thing it had been to join in the party at Tyne [Te]es on Christmas Day.'

[In] addition to her duties as announcer, Valerie Pitts, shown on [the] photograph opposite, was one of the regular interviewers [on] the local news programme, North-East Roundabout. She [lef]t the programme in 1960 to marry James Sargent who was [St]age Manager of the Sadler's Wells Opera Company. The [sto]ry goes that some time after they were married, they were [in]vited to a grand event where guests were announced on [arr]ival. The doorman recognised Valerie immediately and [an]nounced,

[L]adies and Gentlemen, Mr and Mrs Pitts.'

[Va]lerie was horrified and whispered to the doorman, 'No, it's [Sa]rgent.'

[Re]d faced, the doorman gave his revised announcement,

[Se]rgeant and Mrs Pitts.'

Much later, Valerie married the famous conductor Sir Georg Solti.

Tyne Tees announcer Jon Kelley, shown in the photograph below, had the enviable task of travelling around the world with a camera crew filming for a Tyne Tees series called 'Faraway Places' which was screened in 1961. Produced by George Adams, the programme featured items from the West Indies, Malta and New Zealand. Not such a glamorous assignment for Mike Neville in 1962, however. He had to tramp up and down the banks of the North-East's three rivers for the filming of the trio of documentaries called 'Your Heritage'.

On the following pages, some of Tyne Tees announcers recall their memories of the early years of Tyne Tees Television. I am deeply grateful for their contributions towards this book and, it was a terrific thrill for me to actually meet and chat with, Tom Coyne, Mike Neville, Bill Steel, George Taylor, and David Hamilton.

[S]ome of Tyne Tees' early presenters.

[L]to R: Valerie Dennis, Tom Coyne, James Lloyd, Jon Kelley and Margaret Robinson (Secretary).

Adrian Cairns

His face and voice were known by millions of viewers in the North-East and many described him as Mr TTT. He had a friendly, soothing style of presentation and most viewers felt at home with him linking the programmes. Adrian's most vivid memories of Tyne Tees are from the programme 'Star Parade' which he presented on most of the 237 editions. The programme featured excerpts from and news about the latest cinema films. Adrian wrote to me from his home in Bristol where he lives with his wife Laura. He recalled some memories of 'Star Parade'.

> **7.0   STAR PARADE**
> this week features films starring
> **ROBERT BEATTY**
> including his latest, *Shake Down*
> *Introduced by* ADRIAN CAIRNS
> *Edited by* FRED TUCKER
> *Directed by* BERNARD PRESTON
> **A Tyne Tees Presentation**

'It's difficult to select which name to drop or which location or studio visit to describe. The honours should go to Fred Tucker, then TTT Head of Film, who organized the programme content. As presenter of the programme, I did the interviews and scripted the film intro's and links. I remember when 'Lawrence of Arabia' opened in Newcastle, in order to review it on the programme the following night, one of the major cinema screened a special showing for myself alone at midnight. wife Laura joined me, and there we were, centre circle in vast empty auditorium, and on the Cinemascope screen endless desert before us with that interminably exciting s of Omar Sharif trotting towards us from the shimmer horizon on his camel. As it happened, Omar Sharif (thought!) caused Laura to faint (or was it the heat, or the f unit food?) when we met him on location in the plains north Madrid on the set of 'The Last Days of the Roman Empi The enormous reconstruction of the Roman Forum and oth buildings and statues was a tourist attraction for years af the film was finished. The film starred Sophia Loren, Alec Guinness, and Stephen Boyd as well as Sharif, but first two were unfortunately not on call the day we were the Instead, we witnessed the clash of the Roman and Pers armies on horseback, between which I was able to sna interviews with Boyd and the highly respected director, late Anthony Mann.

The 'Star Parade' unit had another, trip abroad to Gran Cana where Sir Cliff Richard and the Shadows, Susan Hampsh and Walter Matthau were shooting 'Summer Holiday' (or w it 'Wonderful Life'?) among the sand-dunes of Maspalom

Adrian Cairns and Fred Tucker (right) chat with Richard Harris at Elstree Studios. *Picture: Associated British Picture Corp*

Mentioning Sir Cliff Richard reminds me of the time that we invited members of both his fan-club in the North East and that of Elvis Presley to Studio One together. Both singers had films out in the same week and I had to be very careful in both viewing them and talking to the fans not to upset either party. They were seated apart, separated by a wide gangway in the studio (for the camera-dolly to run in, and me with my hand-microphone) and it was just as well as feelings and allegiances were running high on either side!

Finally, I cannot leave 'Star Parade' without mentioning what, at the time, was one of our better scoops. Getting in to Highbury Studios in North London when the Beatles were making their second film there ('Help!') was like getting into Fort Knox. The gates outside were besieged by hundreds of teenagers, and we had to convince some rightly tough security people that we really were invited. Lennon was the 'hard one', cynical and lethal about any questions, McCartney was charming and amiable as ever, and George and Ringo said as little as possible. Only a few years ago, I heard from relatives in the United States that they had seen me interviewing the Beatles during a documentary about the group which had obviously dug up the old 'Star Parade' material from somewhere.

'Spike Milligan caused a bit of a stir when he visited Tyne Tees Studios. He had been appearing on the 'One O'Clock Show' and generally causing mayhem by interrupting everyone's act. When the show ended, I was reading the news in one of the smaller studios and in walked Spike and interrupted transmission. It might have been funny if I hadn't been reading about a bus crash at the time.'

Adrian left Tyne Tees in 1964 to join the Bristol Old Vic Theatre School as Assistant Principal. The school has an international reputation for training actors, and its roll-call of ex-students reads like a star line-up from today's profession, including two Oscar winners, Jeremy Irons and Daniel Day-Lewis and other Award winners such as Miranda Richardson, Tim Pigott-Smith and Jane Lapotaire. Many other ex-students of the school are often seen on television and regularly at the National Theatre and Royal Shakespeare Company.

Adrian had intended to stay only five years at Bristol, but such were the attractions of the area, and the genius of his original colleague, the late Nat Brenner as Principal, that he stayed on for 25 years. Meanwhile he continued his 'other' career (by agreement), playing small parts for TV films, and doing frequent voice-overs for both ITV and BBC in the West. In 1979 Adrian became Associate Principal of the Bristol Old Vic Theatre School with Chris Denys, and eventually, at 65, he retired from the school in 1989. He continues regular initial audition sessions in London for aspirant students at the school, and does a little acting himself when asked. Recently he has appeared in 'Eastenders' as a University Chancellor giving Michelle her degree and in 'Kavanagh Q.C.' as a judge. Adrian recently worked for a new young director playing 'God' as a film projectionist - a strange epitaph to 'Star Parade'. In November 1998 Adrian will be seen acting with Juliet Stevenson in Carlton Television's remake of 'Cider with Rosie'.

Alongside his professional work, he continues writing, mostly on philosophical themes (especially the nature of time), having had a number of articles and pamphlets published. In 1996, he completed a major work, 'The Making of the Professional Actor: a History, an Analysis, and a Prediction', which was published in hardback by Peter Owen Publishers. Another work which is in progress is a wartime journal edited in fifty year's hindsight.

Laura Cairns

Adrian's wife Laura appeared in Tyne Tees productions such as the 'Jimmy James Show' and the 'One O'Clock Show' from time to time. She ran 'Laurian Limited' which was a Tyneside model agency in the early 1960's. She is now a freelance casting director.

Tom Coyne

Before joining Tyne Tees, Tom Coyne had made many broadcasts on BBC. He started his radio career on 'Children's Hour' at the Leeds and Manchester studios. He was heard in many BBC radio plays, documentaries and he compered the last series of the radio show 'Wot Cheor Geordie' which was a lunch-time show starring Bobby Thompson.

Tom's first duty in front of camera at Tyne Tees was to read the first ever Tyne Tees local news which went out on Thursday 15 January 1959 at 6:05pm just before Adrian Cairns interviewed the Prime Minister, Harold Macmillan. Tom was a very popular personality and a bit of a 'heart-throb' for many younger viewers. My wife clearly remembers him visiting her youth club in the early 60's and getting his autograph. I met Tom and his wife Pat when they were visiting the North-East. Tom told me about his first experiences at Tyne Tees.

'Hello again!

The letter from 'Black Television' invited me to London to audition for the job of Announcer with the new TV company which was to be launched in the North-East. What would they ask me to do? My work on BBC Radio had always been scripted, but surely on TV they would expect me to ad-lib if things went wrong.

On arrival in London on that July day in 1958, I bought a copy of the TV Times. London already had its own Commercial Television station and I thought I'd have a look at what they were showing that evening. The most heavily featured programme was about the closing of the Harringay Boxing Arena. As a keen fan of boxing, I thought, if they asked me to ad-lib, I'd talk about this programme just as if I was going on the air to plug it that night.

The hired studio in London where the audition was held was a grim place with simply a desk, a camera, a flood of lights, and a large clock. Hidden away in a control room were George and Alfred Black and the new station's Programme Controller, Bill Lyon-Shaw. It was the voice of Bill Lyon-Shaw which gave the instructions,

'Let's hear you read that script on the desk in front of you.' The script read, the voice boomed out again.

'Now, do you see that clock in front of you? We are going to set it to run for a minute. We want you to talk about anything you like for a minute and try to come out on the second.'

I had been practising ad libbing to time ever since the invitation to audition had arrived.

'I'll talk about one of the programmes on ATV tonight just as if I was on the air promoting it.' I replied. My practice sessions had been worthwhile. I came out on the second. The voice came over the speaker again,

'You've got the job. We'll drop you a line about the starting date.'

The starting date turned out to be the 1st December 1958 six weeks before the station, which was now called Tyne Tees Television, went on the air.

The Tyne Tees studios were like Bedlam as new directors, camera crews, studio crews and announcers met new colleagues, sorted out offices and began the process of settlin in to the TV Centre which was still overrun with the builder The announcers were Adrian Cairns, Sally Morton and myse Jimmy Lloyd was to join us before the station went on the a By the morning of December 2nd our voices were bein broadcast by the transmitter over slides and stills informin the people of the North-East what to expect when Commerci Television came into their lives.

The six weeks which followed were a period of enjoyabl activity culminating in the launch of the new service o Jan.15th, 1959. After the Duke of Northumberland ha officially opened the Station, the first programme took viewer on a roving tour of the studios with Sally Morton. During thi programme Adrian introduced myself and Jimmy Lloyd to th viewers. The whole evening which followed was one c controlled panic as one crisis seemed to follow another.

read the first ten minute news bulletin from the Presentatio Studio. Nothing had been timed and halfway through the new the director realised that we were in grave danger o overrunning.

Two minutes before the end of the news I had to introduc film of the Prime Minister, Mr. Harold Macmillan's visit t the North-East, do a voice over, and then hand over to Adria Cairns who was interviewing Mr Macmillan. As we had n earpiece communication in those days, the floor manager, Bo Hughes, crawled along the floor below camera shot, leane against the Desk, and in a loud whisper instructed me to 'Cu to bloody Mac.'. I then searched through the news script i nt of me until I came to the item on Mr Macmillan's visit to North-East and went into the introduction to the film.

e Prime Minister, the Rt. Hon. Harold Macmillan has spent day in the North-East and his tour began with a visit to the sside ship yards.'

at was when things began to go wrong. Up came a film of ly Smart's Circus.

next job on the launch night was to take part in 'The Big ow' at 7 o'clock. That too had its exciting moments which rian Cairns writes about in another part of this book. The nch of the new service was also the launch of my TV career d the day hadn't finished yet. I presented a programme ich I think was called 'Meet George and Alfred Black' which d the story of the Black family and their associations with ow business and the North-East. Before I left the studios on t opening night I looked down from the gallery steps at the shop of Durham who was speaking his Epilogue to bring first day's programmes to a close. The studio was packed th massed North-East choirs waiting to sing Handel's llelujah Chorus. I left the studio and took a taxi to my me in South Shields.

ell!' I said to my wife as she opened the door. 'How did the st day go? I've been heavily involved but, of course I haven't en any of the programmes.'

ell come into the lounge,' she said, 'and watch the Epilogue; Bishop is still talking.'

e Bishop had long overrun his scheduled five minutes. I'm d that some members of the choirs had fainted from the at as the Bishop warmed to his theme.

ne Tees Television was well and truly launched.'

m is best remembered for 'North-East Roundabout', a local ws programme which was first transmitted on Friday 16 nuary 1959. It was broadcast once a week at first but later ent to five nights a week. He presented the programme until final edition on Good Friday 1964. The opening sequence as film of a carousel with the camera moving closer and oser to the roundabout until a sort of stroboscopic effect as produced. A camera in the studio abbed across a roundabout set and the oduction people in the box cut from the lm to the studio camera which entually found Tom. The effect was uite stunning in those days and emonstrated the innovative style of the oduction staff. The roundabout set in e studio, however, was a little Spartan onsisting of wooden poles linked gether with rope. Still, money was carce in those days.

Much later, the opening scene was where Tom walked past large notice boards while the signature tune was playing. When the music stopped, Tom would welcome the viewers and introduce the first guest. Tom remembered the night when his first guest was Sir Arthur Bliss. He recalled the opening scene.

'Sir Arthur was Master of the Queen's Music and had written the music for many Royal events. We decided to substitute the normal signature tune with one of the fanfares from the Coronation of Queen Elizabeth II. We played the wonderful fanfare, I walked past the large boards, and as the music ended I said, 'Good evening. Our regular viewers may have noticed that we have changed our signature tune tonight to the fanfare composed for the Coronation of Her Majesty the Queen, by our first guest this evening, Master of the Queen's Music, Sir Arthur Bliss.'
He looked up at the camera and said,
'I didn't write that one you know.'

One of the nicest regular guests on 'North-East Roundabout' was Prime Minister Tony Blair's father, Dr Leo Blair. Dr Blair was a lecturer in law at the University of Durham. He used to appear on the programme quite regularly and answer viewer's questions on legal matters. He was a lovely man and a treat to work with. He was adopted as a prospective Conservative candidate, would you believe?

When people ask me who was the most interesting person I interviewed on the Show, I always reply, 'Bella Mathison', a Cullercoats fish-wife. In the early years of Tyne Tees, she was in her 80's and she had saved up enough money to buy a lifeboat. She was awarded the BEM. She used to appear on the Show dressed in her 'fish-wife outfit' and had the loveliest Northumbrian 'roll' you ever heard. We hit it off so well, and had so much fun, that she was asked back onto the show about four or five times. She was wonderful.'
On one edition of 'North-East Roundabout', Tom had the privilege of interviewing Sir John Gielgud and Sir Ralph Richardson who were appearing at the Theatre Royal at the

om Coyne in 1959 on the set of the cal news programme, 'North-East oundabout'.

6.40 NORTH-EAST ROUNDABOUT

A weekly magazine that takes you round about the North-East and casts a lively eye on events of the week
Introduced by TOM COYNE
Produced by H. K. LEWENHAK
A Tyne Tees TV Production

6.55 GUN LAW

starring
JAMES ARNESS
·with·
Dennis Weaver
and
Amanda Blake

Meet The Law of the roughest town in the Wild West—Marshal Matt Dillon of Dodge City

7.25 EMERGENCY—WARD 10 INTRODUCTION

7.30 EMERGENCY—WARD 10

with
CHARLES TINGWELL
and
BARBARA CLEGG

CAST INCLUDES :

Chris Anderson	**Desmond Carrington**
Nurse Julie Wayne	**Jean Aubrey**
Jane Graham	**Ann Sears**
Jake O'Dowd	**Shaun O'Riordan**
Dr. Latimer	**John Carson**
Dr. Whittaker	**Robert MacLeod**
Alan Dawson	**Charles Tingwell**
Sister Stevenson	**Iris Russell**
Peter Harrison	**Peter Howell**
Nurse Jo Buckley	**Barbara Clegg**

Script by MARGOT BENNETT
Original idea by TESSA DIAMOND
Designed by VIC SYMONDS
Directed by CHRISTOPHER MORAHAN
Produced by ANTONY KEAREY
An ATV Production

8.0 TAKE YOUR PICK

starring
MICHAEL MILES
who invites you to a half-hour of fun and excitement
Directed by AUDREY STARRETT
Produced by Arlington Television and Radio Ltd., for Associated-Rediffusion
An Associated-Rediffusion Network Presentation
(See Page 19)

8.30 THE ARMY GAME

starring
MICHAEL MEDWIN
ALFIE BASS
with

Bill Fraser	**Norman Rossington**
Ted Lune	**Frank Williams**

Written by SID COLIN, LARRY STEPHENS,
MAURICE WILTSHIRE *and* LEW SCHWARZ
Designed by STANLEY MILLS
Directed by MILO LEWIS

9.0 TELEVISION PLAYHOUSE

presents

MAXINE AUDLEY
PETER GRAY
YOLANDE TURNER
GORDON CHATER
in
PRIVATE LIVES
by Noel Coward

Adapted for television by NICHOLAS PALMER

CAST :

Elyot Chase	**Peter Gray**
Sibyl Chase	**Yolande Turner**
Victor Prynne	**Gordon Chater**
Amanda Prynne	**Maxine Audley**
Louise, the maid	**Brigid Panet**

Settings by PAUL MAYO
Directed by LIONEL HARRIS
An ATV Production by H. M. Tennent
(See Page 17)

10.0 NEWS

The facts—first and latest—from **ITN**

10.15 THE MELODY DANCES

with
CYRIL STAPLETON AND HIS BAND
Set designed by PEMBROKE DUTTSON
Produced by DICKY LEEMAN
An ATV Production

10.45 SPORTS DESK

Introduced by
GEORGE TAYLOR
News of tomorrow's big matches
Edited by BRIAN HARRISON
Produced by RAYMOND JOSS
A Tyne Tees TV Production

11.0 COOL FOR CATS

Modern music presented in the modern manner
Introduced by
KENT WALTON
Discs arranged by
KER ROBERTSON
Choreography by DOUGLAS SQUIRES
Designed by SYLVA NADOLNY
Directed by BRIAN TAYLOR

11.30 THE EPILOGUE

by **Father Paschal**

Close down

The schedule above details the first Friday night's viewing on Tyne Tees Television and shows the very first edition of North-East Roundabout introduced by Tom Coyne. Many readers will remember the routine; put the cat out, bring the dog in, make sure you have plenty of coal in, put the draught excluder along the bottom of the living room door and now that the week's work is finished, settle down for a good Friday night's telly on TTT. ATV's Emergen** Ward 10 had been running since 1957 so a 5 minu** introduction was screened for TTT viewers. It was ITV** first hit soap opera and ran for 10 years. Take Your Pi** had started even earlier in 1955 and ran for 13 years. T** programme was revived in the 1990's with Des O'Conn** as the new Quiz Inquisitor.

e. Tyne Tees arranged for a Rolls Royce to convey
distinguished guests from the Theatre to the studios.
two celebrities had never been to Newcastle before
on the way to the studios, they asked Tom if they
ld stop at the Quayside for a while so they could
a short walk by the legendary 'Coaly' Tyne. While
three were walking along, a 'canny' Geordie woman
tted Tom, crossed the road, and announced,

you're Tommy off the telly. How ye doin' pet? Can
ave ya autograph on this newspaper?'

n was embarrassed enough by that experience, but
en the woman asked if Sir John and Sir Ralph were
one important in show business, he was lost for
ds.

another occasion Tyne Tees were filming in Gibraltar
Tom was interviewing some of the British Soldiers
re who had requests for songs to be sung on the 'One
lock Show'. The crew were filming from a vantage point
h up on the Rock. A few hundred feet down was Gibraltar
son and you could see the convicts in the exercise yard.
m started his interview with one of the soldiers and suddenly
eordie voice was heard echoing from the prison yard.
y! Are ye Tom Coyne? What are ye deein here?'
was one of the prisoners in the exercise yard who was
viously from Newcastle. Tom explained that they were
ning soldiers requests for the 'One O'Clock Show'. The
nate shouted up to Tom.
in ye ask George Romaine if he'll sing one for me mother.'
urned out that he was a merchant seaman who was in prison
a few days because he'd been in a pub fight.

Jim Dumighan was researcher for 'North-East Roundabout'
for a while before he moved on to a highly successful career
with the BBC. Jim heard on the grapevine that the American
film star Rod Steiger was on a flying visit to Newcastle to see
his wife Claire Bloom who was starring in a play at the Theatre
Royal. He had arrived in the City without any UK currency.
It was quite late and when Jim telephoned Rod to invite him
onto 'North-East Roundabout' he was more concerned about
his lack of cash than appearing on local TV.
'Yes I'll appear on your show,' Rod agreed, 'for twelve English
pounds. But I want paying in cash, now.'
Jim was ecstatic at having won such a 'scoop' for only £12
and hurried 'round to the Royal Station Hotel with the money.
Rod came on the show that night and Tom Coyne was delighted
to interview him. Jim was ticked off by his boss for 'over-
spending' the petty cash.

Tom also presented the programme 'Spotlight' which focused
on controversial issues of the day. It was a pioneer in presenting
such issues as birth control, the social security system, and
river pollution. The programme was edited by Leslie Barratt
and the producer was 'Lew' Lewenhak. One special edition of
'Spotlight' in 1959 interviewed some of the NATO leaders on
the eve of the Parliamentarian's Conference. It was Tyne Tees'
first networked programme and was also their first outside
broadcast. It was transmitted live from Church House
Westminster and Tom's role was to give a resume of the history
of NATO and to introduce the chairman, Bob Boothby.

Tom recalled his memories of a time when TTT produced a
film documentary of the Durham Miners' Gala.
'In 1960, when the Durham Miners' Gala still attracted many
thousands of people, Lewenhak made a special film using, I
think, about six film crews. We set off with packed meals
early on the Saturday morning to film one of the miners' brass
bands starting off for the day. I was stationed in the window
of the Conservative Association offices opposite the County
Hotel where Hugh Gaitskell and the other Labour leaders were
making their speeches from the balcony. The Programme was
filmed until the sun went down and the crowds dispersed at
the end of Gala Day. While the late filming went on, I returned
to the studios with the early rushes to present a live trail of the

Jack Clarke was one of the interviewers on 'North-
East Roundabout'. He was noted for his no-nonsense
'In Depth' interviews.

Donald Sinden presenting 'The Viewer' awards Friday 4 March, 1960. Philip Jones (left) was 'Producer of the Year', Shirley Wilson 'Fem Personality of the Year', and Tom Coyne (right) 'M Personality of the Year'. The Award ceremony to place at the Empress Ballroom in Whitley Bay.

programme which was to go out at lunch time the following day. Lewenhak returned to the studio and worked right through the night editing the film from six camera crews. The programme, without rehearsal, went out the next day and I did the live commentary and interviewed a senior churchman about the religious significance of the day.'

'Coronation Street' at TTT

Tom told me an interesting story about the time that 'Coronation Street' was actually produced at Tyne Tees studios at City Road. At some time in 1963, all of the Granada TV studios were occupied during the production of the opera, 'Orpheus in the Underworld'. Most of the sets for 'Coronation Street' were dismantled and transported to City Road. Tom particularly remembers taking Violet Carson (who played Ena Sharples) and Doris Speed (who played Annie Walker) to the Egypt Cottage pub for a drink. He had worked with both artistes on BBC 'Children's Hour'.

Tom left Tyne Tees Television on Good Friday 1964 and joined the BBC the following Tuesday to present the nightly news magazine in the Midlands. He stayed with the BBC for more

than 16 years. During this time he was also one of presenters of 'Nationwide' for more than ten years wh he met up with Mike Neville from time to time.

He actually started the BBC programme 'Pebble N At One' with other Tyne Tees exiles Bob Langley a Marion Foster.
He presented the first series of 'Top Gear' with Ang Rippon and for three years played Gordon Armstro in 'The Archers'.

In 1980 he returned to Tyne Tees for four years presenti 'Northern Life' and the fully networked programme Better Read'. In the past few years he has been a boardroo director of a TV production company and presenter of weekly programme 'Contact' for Central TV.

4.40 INFORMATION DESK

An Advertising Magazine
featuring
KENNETH HORNE
with
Vincent Goodman   Patricia Allison
Designed by JOHN DINSDALE
Produced by BERNICE DORSKIND
A Tyne Tees Production

Tom's wife Pat (Patricia Allison) co-presented the Tyne Tees advertising magazine 'Information Desk' with Kenneth Horne. The programme was transmitted on a Sunday afternoon and was later called 'Trader Horne'.

Tom Coyne in 1998 checking the text of one of the earl drafts of 'Memories of Tyne Tees Television'.

••

.25   CISCO KID
starring
DUNCAN RENALDO
as Cisco
and
LEO CARRILLO
as Pancho

hen Cisco and Pancho call at a ranch owned
Turk Martine, a young hothead, they are
ed on by Turk who believes they are the men
no earlier had attempted to kill him. Sub-
quently, Cisco and Pancho are told by Turk
at he believes Jim Turner, a banker who
lds a mortgage on his ranch, to be behind the
urder attempt—the motive being the dis-
very of oil on the ranch

.55   NEWS
Keep up to date with ITN

.5   NORTH-EAST NEWS
The latest from Tyne Tees newsroom

.15   NORTH-EAST ROUNDABOUT
TUESDAY EDITION
nightly magazine that features people in the
orth-East and takes a lively look at events
rious, humorous and curious
Introduced by **TOM COYNE**
Interviewers :
ALERIE DENNIS   JACK CLARKE
Edited by JOHN BARRETT
Designed by JOHN DINSDALE
Directed by AUD PENROSE
A Tyne Tees Television Production

.30   SAILOR OF FORTUNE
starring
LORNE GREENE
as Grant Mitchell
in
STRANGER IN DANGER
CAST:

Kadir .... **Esmond Knight**
ram .... **Philip Leaver**
rnot .... **Christopher Lee**
cki .... **Lisa Daniely**
ssim .... **Gordon Needham**
rgt. Major .... **Humphrey Heathcote**
Directed by MICHAEL MCCARTHY
Written by LINDSAY GALLOWAY

hen Mitchell (" Mitch ") walks into Bab-Esh-
aul he walks into a load of trouble in the
ape of El Kadir, the Sheik. Mitch is looking
r Bon Curtis who has disappeared and the
eik has strong reasons for not letting Mitch
d him

.0   PENCIL AND PAPER
e quiz show which allows viewers to com-
te amongst themselves to test general know-
ge and I.Q
Introduced by
AW TAYLOR and GWYNNETH TIGHE
*or full enjoyment viewers should have
ncil and paper to hand)*
swers to the HANGOVER QUESTION
should be sent to :
angover Question, *Pencil and Paper*, 17 Great
umberland Place, London, W.1
Directed by DINAH THETFORD
Produced by JOHN IRWIN
An ATV Production

7.30   EMERGENCY—WARD 10
with
CHARLES TINGWELL
JILL BROWNE   RICHARD THORP
JANE DOWNS
CAST INCLUDES :

Peter Harrison .... **Peter Howell**
Derek Bailey .... **Brian Nissen**
J. Maxwell Rennie .... **John Longden**
Sister Phillips .... **Yvette Wyatt**
Mr. Mackie .... **Thomas Heathcote**
Norman Farley .... **Alan Browning**
Penny Foster .... **Margo Andrew**
Alan Dawson .... **Charles Tingwell**
John Rennie .... **Richard Thorp**
Audrey Blake .... **Jane Downs**
Carole Young .... **Jill Browne**

Script by JEAN SCOTT ROGERS
Original idea by TESSA DIAMOND
Designed by LEWIS LOGAN
Directed by JOHN COOPER
Produced by REX FIRKIN
An ATV Production

8.0   MESS MATES
starring
VICTOR MADDERN   SAM KYDD
as Tug Nelson   as Croaker Jones
ARCHIE DUNCAN   FULTON MACKAY
as Capt. Biskett   as Willie McGinniss
and
DERMOT KELLY
as Blarney Finnigan
in
THE NEW BROOM
Written by TALBOT ROTHWELL
Designed by STANLEY MILLS
Directed by KENNETH CARTER
A Granada Production

8.30   ADVENTURES IN PARADISE
starring
GARDNER McKAY
in
THE ARCHER'S RING
with guest stars
ANNA KASHFI
WAYNE MORRIS
CAST :

Adam Troy .... **Gardner McKay**
Monique Le Febure .... **Anna Kashfi**
Sam Agnew .... **Wayne Morris**
Geoffrey Carey .... **Murray Matheson**
Red Wickham .... **Paul Comi**
Oliver .... **Weaver Levy**
Daphne .... **Moyna Macgill**
Driver .... **Manuel De Pina**
Taku .... **Jerado De Cordovier**

Produced by RICHARD GOLDSTONE
Executive producer : DOMINICK DUNNE
Directed by BERNARD GIRARD

A pretty young Chinese girl, Monique Le
Fabure, approaches Adam Troy to charter *The
Tiki* in order to search for her grandfather.
The story she tells Adam is that a group of
old Chinese men, together with their valuable
possessions, were going back to their island
home to spend their few retiring years. They
were on an Atoll Airways flying boat, which
apparently disappeared, supposedly sunk. But
she says that she knows something is afoot

YOUR KIND OF MUSIC
one of the most popular network productions ever undertaken by Tyne Tees Television, makes its return to Channel Eight
soon

MR. BILL LYON-SHAW
programme controller of TTT, has written
an exclusive article for
THE VIEWER
about this programme and others coming
your way soon. Make sure you get next
week's " VIEWER "—order it now !

9.25   NEWS
ITN brings you foreign and home news

9.35   PLAY OF THE WEEK
presents
MARGARET LEIGHTON
LOUIS JOURDAN
in
GASLIGHT
By PATRICK HAMILTON
CAST :

Mrs. Manningham .... **Margaret Leighton**
Mr. Manningham .... **Louis Jourdan**
Rough .... **Lockwood West**
Elizabeth .... **Molly Urquhart**
Nancy .... **Joanna Vogel**
The gaslight dims, footsteps vibrate. Confused
by her husband's dominant personality, Mrs.
Manningham suppresses her fears and sus-
picions. Ex-Detective Rough reveals the
strange truth that has been obscured for so
many years

Designed by REECE PEMBERTON
Directed by GEORGE MORE O'FERRALL
*An Anglia Production networked
by Associated-Rediffusion*
(See Pages 8 and 9)

11.5   NEWS HEADLINES

THE EPILOGUE
by the **Rev. T. D. Bell**, St. Luke's Church,
West Hartlepool
Close down

James Lloyd

'When I got the 'phone call I was an actor, married to a young dancer. We had just bought a flat in Brixton, determined to stay in London to seek fame and fortune in the West End theatre. The 'phone call came from my agent who said that George and Alfred Black were looking for an announcer to join the presentation team for their new television station in Newcastle upon Tyne.

Now I had absolutely no intention of leaving London or of working in television, but in those days young actors didn't say 'no' to George and Alfred Black, so I went to the Tyne Tees studios determined to do my worst and not get the job. Looking back, I suppose my flippant approach to the audition must have come over as some sort of confidence in front of the camera. Whatever the reason, they offered me the position.

The whole atmosphere in the studios was so exciting that I decided there and then to abandon my ideas of fame and fortune in the London theatre and to throw in my lot with this new enterprise; joining Adrian Cairns, Tom Coyne and Sally Morton in the team of announcers.

I arrived as the concrete was setting and found the building bursting with young enthusiasts, most of whom knew as little about television as I did. Even before the station opened, the announcing team caused quite a stir; we took it in turns to be driven around the region's towns and villages in the impressive Outside Broadcast van, showing the flag to the locals. That was just about all we could show them as the van had no equipment in it, but it did put us one up on the BBC who until then had considered that the North stopped at Manchester.

Opening night saw me in Continuity, ready to cover any gaps between programmes with nothing between me and disaster but a copy of 'The Viewer' and a far from confident smile. In those days many more programmes were 'live' so you were never sure when you were going to be called upon to fill a gap. It was rather like being in a war; long periods of boredom, interspersed with moments of terror.

In the 'most embarrassing moment' category, it took me a long time to live down the occasion when I was covering an afternoon of horse racing. As I couldn't leave the studio, I was enjoying a lunch, brought down from the canteen, at the announcers' desk; so when the Transmission Controller pushed the wrong button, instead of a commercial break, the whole of the North-East of England saw me sitting there quietly eating sausage and chips!

One of the joys of working with the station was that there were plenty of opportunities to work on programmes. For me, it included everything from interviewing film stars for 'Star Parade', to stooging for Larry Parker and his rabbit on 'Happy-Go-Lucky'.

On one occasion I was co-presenting a live programme from a Joblings glass works in Sunderland with Shaw Taylor. Faced with a five minute under-run we ad-libbed for as long as we

James Lloyd, one of TTT's three regular newscasters, puts over the news in a human yet dignified manner

could until, running out of ideas, Shaw took a yard of a which we had seen being made and poured it over me. Perha as a placatory gesture, a couple of weeks later he recommend me to the Programme Controller at ATV and in 1961 I mov to Birmingham, my place at Tyne Tees Television being fill by a new boy called David Hamilton.

In the 60s and early 70s I returned many times to Tyne Tees a relief announcer, as a reporter on news programmes, a presenting shows like 'Three Rivers Club' and 'This is Yo Town'. Later, when I got involved in folk music and chang my name from James Lloyd to Jim, I came back again as Edi of two folk series: 'Walk Right In' with Wally Whyton, a 'Sing Out' with The Settlers.

Looking back, I remember those early days as the most exciti of times and I am truly grateful for my two years as sta announcer with Tyne Tees - they changed my life. I never g to be a star of the West End stage, but I did have a lot of fu

---

Popular Songs of the Time

'The Day that the Rains Came' - Jane Morgan

'Hoots Mon' - Lord Rockingham's XI

'Come Prima' - Mario Marini

'Come on Let's Go' - Tommy Steele

'It's Only Make Believe' - Conway Twitty

...lly Morton

...ly Morton, whose father was Managing Director of the ...neside engineering company Clarke Chapman, began her ...ucation at La Sagesse School in Jesmond, Newcastle upon ...ne and later won a scholarship to study drama at the ...iversity of Bristol. She was one of the original team of ...r announcers at Tyne Tees and at 21, was the youngest ...senter on British Television. She acted as host on the ...ving camera tour of the studios during the very first ...ogramme on Tyne Tees. Sally told me about that first night.

...ke Adrian Cairns, I have vivid memories of the opening ...ht at TTT as I presented the first programme that the viewers ...w on their screens. After Adrian's opening announcement, ... Duke of Northumberland declared us open and pressed ... button to put us 'On Air' officially. Then, my most vivid ...mory - as he did so, the other camera swung round to point ...wn the full length of Studio 1 to where I was standing waiting ...give the viewers a tour of Studios 1 and 2 and to introduce ...me of the important people connected with the station. That ...mera track down the long studio seemed to be in slow motion, ...was alone, on television, live, for the first time - help!

...ave another vivid memory of that programme - when I came ... move to speak to one of the Board members, I found that ... cable connected to the microphone concealed in my bra, ...s trapped under one of the camera dollies. As I tried to ...ove, the cable remained trapped, and I could feel the ...crophone slipping slowly down my cleavage! Ad-libbing ...e mad, I gave the cameraman, George Adams, a panic ...icken glare and eventually he got the message, moving the ...mera to one side to allow me to continue my tour of the ...dios.

...lly Morton with John Dinsdale (Head of Design) judging
painting competition for children which was organised
... staff of The Viewer magazine. The winners were invited
... visit the TTT studios and were presented with boxes of
...ints.

My most embarrassing experience came one Saturday afternoon when I was sitting in the continuity studio where I was duty announcer. I had half an hour before my next announcement while a programme of Popeye cartoons was in full swing. Unfortunately the film broke and the Transmission Controller, with no warning, switched to the continuity studio. Several thousand viewers saw me at my most relaxed, leaning back, feet on the desk and painting my fingernails. Few people in television have ever moved so fast! As you can imagine the press had a ball but judging by the jammed switchboard, the viewers loved it!

I never cease to marvel at how lucky I was to be chosen from thousands to be the first female announcer on Tyne Tees Television. Looking back over the years at all that's happened since, undoubtedly being in at the birth of the station was one of the most exciting and privileged experiences of my life.'

Big News Stories of early 1959

* Buddy Holly killed in a plane crash.

* Fidel Castro takes over Cuba.

* Winter fog cripples transport throughout Britain.

* Racing driver Mike Hawthorn killed.

Mike Neville MBE

Mike's first engagement at Tyne Tees Television was actually as an actor a few months after the station first began. Mike recalled,

'I was coming to the end of a summer season at Bridlington and had begun the usual round of writing to television companies seeking work. You very rarely got a reply - it was very bad for actors in those days. However, Bill Lyon-Shaw, the Programme Controller at Tyne Tees replied, asking me to call and see him when I got back to the North-East. Within minutes of meeting Bill I was offered a part the very next night in the children's programme 'Happy-Go-Lucky' with Jack Haig and Len Marten. Somebody had dropped out and would I care to play a policeman, 'live', the next night? Yes I would!' During rehearsals I had to deliver my one and only line and then walk across the set. I started walking as I said my line and the Floor Manager, who had received instructions in his headphones from the Director said to me,

'Director's compliments, but can you say the line before you start to walk.'

I found out later that the Director's compliments were,

'Will you tell that * * @!! * *! actor that he's not on the **@!!**! stage now! Tell him to stand still when he says the **@!!** line!!'

Bill then took Mike to meet producer David Croft, later to become a household name as producer/writer of such classics as 'Allo, Allo', 'Hi-de-hi', and 'Dad's Army'. David was about to rehearse a new comedy series called 'Under New

Management', about a pub called 'The Three Pilchards' starri Glenn Melvyn, Danny Ross, and Mollie Sugden. David sa that the programme was fully cast apart from a policema and honestly, Mike didn't look like a policeman. Bill laugh and said, 'Well he's playing one in 'Happy-Go-Lucky' tomorro night!'

This photograph was tak from The Viewer 7 Novemb 1959 and shows the cast a some of the producti personnel of TTT's 'Und New Management'. Moll Sugden appeared in anoth David Croft production ma years later when 'Are Yo Being Served' was screened the BBC. Danny Ross remembered as Alfie (Oh n leg!) Hall in 'The Clither Kid'.

Tom Kilgour and Judi Gibson made gue appearances in 'Under Ne Management'.

When Glenn Melvyn invited his friends to pop in and have one after a recent broadcast of " Under New Management" there was a ready response. Among those " called to the bar" were : (1) cameraman Derek Brady (2) designer John Dinsdale (3) Danny Ross (4) floor manager Denver Thornton (5) Bill Moore (6) Anne Moore (7) producer David Croft (8) property man John Corbett (9) Glenn Melvyn (10) Mollie Sugden (11) Les Frankcom (12) Michael Neville (13) Jerry Verno (14) Ian Fleming (15) Graham Stark

...vid invited Mike to rehearsals in a nearby church hall that ...ening. Mike continued his story.

...y opening - if not only - line was, after a comedy explosion, ...ay, what's that door doing down there on the floor?' I was ...desperate for the job and I felt I had to make an impression, ...I unashamedly did the line 'a la Kenneth Williams'.
...hat?' said Glenn Melvyn, off-script.
...I repeated the line the same way.
...ight!', said Glenn, 'we keep that in, exactly as it was said, ...cluding my 'what?' and the repeat of the line.'
...d this daft copper found himself written-in for the rest of ...e series! Sometimes there wasn't a line but something daft ...ppened to him. They used to pay me for rehearsals even if ...wasn't there. If I had no lines it was pointless turning up and ...was very generous, very kind. I thoroughly enjoyed it; I ...as a 22 year old actor and was able to meet people who were ...g names then. Stars like Cardew Robinson, Graham Stark, ...rthur English, Jack Douglas and Hugh Lloyd who were ...ing a double act at the time. They came and guested on the ...ow and I knew all these people from the comic 'Radio Fun' ...d I remember talking to Cardew during rehearsals and I ...id, 'Blah blah blah ... Douglas.'
...e said, 'How did you know that?'
...now what?' I replied.
...ou called me Douglas.'
...es!' I replied, 'Douglas, Cardew the Cad Robinson.'
...hat was the title of the 'Radio Fun' strip.)
...ardew said, 'That's absolutely marvellous; I dropped all that ...ars ago and changed it to just Cardew. How wonderful to ...eet someone who remembers that.'
...was thrilled to meet all those lovely people and to be working ...well.'
...fter that experience Mike returned to repertory work for a ...uple of years. He continued his story.

...was living in Wimbledon, lodging with the lady who later ...came my mother-in-law. I was out of work at the time and ...received a telephone call saying Tyne Tees were looking for ...announcer, so I wrote to them and had to attend a meeting ...London. Chief Announcer Adrian Cairns interviewed me ...d I was so nervous. You know, you plan everything in your ...ind and when I went to the interview I forgot everything. I ...dn't even tell them I was from the North-East. I received a ...tter inviting me to an audition and it turned out I was in the ...nal eight out of 200 applicants. I was sat down in front of a ...amera with a clock underneath and given a copy of 'The ...iewer'. I was told to talk for 45 seconds. I talked for 55 ...conds and they said, 'Do you want to try it again?' This time ...talked for 35 seconds. So I thought that's it! I'm wasting ...eir time. There's no chance of getting it; but I did, which ...as nice.

...o in 1962 I was offered a permanent post at TTT as ...ontinuity man and newsreader. I had to link one programme ...the next and fill in if a programme had underrun. I was on ...uty one Sunday night and the Palladium Show was on, and ...at went out live. On that particular night it was underrunning ...orrendously by about ten minutes. I imagined that dozens of ...ontinuity announcers like me up and down the country were

saying, 'Keep going!' I remember Frankie Vaughan was on and he was singing his last song. He was obviously getting a 'spread' signal from someone and eventually they finished about five minutes light. I was down to talk for 40 seconds already, so I had a total of five minutes 40 seconds on camera. There I was talking to this tiny camera just dredging stuff up. 'And on a week on Friday you can see episode No43 of .....'
It certainly exercised the mind. There weren't any buttons you could press to run a trailer or something; it was your job to fill in.

It was this strange thing - talking to a clock. For the last 37 years I've been talking to a clock. But it's made me obsessional with time and my watch must be accurate. I used to have a digital watch. My wife used to say,
'What time is it?'
I would say, ' 9:43 and 10 seconds.'
'So you mean nearly quarter to ten, then,' she'd reply.
I have an analogue watch now but it's got to be accurate. A while ago I was talking to my dentist and I said that I had a new watch which was losing five seconds a day and was really getting on my nerves.
'Five seconds a day,' he said. 'What's five seconds a day?'
'It's 15 or 20 words! That's what five seconds is.'

You used to get a running order each day and sometimes, if you were talking over slides, it would be scripted by a continuity script writer. Bob Langley was a continuity script writer at one time. If you were in vision, the script just said '19 seconds' typed in black, and that meant you had to ad lib. When I first started, I used to write down say 19 seconds of words and Jon Kelley, who was an announcer then, said that it was not the best way because your mind locks onto that and if there's an overrun or underrun it's much more difficult to fill in as your brain is telling you to say the thing you've written. If you don't write anything down but just have a loose idea in your mind about what you want to talk about, then you can stretch or cut at will and it's much easier. He was perfectly right and I never wrote down anything after that. Jon Kelley married Wanda, who is Bill Lyon-Shaw's daughter. I went to the wedding; it was marvellous. Jon was an actor - he popped up again later in UFO which was like Thunderbirds only with people instead of puppets. I haven't heard from him for years.

Well, I'd been doing the continuity job for about 18 months and Tom Coyne was doing the local news programme, 'North-East Roundabout' when Arthur Clifford became the new Programme Controller. I was called into his office one night just before I went onto the late shift. In half an hour I think I said, 'Good evening Mr Clifford, thank you Mr Clifford, goodnight Mr Clifford.' 'cause Arthur was a lovely man. So cutting it down, he said that they were changing the local news; it was going to be longer, it was going to be called 'North-East Newsview', and I'd be doing it. So I said thank you very much. 'Newsview' ran for 45 minutes, three nights of the week, and on Wednesdays and Fridays ran for an amazing 55 minutes. The opening shot was from a camera mounted 20 feet high on the wall. I had to stand on a jagged arrow painted on the floor and gaze up at the camera. I remember being made fun of in

MONDAY

Continued from Page 14

5.5 SEEING SPORT

Lawn Tennis with PETER LLOYD

In the first of a new series from the R.A.F. Station, Stanmore, Middlesex, ex-Davis Cup player **Tony Mottram**, and **Joy Mottram**, ex-Wightman Cup player, will be giving instruction in forehand and backhand drives

An ATV Production

5.25 SPACE PATROL

The Unknown Asteroid

Tyne Tees Television Presentation

5.55 NEWS

6.5 NORTH-EAST NEWSVIEW

A nightly round-up of the North-East day with
News . . . Sport . . . Weather . . . People . . . Opinion . . . Events
Introduced by
MICHAEL NEVILLE
Newscasters:
BOB LANGLEY
JON KELLEY
Reporters:
PHILIP McDONNELL
JACK CLARKE
VALERIE DENNIS
Directed by DON GOLLAN
Executive producer: TERENCE WYNN

A Tyne Tees Television Production

6.45 SPORTS EXTRA

swings its cameras into action and records, interprets and comments on Sport in the North-East and introduces the men and women who make the sporting headlines
Tonight's Special:
The Tour of the Border Cycle Race
Introduced by **GEORGE TAYLOR**
Programme editor: FRANK KILBRIDE
Directed by BERNARD PRESTON
(See Page 3)

7.0 DISCS A GOGO

KENT WALTON
welcomes you to
Gogo's
Guests:
ALMA COGAN
IAN McCULLOCH
THE MOJOS
JACKIE and JILL
Produced by CHRISTOPHER MERCER
A TWW Production

7.30 CORONATION STREET

CAST INCLUDES:
Dennis Tanner .... PHILIP LOWRIE
Elsie Tanner .... PATRICIA PHOENIX
Laurie Frazer .... STANLEY MEADOWS
Jerry Booth .... GRAHAM HABERFIELD
Myra Booth .... SUSAN JAMESON
Kenneth Barlow .... WILLIAM ROACHE
Valerie Barlow .... ANNE REID
Frank Barlow .... FRANK PEMBERTON
Jack Walker .... ARTHUR LESLIE
Annie Walker .... DORIS SPEED
Ena deputises for Martha, and Len and Jerry have a busy night
Produced by MARGARET MORRIS
Directed by MILO LEWIS
A Granada Production

8.0 CRANE

PATRICK ALLEN
SAM KYDD
GERALD FLOOD
in
Murder is Waiting
CAST INCLUDES:
Raswani .... BASIL DIGNAM
Orlando .... SAM KYDD
Crane .... PATRICK ALLEN
Halima .... LAYA RAKI
Mahmoud .... GERALD FLOOD
Because somewhere in Casablanca there is a ruthless killer, Crane receives an unexpected invitation
Produced by JORDAN LAWRENCE
An Associated-Rediffusion Production

8.55 NEWS

9.10 PLAY OF THE WEEK

GEORGE MURCELL
HAROLD GOLDBLATT
and introducing
ANNIE ROSS
in
Where Are They Now?
CAST INCLUDES:
Vincent .... PATRICK WESTWOOD
Walter Kells .... GEORGE MURCELL
Ellie Dafoe .... ANNIE ROSS
Santiaga .... MARIA LAWTON
Otis Dafoe .... HAROLD GOLDBLATT
When Walter Kells flies down to Mexico to see the old movie maestro, all he wants is an interview. But what he gets is some very curious behaviour from the old man and his daughter
Directed by ROBERT TRONSON
An Associated-Rediffusion Production
(See Pages 8 and 9)

10.40 SOMETHING TO SAY

DANIEL FARSON
talking to
LORD ROBENS
Film editor: JOHN ZAMBARDI
Research by SUE TURNER
Programme editor: BRYAN FITZJONES
Directed by RANDEL BEATTIE
An Associated-Rediffusion Production
(See Page 8)

11.10 NEWS HEADLINES

11.12 NORTH-EAST NEWS HEADLINES AND WEATHER FORECAST

Bringing you the latest news headlines from the newsroom of Tyne Tees Television, up-to-the-minute weather forecast

11.15 UNIVERSITY CHALLENGE

This week
PETERHOUSE COLLEGE, CAMBRIDGE
versus
LEEDS UNIVERSITY
Chairman: **BAMBER GASCOIGNE**
Directed by PETER MULLINGS
Produced by PAULINE SHAW
A Granada Production

11.45 (approx) THE EPILOGUE

from
" *The Exhortations of Father Zossima*
by FYODOR DOSTOEVSKY
read by **Maxwell Deas**

Close down

Michael Neville in Tyne
Tees Television's
'Newsview' studio in 1964.

...e canteen for that. When I ...proached, people would ...ok up at the ceiling and say ...Morning Mike'.'

...1963 Mike was voted 'Male ...ersonality of the Year' by ...aders of 'The Viewer' ...agazine. He appeared on the ...ne O'Clock Show' in ...bruary 1964 to receive the ...ward which was presented ... Kenneth Horne.

...he programme schedule ...own on the opposite page ...as for Easter Monday, 30 ...arch 1964 and it shows the ...rst edition of 'North-East ...ewsview'. One of the ...ewscasters on the ...ogramme was Bob Langley ...ho later teamed up with

...oderick Griffith to present 'Newsview' when Mike joined BBC ...orth-East.

...ike's contribution to local television at BBC North-East is ...gendary and his 'Geordierama' performances with George

House go down in the history books as classic Tyneside comedy.

In 1996 Mike accepted an offer to return to Tyne Tees Television after 32 years with BBC North-East. He now heads the news presentation team on the 'North-East Tonight' programme which is transmitted from 6pm until 7pm on weekday evenings. The programme, which had only been on the air for six weeks, was voted 'Best Regional News Programme' in the Royal Television Awards of 1996. Mike attended the ceremony at the Hilton Hotel in London to accept the award on behalf of the news team. When I spoke with Mike about the award and 'North-East Tonight', he praised the innovative techniques of the production staff and the variety of items featured on the programme.

In January 1998 'North-East Tonight' won a World Medal for the Best News Magazine Programme, at the New York Film and Television Festival. Tyne Tees Television won the award in competition with over 2500 entries from around the world. Mike was literally lost for words when the news was presented to the viewers of 'North-East Tonight' by Weather Presenter, Bob Johnson.

In 1996, Mike Neville returned to Tyne Tees Television to present the local news programme: 'North-East Tonight'.

Bill Steel

Bill Steel is remembered as Chief Announcer at Tyne Tees and Presenter of the news magazine 'Northern Life'. His career with Tyne Tees started long before that, however, as Assistant Transmission Controller.
Ian Westwater and I met Bill at the Imperial Hotel in Jesmond and Bill told us how it all started.

'I recall my first interview with Howard Thompson. I'd written a letter applying for the job and he asked me to go and see him for the initial audition. What I didn't know then was about three or four hundred people were applying for the same job, which might have put me off a bit. Anyway, I got through to the next round of interviews and then on to the final selection list and that was on a Sunday morning. I remember it was raining and I got to the station at about 10 o'clock. Howard came downstairs to see me and he had a clipboard and a stopwatch, which to me seemed very glamourous at the time. Anyone who had a clipboard and a stopwatch, well that was showbiz. I was a young trainee accountant with the General Electric Company, with the hard collar and the old college tie on. Howard said,
'It's so nice to see you. Would you mind coming back at 11 o'clock as I'm trying to get the station on the air?'
I remember that phrase vividly as it sounded like he was going to kick-start a motorbike or something. With his clipboard and stopwatch and getting the station on the air, I thought I was in Hollywood. I remember walking along the Quayside and thinking, 'This is an important day in my life if this comes off.' And by God it was. I went back and saw Howard, he showed me the control room, and that was the first time I had seen a control room. Nigel Birch was there, a couple of others, and I watched Tony Sandford operate the desk. He said, 'That's the job you'll be doing, mixing sound and vision and assisting the Transmission Controller, and getting the station on the air.' He asked if I thought I could do it. I said, 'Show me how and I'll do it faster than you.'
So he said,
'The job's yours; start in a week's time.'
And that was my entry into Tyne Tees Television thanks to Mr Thompson. I'm eternally grateful to him.

It was Assistant Transmission Controller John Dightam who trained me for the job. He was an ex-RAF instructor and was keen to bring me up to the mark so he could become Transmission Controller. He was smashing; a blood Yorkshireman who made Fred Trueman sound like Noel Coward. He used to pull my leg unmercifully, but he was a good teacher.

I nearly lost my job a couple of weeks later. Tony didn't turn up one Sunday morning, so I was in charge; a young apprentice, and a bit green. We were networking, that means our church service was going throughout the UK. I knew Tony had probably slept in, so I went ahead and did it all myself. I co-ordinated with OB and with all the controllers throughout the country. I didn't want to get Tony into trouble so I didn't ring anyone to say he hadn't turned up. I got the biggest bollocking in my life for that. I got a letter from management saying, 'It

would be a shame to put a blight on such a promising care_ so early.' Tony never forgot how I had covered for him a_ years later he bailed me out when I was in a bit of troub_ There aren't many people around like that now. I had t_ greatest respect for Tony and still do.

A year or so later I became Transmission Controller whi_ was unheard of at the age of 23. The job was normally do_ by people 30 or older. Sometimes I would start work ve_ early in the morning and would park my car right outside t_ front door of the studios and dash upstairs to 'get the stati_ on the air.' I would get a call from security saying,
'The MD Tony Jelly wants you to move your car from h_ space.'
I thought, 'What a nerve! How can he say a piece of Ci_ Road is his space. He should have come in earlier.'

They were auditioning for a new voice-over man. It was Jimn_ Nurse who was Head of Sales then and he wanted a new voic_ over man as the one they had was awful. Jimmy said the_ were holding auditions and he asked me to pop down. It w_ Adrian Cairns and Jimmy who were auditioning and I got t_ job; five sessions, sometimes ten sessions a week. I rememb_ going to Jon Kelley and saying that I'd got the voice-over jc_ and I was a bit concerned as I hadn't been to drama schoc_ Jon offered to give me a three year course in three weeks, _ his bed-sit in Jesmond. He was very kind to me as most peop_ are in this business.'

Ian Westwater interjected and recalled that where most voic_ over people could average three words a second; Bill coul_ achieve five words a second and still have a 'smile' in his voic_

...ll continued his story.

...was working with some good guys like Adrian Cairns, Jimmy ...oyd, and David Hamilton, who helped me with voice-training ...d approach. I used to try and work to order. At first I ...ould do a straight commercial read and then I listened very ...refully to what the customer wanted. The client might say ... wanted it speeded up a little or slowed down, a bit more ...thority, or a bit more 'smiley'. That's what I got paid to do, ...d you had to do it very quickly as studio time is expensive. ...you can do what the client wants quickly, then they are very ...ppy, and there's a chance you'll be used again.

...lid voice-over for a lot of years; I did about 10,000 ...mmercials in all. Several years later I was asked to do a ...sion commercial for Philipson Studios. Phil Harland used ... be the producer there and this guy used to look like every ...m producer/director you've ever seen in a movie. He had a ...ard, a sleeveless pullover, and checked trousers. He rang ... up and said he was doing a commercial for paint; I think it ...s Leveys. We filmed on the Town Moor, I was dressed up ... football strip, and I had to run and kick a football. Phil ...id,
...ue Bill.'
...ame rushing in like Alan Shearer, kicked the ball with all ...y might and it hit the camera. You should have heard the ...nguage from the Director. That was my first film commercial.

...y contribution to the swinging 60's on Tyne Tees was when ...osted 'Songs for the Swinging Sixties' in 1965. I was actually ...t of vision - it was like radio on television. It doesn't sound

6.35 SONGS FOR THE SWINGING SIXTIES

With an ear-catching mixture of Ballad, Blues, and Beat, **LONG JOHN BALDRY** and his friends get together to give a new twist to the songs of the 1960s . . .

Our guests:

THE STEAM PACKET
featuring
LONG JOHN BALDRY
ROD STEWART
JULIE DRISCOLL
THE BRIAN AUGER TRINITY
Introduced by **BILL STEEL**
Designed by MALCOLM DAWSON
Produced by ANNA K. MOORE
A Tyne Tees Television Production

...ery novel now but it was very innovative then. It was Anna ...oore who produced the show and we had many of the big ...ames of the time; Dusty Springfield, Anita Harris, Long John ...aldry, Rod Stewart, and Karl Denver, to name a few. The ...ow was recorded as live before a studio audience and we ...ould do 'radio type' links between the songs which were ...gued. Some time later the Programme Controller, Arthur ...lifford asked me to do a 'warm-up' for 'Geordie Scene'. My ...b was to be on the studio floor, talk to the audience and get ...em all fired up ready for the compere Dave Eager. I used to ... the audience into a frenzy ready for the acts coming on. I ...as well pleased with the results. One night I was in the ...gypt Cottage pub and Arthur Clifford came in and said to ...e,
...Vhat a big improvement there's been on 'Geordie Scene', Bill.

What I think we need from a compere on 'Geordie Scene' is someone who can get the audience all worked up like that.'
I said, 'Yeh!'
'Someone that the kids will respond to.'
I said, 'Yeh!'
'Someone that they all recognise immediately.'
I said, 'Yeh!' and thought, 'This is going to come my way.'
And then he gave the job to Dave Lee Travis.
I walked home that night very disappointed. I suffer from being invisible from time to time. To Arthur I was totally invisible. He just did not see what I was doing.

Around about 1967 I got a call from ABC Manchester. It was David Hamilton and he said that they had a vacancy for a news reader in Manchester. So I went down for the audition and they took me to a studio. I asked if they were going to record it and they said,
'No, you're going to do the audition live on air.'
So it can't have been too bad as I got the job and stayed for three years in Manchester and then Birmingham. I was still doing my job as Transmission Controller at Tyne Tees by the way. I was burning the candle at both ends and the middle. ABC then became Thames TV and David Hamilton and I were working there together. At Tyne Tees I was still Bill, the Transmission Controller doing voice-over commercials. I remember Chris Palmer used to go down to London, sometimes see me on TV there, and come back to Tyne Tees and say to people'
'Why aren't we using Bill here?'

Tony Sandford took over the Promotion Department and he asked me to do a couple of shifts on continuity which was voice only at the time. When Peter Moth became Head of News, he invited me to be Chief Presenter of the magazine programme 'Northern Life'. Around about the same time I got a telephone call from Geoff Coates who used to be a BBC producer. He said that he wanted me to work at Metro. Well I thought it was a Paris Underground. He said that it was a new radio station in the North-East, he was Programme Controller there, and he wanted me to present the Breakfast Show. I said that I didn't know the Top 20. He said that I'd be alright, and could I do weekends. So I was doing Thames newsreading, Tyne Tees Television Transmission Controller, voice-over commercials, and now I'm also doing the weekend Breakfast Show on Metro Radio. Within four weeks I was doing six Breakfast Shows a week. I then had to make up my mind what to do, as I couldn't do it all. So I sat down and thought about it and decided I had to let go of the job as Transmission Controller. I got a very nice contract as the main Presenter on 'Northern Life' which ran for four years. I had to drop the commercials but I did a lovely deal with John Tonge where he paid me for not doing them. John was a very logical man; you couldn't put one over on John Tonge but I think I did. I said that I couldn't do the voice-over commercials and present 'Northern Life' at the same time. He said that I was right as it was company policy.
'Therefore you'll have to pay me for the money I've lost,' I reasoned.
'Tell me that again.' replied John rather puzzled.

Bill Steel in the 'Northern Life' studio. The cameraman is Richard Edwards.

He came back from lunch and said that I was right, so I got paid for not doing the commercials.

The Breakfast Show on Metro actually won awards and I had to go to London and lecture about the Show. The 'Northern Life' show also did really well.

Andy Allan became Programme Controller and he wanted me to pump up the promotion output. He wanted me to be Chief Announcer. I asked him what it entailed. He said that it was twice the money I was getting so I said, 'That'll do very nicely.' I did the Chief Announcer's job until July 1996; about 15 years in total.

One vivid memory I have of Tyne Tees is when the studio caught fire. I was reading the morning news and the studio went up in flames. What had happened was the cleaner had put the curtains over the big arc lights and they had been smouldering since six o'clock. I walked in and I thought it smelled a bit funny. I sat down and started to read the news, and the smoke was getting higher and higher. The viewers were not aware of it as the smoke was not yet in shot. I looked at my monitor and thought, 'When the smoke comes into shot I'm going to have to say something.' So I kept on going, and then suddenly there was a flash, and flames leapt up the curtain. Through the studio window all the faces were there with their noses pressed up against the glass. The studio firemen with their axes were there behind the glass and I thought they mean bloody business. I finished the news, the credits rolled, and I went out of that door like Seb Coe. One of the lads got smoke inhalation and was off work a couple of weeks. For a while we kept the studio carpet with all the burn marks, and during studio tours they would show visitors the piece of carpet and say,

'This is where Bill Steel stayed at his post and continued to read the news when the studio caught fire.'

I remember interviewing Johnny Nash; he was a lovely man. He was very nervous about interviews; his manager said that he hated them. But I made him relax, it was a great interview, and he stayed for lunch. I remember he repaired my cigarette lighter; I was most touched. I still get letters from him.

Arthur Askey was another nice memory at Tyne Tees. I interviewed him with only a minute's notice. I was walking down the corridor, Arthur just happened to be walking along, and I asked him if he would talk with me on TV. I was doing continuity announcing at the time and I had a five minute spot

coming up. Arthur said that he'd love to chat and asked ▮ when. I said, 'In about 30 seconds!'

We ran down the corridor, rushed into the studio, and I spo▮ with the Transmission Controller. I told him I had the gr▮ Mr Askey here and I'd like to interview him. I had the m▮ delightful chat; it was wonderful.

Alongside my television presenting work at Tyne Tees, I h▮ been able to develop a theatre career as an actor. Sir Camer▮ Mackintosh started me off by asking me to take over fr▮ Ned Sherrin in 'Side by Side by Sondheim' which was a b▮ break for me. I acted alongside Mark Wynter, Sally Smi▮ and Jill Martin. It was a nationwide tour and I played at t▮ Theatre Royal in Newcastle. Some time later, Jack Dix▮ rang me and asked me to play Professor Higgins in 'My F▮ Lady'. It was a lavish production with the original Dru▮ Lane set and a 13 piece orchestra. I also played the lead r▮ 'Herbie' in 'Gypsy' and also appeared in a revival of 'T▮ Dancing Years' at a theatre in Ashington.

I left Tyne Tees in July 1996 to further develop my acti▮ career. My agent Dave Holly and I got together and he sa▮ 'It's about time we concentrated on your television acti▮ career.' He rang me in August to say they were casting f▮ Catherine Cookson's 'The Rag Nymph' and could I go for ▮ audition. Some time later I found I had won a part, not t▮ part I had auditioned for but a much better role as Mr Spong▮ So that was my first TV film. Not a huge part but a nice on▮ In January my agent said that they wanted to see me ▮ Manchester for 'Coronation Street'. They had a new charact▮ Alan McKenna's father, and they wanted to meet me. He sa▮ that they meant business because they were going to pay ▮ expenses, which doesn't normally happen. I met the Casti▮ Director at Granada and we chatted for a while about the 'Stre▮

Bill Steel the actor in 1998.

walked through the door my wife said that my agent had rung at five past two saying, 'Congratulations you're Bernard McKenna in 'Coronation Street'.' What a break! So it was a happy time in the Steel household that night. The next day the 'phone started to ring; it was make-up, and then wardrobe, asking me to go down to Manchester. What an experience! You know the corner shop where Rita works? well just next door and up the stairs is the Wardrobe Department. The 'Street' was open to the public that day so there were lots of people milling about. I was shown my rack of clothes which had a label on it - Bernard McKenna. Next to my rack of clothes was Mike Baldwin's. Next to that was Curly's rack and so on. The Director came down to see me and asked if I would like to meet the 'family'. Directly opposite the corner shop is a very non-descript window which is a two-way mirror; you can't see through it from the outside. Behind that is the Green Room where the cast take a break. We went through the door and there were the members of the cast, all the faces you see on the show, reading their scripts ready to go on camera. Mavis came over and welcomed me, then I met my stage son Alan and his girlfriend Fiona. I watched some of the production which took place in the huge set of the Rover's Return and Mike Baldwin's flat; it was very impressive as they are all high quality actors. A couple of weeks later I was on set doing it myself.'

...d the part. They took a photograph of me and said, 'We'll ...t you know.' I couldn't make the recall a week later so my ...ext meeting was at London Weekend Television on the South ...ank adjacent to the National Theatre. I'd studied Alan ...cKenna's role and had an idea what sort of character his ...ther might be. I met the Director Garth Tucker and the ...asting Director Judi Hayfield who had come down from ...ranada. A script appeared, we discussed what the role should ...e, and then we did the 'read' with Judi reading the other parts. ...he audition ended at 2pm and I went for a cup of tea in the ...anteen. I remember looking across the river at St Paul's ...athedral thinking, 'Shall I stay in ...wn and ring David Hamilton up for ...couple of 'bevvies' or should I go ...ome.' I thought, 'Well if I don't get ...e part I was jolly close to it.' I ...aught the train home and when I

Among Bill's many claims to fame are his voice-over contributions to Hughie Green's shows such as 'The Sky's the Limit' and 'Double Your Money'.

Bill is currently a presenter on Century Radio where he hosts the early morning shows Monday to Thursday. He also presents the Saturday afternoon show, (music and sport) and the Sunday afternoon show. He is also Director of 'Media Manners' a media training company.

A scene from episode No 4236 of 'Coronation Street' which was transmitted on Sunday 27 July 1997, shows Bill Steel as Bernard McKenna and his stage wife Mary (Madalaine Newton) hearing some important news from their son Alan McKenna (Glen Hugill) and Fiona (Angela Griffin).

Picture by kind permission of Granada Television.

George Taylor

George Taylor began his career at Tyne Tees Television as the station's first Sports Presenter and continued in their employment for 26 years, eventually becoming Head of Sport, but his long association began a few months before the station actually went 'on air!' George told me about the early years.

'It was while working as a staff sports writer for the Daily Mirror, based in Newcastle and covering the entire North-East region, that we heard of the impending arrival of commercial television to be based in the City. The news was announced at a Press conference at the Station Hotel, and made me think that perhaps, when the station was functioning, sport would obviously have an important role within its programming. The prospect of being asked for the odd contribution prompted me to write offering my services, on the strength of just one television appearance to my credit!
That had come about when a BBC programme -'Sport in the North', hosted by the Rugby League writer and broadcaster, Eddie Waring, had left its normal studio base and travelled to Tynemouth. Because of my connection with the Daily Mirror, the BBC invited me to do a two minute insert on 'Sport in the North' live from the Plaza Ballroom, Tynemouth. The BBC had brought a camera crew there for a live edition of the '6:5 Special'. I had to gather all the news about the Sunderland and Middlesbrough matches that day, and give a live, two-minute report from the Plaza, just before the '6:5 Special' went on the air. When we arrived at the Plaza, the queue around the building was enormous. They were all young kids waiting to go into the music show. We pushed our way to the front and said to the security guy that we were doing a sports broadcast from there. He laughed and said that he had heard every excuse in the book to get past him, but ours was the best yet, and he told us to clear off. Fortunately, I had a letter from the BBC with me which convinced him that we were genuine, so he let us in. When we approached the crew they were rehearsing for the '6:5 Special' and no-one wanted to know about some daft sports reporter who was going to do a spot just before the show. The producer saw me and said, 'You're not the usual guy. Have you done this before? What's your 'in cue'?'
I hadn't a clue what he was talking about. I did my spot and the producer said,
'I thought you said that you'd never done this before.'
I was quite flattered to hear that from a BBC producer. On Monday morning Eddie Waring rang me to thank me for a very nice report and ironically enough, for a man who used to stumble his way through commentary, gave me some friendly advice and declared,
'Watch your diction, lad!'

Having had that taster, when Tyne Tees Television were setting up, I filled in an application form thinking that I might be able to write a sports report for them from time to time to supplement my Daily Mirror income. I received a letter asking me to attend an interview at TTT's office in Northumberland Street. I did my research on the Black Brothers before I went to the interview and at the end, George Black said,
'You've come here to be interviewed and it's ended up with

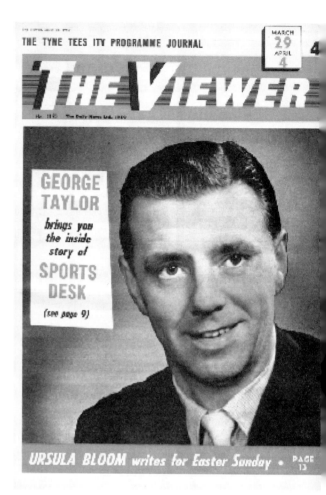

you interviewing me.'
I was asked to go to an audition at the studios on City Road and I can remember the place was still being built and there were carpenters banging away while we were talking.
The interview went well, to the point of being offered staff post as an announcer and news reader, an offer which I declined. It was sport or nothing - sport won. So began the happy association that was to last for many years.

It was a hectic and an amateurish beginning, one has to say, while the teething problems were sorted out. Sports Desk became a lively, and well liked 'infant'; first in a family of ever growing sports productions. You name it - we did it.
Unflagging enthusiasm, sheer bloody-mindedness, almost total cooperation from just about every sporting body we ever approached, encouragement from viewers, staff members and participants alike enabled us to show North-East sport as it had never been seen before, or in many cases, since.
We featured archery, bowls (both carpet and indoor), cricket, darts (and who could forget the 'Double Top' series) athletics, basketball, snooker, speedway, squash, greyhound racing, quizzes, target golf, and a host of other events as well as a weekly half hour round-up of events, topics, big name interviews and action. All this reflected an extremely committed local television involvement throughout the region.

In the early 60s there was a major breakthrough in that it was the first time we were allowed to transmit recorded highlights

League Football. The news came as something of a shock say the least. One of the programme directors, later to be olved in the productions, casually remarked in the canteen e afternoon, just before the actual coverage was to begin, t I would be commentating on the games.

most of the grounds we went to, we were stuck in the corner th a film camera. We also had the problems of changing a l - someone would score a goal right in the middle of a reel ange. Much later we bought an outside broadcast unit with R and things became a bit more sophisticated. In 1966 our meras covered the World Cup from Roker Park and ddlesbrough. I was interviewer for the network and among teams playing were Chile, North Korea and Italy. I was d that I was stand-by commentator on the North Korea - ile match. I thought it was a wind-up. I was up all night rning the names of the Korean team. Eventually I thought, 'ho cares anyway whether it is Pang Yong Sing, Hoo Lan oo or Sang Yang Ling.' rtunately, I wasn't asked to do it.

om time to time, we would have announcers on trial and one ght we had a chap reporting on horse-racing. After rehearsal, adjourned to the Egypt Cottage for a swift half before nsmission. We seemed to lose the racing chap and we ught that he must have stayed behind in the studio to learn s lines. When we returned to the studio, he had been in the rong pub and it was obvious that he had drunk one too many. me transmission, he made a right hash of it. He was slurring s speech, mispronouncing some of the words in the report, d then started getting the name of the horse mixed up with e name of the rider, making a complete mess of the report. e final line was to give the racing tip for the next day and e chap concluded, nd the tip for the 3 o'clock tomorrow is 'Faultless Speech'.'

had some fun doing things other than sport. There was a ogramme called 'Northern Life' which was transmitted before e ten o'clock news. Having been involved with the army at e stage of my career, I was given a book to read called 'The even Faces of War' by a woman called Martha Gellhorn ho was married to Ernest Hemingway. She was an author some repute, and it was an interesting book. I was given e job to interview her and I was going to take her to task out her attitude towards the Vietnam War. The programme as live, and my spot was the last one in the running order, so was the buffer. If the programme overran then I had to cut; it underran, I had to take up the slack. About five minutes fore we went on the air she was shown into the studio while ere was a film playing. I was introduced to her; she was a oman of about 70 and was dressed in a black cat suit and a ll length mink coat. She shook my hand and said, You've read my book? You have some questions about it? ine!' he Producer said, 0 seconds to go George.' 5 seconds.' Martha leaned over and said, One word about Hemingway and I'll walk out.'

One of the questions I was going to ask her was whether Hemingway had influenced her writing, so as the interview progressed I thought, 'Shall I risk it?' As it was, we ran out of time and I never asked the question.

I remember on one occasion, John Rickman was doing the racing on Saturday afternoon. He was frightfully 'old school tie' and he always wore a trilby hat. They had just extended the main grandstand at Redcar Racecourse and the man who was mainly responsible was the Managing Director Major Leslie Petch, a very go-ahead man. I remember John came on air and said, 'Welcome to 'World of Sport' here at Redcar. I'm standing in front of Major Petch's marvellous erection.'

Those early days were a joy - going to work was fun, allied to a sense of real togetherness which regretfully tended to be overshadowed in later years. Sophistication came with the electronic age and the microchip, and the magic of those early days now only seems to exist in the memory of those who were fortunate to be there at the beginning.'

George Taylor retired from Tyne Tees in 1984, and after experimenting with radio and Public Relations for a short spell, is back where his heart is - in football. He is Player Liaison Officer with Newcastle United Football Club and loving every minute of it.

George Taylor is now Player Liaison Officer for Newcastle United Football Club.

David Hamilton

David Hamilton had been working as a Continuity Script-Writer at ATV Television in London when he was called up for National Service. He was stationed with the RAF in Germany and an opportunity arose to present a radio show on the British Forces Network in Cologne. That gave him quite a taste for broadcasting and when he returned to his script writing job at ATV, things had changed a great deal and he wasn't happy with his job. I met David in London and he picked up the story from there.

'One of the announcers at ABC TV in Manchester had to take three months leave to visit his sick mother in South Africa, so ABC needed a deputy announcer and I applied. Because of my experience as a continuity script-writer, I was quite familiar with the terminology of television presenting. Many of the other applicants for the job were actors who weren't au fait with the programmes and the schedules. Consequently I got the job. Announcers in those days wore dinner-jackets and bow ties in the evening. I'd never owned a dinner-jacket in my life so I had to borrow one from a guy called John Benson who was a lot taller and slimmer than me. The cuffs came right down to my finger-tips so I had to keep my hands under the desk when I was on camera. Eventually the South African announcer returned and took his job back, but by that time I had begun to like announcing. There wasn't a full time job going at ABC so when a vacancy came up at Tyne Tees, I applied. I went to the audition at City Road and the floor manager was a guy called Denver Thornton. He asked me to ad-lib to camera for 30 seconds about the Palladium Show.

When I wrote continuity scripts, I used a large stopwatch time the announcements, so I took the watch out of my pock and placed it on the desk while I ad-libbed. Later on Denv said that I'd got the job because of the stopwatch - it looked professional. Well I hadn't given it a second thought becau I had always used it when writing scripts. So on 1st Februa 1961 I became a Continuity Announcer at Tyne Tees. On o of my first nights on duty there were 'The Viewer' Personaliti of the Year presentations. Being a cocky, ambitious you man, I said to myself, 'This time next year, I'm going to be t male personality of the year.' I asked myself, 'How am I goi to do it, as I am only an announcer and newsreader?' I thoug I would turn each announcement into a personality spot. devised a cat puppet which I called Tobee and used that liven up the announcements. In the afternoon when there w acres of time and nobody knew how to fill it, I would ch with this puppet. We called it Tobee because no-one was su whether it was meant tobee a boy or meant tobee a girl. T puppet was operated by a guy called Jack Saltman who als gave the puppet its squeaky voice. Jack was a Continui Scriptwriter at Tyne Tees. Years later, Jack became a high respected Producer of documentaries. I wonder if he wou like to be reminded that he was once the voice of a cat!

In the evenings, if I was to introduce 'Emergency Ward 10', would come into vision wearing a white coat and a stethoscop I would move the stethoscope towards the camera and sa something like, 'You don't look too well at the moment. I thir you need half an hour in 'Emergency Ward 10' starting fro now.' If I was introducing 'Wagon Train', I'd be wearing stetson and a lariat and say, 'Howdee partners. We're off

David Hamilton (left) with Tobee the puppet operated by Jack Saltman.

OK Corral now for an hour of Western adventure.'
...as a cheeky young bugger but it did the trick and a year
...er I received the TTT Personality of the Year Award which
...s presented by Dame Vera Lynn. I remember Keith Beckett
...n the Producer of the Year Award. Keith and I did a
...gramme called 'Rehearsal Room' which featured local bands
...h as The Originells, Shorty and Them and of course The
...imals. Keith was a very good director and way ahead of
... time. I used to marvel at his direction. Obviously he
...lised if you were going to 'shoot' pop groups you had to
...ke it exciting. It can't be too static; if the music is lively,
...n the direction needed to be lively.

6.45 REHEARSAL ROOM

Introduced by
DAVID HAMILTON
who will present
THE ORIGENELLS
(This week's group from Whitley Bay)
guest appearance of
CAROL DEENE
A programme designed to give local teen-
age talent an opportunity of appearing on
television
Programme editor: HERBIE BUTCHERT
Produced by KEITH BECKETT
A Tyne Tees Television Production
(See page 3)

**The very first edition of 'Rehearsal Room' screened
by Tyne Tees on Wednesday 1st April, 1964. The
correct spelling of the group's name was Originells.
Geoff Phillips joined the band in 1968.**

...ad digs in Marina Drive in Whitley Bay, just opposite the
...anish City. The landlady there was Mrs Hall who was a
...vely woman and I continued to keep in touch with her for
...any years after I left the North-East. I became friendly with
...ll Steel who was a Transmission Controller and we drank
...ge quantities of beer in those days. One day Bill and I
...cided to take the challenge of drinking a pint of beer in every
...b from Tynemouth to Whitley Bay. There were a hell of a
...t of pubs, but we did it. By the time we got to Whitley Bay
...e were well pissed. I remember I got Bill into broadcasting.
...e thought if I could do it, anyone could do it.

... the early sixties there was a night club in Low Fell called
...e Lido; I don't know if it is still there. There was a very
...tractive lady at Tyne Tees called Myrna Malinski, who
...ndled the booking of the artistes. She rang me up to say
...e Lido had cabaret on three nights a week and she could
...ook me as the compere. She said the fee was five pounds a
...ght which was £15 a week and that was half of my weekly
...age at Tyne Tees at the time. It was a great opportunity to
...ake more money so I accepted the offer. When Adrian Cairns
...ade the roster for the announcers it usually turned out that I
...as not on duty for the nights that the Lido wanted me. But
...e Thursday night I found myself double-booked. I remember
...rmchair Theatre' was on Tyne Tees that night and it ran for
... hour and a half. I introduced the programme and told the
...ansmission Controller I was going to the toilet. I jumped
...to my car, went flying across the Tyne Bridge and up to
...ow Fell, changed into my dinner jacket and bow tie, just in
...ne to introduce the cabaret Dick Emery. I then changed

again, came racing back to City Road, and took my place in
the announcer's studio just in time to introduce the next
programme. To my amazement I got away with it and no-one
ever knew that I'd managed to do the two gigs that night.

Tyne Tees had a tremendous following, with more loyal viewers
than any of the other regional stations. They murdered the
BBC who had nothing to compete with at the time. There would
be fans and autograph hunters on the steps of the studios every
day and it was my first experience of signing autographs and
having fans. They were very 'heady' days. Tyne Tees was a
learning ground for me which has held me in good stead for
the rest of my career. I have a great affection for Tyne Tees as
it was a foundation for forty years in the business. I learnt
how to perform in front of a camera, how to read news, how
to interview, and how to listen to people when conducting an
interview. They were wonderful people at Tyne Tees and it's
probably one of the best times in my career....the pioneering
days!'

**For further reading, see David's autobiography 'The Music
Game', published by W H Allen and Co.**

**David Hamilton presented many other Tyne Tees shows
including:**

'Cue For Sport' (1962)
'Who Knows?' (1963)
'It's The Geordie Beat' (1964)
'The Bright Sparks' (Children's Quiz Show, 1966-67)
'Singalong' (Children's series, 1967)
'Pop the Question' (1968)

**He was also a regular presenter of 'The Viewer'
magazine commercials.**

David Hamilton in 1998.

The Production Staff

Production of a television programme is a complex process. The person in charge of the team which 'makes the programme happen' is called the Producer. He or she is responsible for bringing together the original ideas for a programme, managing the resources which bring it to the screen, and controlling the budget assigned to the production. The production team may include researchers to collect information needed to plan the programme, a Production Assistant which is the Producer's right-hand person, the camera crew and associated staff such as lighting and sound personnel, the Director who controls the actual production process, and the performers or presenters.

Bill Lyon Shaw hand-picked the Production team for Tyne Tees. Some of the people engaged were experienced Production personnel working for stations in the south of England. Many of the staff were new to television, however, and a carefully planned 'melting pot' of Production people was assembled which generated an exciting but highly demanding work culture.

'We were making up the rules of television as we went along.' said one Producer whose career started at City Road in the winter of 1958. The position of Producer was one to which many of the staff aspired. Many Production people were recruited with the promise of a Producer's position 'in a few years'. Many made the grade and produced programmes which were the envy of much larger stations in the ITV network. Some of Tyne Tees Production people went on to become famous names in the world of television; David Croft, Malcolm Morris, Philip Jones, Keith Beckett and Chris Palmer, to mention a few.

The photograph shows Malcolm Morris on the left, who joined TTT as Producer in August 1959. He produced Sir Jimmy Savile's first ever television series when Tyne Tees screened 'Young at Heart' in the early 60's. Malcolm described ** his five years at TTT as the happiest in his life. After working at ABC for a while, he returned to Tyne Tees in 1968 as Programme Controller. A few years later he received an offer from Thames Television which he could not refuse. Brian Tesler asked him to produce 'This is Your Life' which

** For further reading on Malcolm Morris's career see his autobiography, 'This is My Life' published by Virgin Books ISBN 1 85227 599 5

The Fantastic Four: left to right are Producers; Malcolm Morris, Philip Jones, Peter Glover, George Adams.

was to be presented, once again, by Eamonn Andrews and later by Michael Aspel. Malcolm was involved with 'This Your Life' as Producer for almost 20 years.

Philip Jones produced some of the 'One O'Clock Shows' along with many other light entertainment productions at Tyne Tees. He later became Head of Light Entertainment at Thames Television. Peter Glover was from the world of ballet and joined Tyne Tees as Bill Lyon-Shaw's right-hand man. Peter Produced the 'Your Kind of Music' programmes which were classical music productions.

George Adams started his Tyne Tees career as Senior Cameraman and trained many new recruits to become 'gentlemen of the cameras'. He was later promoted to Producer and was voted Producer of the Year in 1960 by readers of 'TV Viewer'. He was responsible for programmes such as 'Your Outlook', 'One O'Clock Show', 'Request Time', 'Star Parade' and 'Glamour Trail'.

Canadian-born Bernice Dorskind studied acting and production at the Bristol Old Vic before working as a Production Assistant when ITV first started in 1955. She was offered the post of Producer when Tyne Tees first started and soon made a name for herself by producing many of Tyne Tees light entertainment programmes. Another Canadian-born TTT Producer was Don Gollan who produced some of Tyne Tees' 'Ad Mags' , 'One O'Clock Show' and local news programmes.

Anna Moore had worked for the Black Brothers in theatre as a Soubrette and had worked with big names such as Max Bygraves, Sir Harry Secombe, Tony Hancock, and Jimmy Edwards. The Blacks encouraged her to enter the world of television.

'Typing up scripts or transmission logs is not for me,' she replied

ft to right are:
an Chaplow -Production Assistant,
d Penrose - Director, and Anna
oore - Vision Mixer.

en George Black discussed the jobs
ailable. Television production appealed
her and she became one of Tyne Tees'
st trainee vision mixers working with
d Penrose and Agnes Hughes. She loved
sic and had played the xylophone,
sequently she was assigned many of the
sic productions. She later became a
oducer and was responsible for
grammes such as 'Star Parade', 'Happy-
-Lucky' and 'Songs for the Swingin'
s'. She recalled that in the early 60's
istes were allowed to mime to their latest
ord and Tyne Tees invited many of the
pop artistes to appear on the shows for
princely sum of 15 guineas. When a chance of booking a
w group called 'The Beatles' arose, she turned the offer down
the 'fab four' wanted 15 guineas each and their train fare.
nyway,' she said at the time, 'they are a funny looking lot.'

ith Beckett was no stranger to showbusiness when he joined
ne Tees in the early 60's. He had been in showbusiness
ce the age of 13 and had acted, danced and even tried his
nd at light comedy. Before joining Tyne Tees he had been
emier Dancer at the National Ballet Company. Keith adapted
e ballet 'Petrushka' for television and danced the part of
trushka on the Tyne Tees' production of the ballet screened
Monday 28 March 1960.
ith also appeared in the Tyne Tees light entertainment
oduction 'Sunshine Street' which was written and produced
David Croft and transmitted in the early 60's. Keith
came a Producer and was often responsible for the dance
rection on the classical music programme 'Your Kind of
usic'. He was voted 'Producer of the Year' by readers of
he Viewer' in 1961 and was presented with his award by
ame Vera Lynn. Keith Beckett died in 1998.

t Johns described himself as a 'Cosmopolitan Irishman' when
was interviewed by Bob Stoker for a 'Viewer' article in
60. Before joining Tyne Tees as Producer he had enjoyed
eventful career in showbusiness. He had been a straight
tor, a theatrical producer, a variety comedian, a TV studio
anager and a director. He had also gained experience as a
levision interviewer in the Granada Television programme
eople and Places'.

ne Darling, (now Jane Summers) daughter of Tyne Tees Vice-
hairman Claude Darling, joined the Company in November
58 as trainee Production Assistant to Producer David Croft.
e remembers working with David on many of the 'One
'Clock Shows' which were initially transmitted live five days

STUDIO THREE - production team at work

a week. David produced the show alternately with producers
Philip Jones and Bob Reed.
Bernard Preston joined Tyne Tees in August 1959 as a trainee
Producer/Director. He had been Communications Engineer
at Associated Rediffusion on the opening night of ITV in
London and later worked for ABC Manchester as Outside
Broadcast Planning Engineer. At Tyne Tees he was mainly
responsible for directing sports programmes such as 'Sports
Desk' and 'Cue for Sport' but recalls directing the 'One O'Clock
Show' from time to time. One day Terry O'Neill and Austin
Steele were acting in a comedy sketch that went terribly wrong.
Terry was playing the part of a grocer who was rushing up
and down a set of step ladders, when he fell and gashed his
leg. Bernard knew something was wrong when the station's
nurse came into shot which was not in the script. Terry had to
be rushed to hospital and Bernard remembers how versatile
the cast were in that the programme was able to continue with
Terry's colleagues taking over his role for the rest of the Show.

Bob Herrick joined the company as Stills Photographer but
soon became Film Cameraman. He recalls a time when he
was filming the arrival of an Inspecting Admiral on HMS
Calliope. He was using a clockwork film camera and without
warning the main spring suddenly broke with a deafening
'crack'. The Admiral thought that someone had shot at him
and dived for cover!
Bob, along with his colleague Norman Jackson, won the 'British
Television Newsfilm of the Year Award' in 1965 for their film
of 'Lord Robens Ambush'. Bob was promoted to Head of
Film that same year.

I am greatly indebted to the people whose stories are presented
on the following pages. I would like to thank them for taking
time to meet me and recalling their memories of Tyne Tees
Television.

Philip Jones OBE

'I joined Tyne Tees Television when the station first went on the air. I had been working for Granada Television in Manchester as a light entertainment producer for the previous three years but, having met George and Alfred Black and Bill Lyon-Shaw, and hearing of their plans for the new TV station, I was happy to accept a job as Producer/Director in the Light Entertainment department.

So, my wife Florence, my little boy Pip, and I all moved to Newcastle upon Tyne. The North East was new territory to us but we knew of the Geordies' legendary friendliness and hospitality, and this certainly was true.

My first brief was to launch a lunchtime entertainment show. In those days several of the regional ITV companies produced midday magazine shows catering very much for local audiences and tastes. In Birmingham, ATV's long-running series was 'Lunchbox' while from Glasgow, Scottish Television produced 'The One O'Clock Gang'.

Thus was born TTT's 'One O'Clock Show'. The Blacks and Bill Lyon-Shaw with his many years' experience in the theatre and in television both at the BBC and at ATV, had assembled a talented team of performers. Leading the comedy team was Terry O'Neill (with Cinders, his singing dachshund!), Austin Steele and Len Marten. The resident music group was led by Dennis Ringrowe with singers Chris Langford, Shirley Wilson and George Romaine. The bulk of the sketch -writing in the early shows was by Lisle Willis and Dan Douglas. For all of us it was an exciting and demanding challenge to produce a forty minute show five days a week but we all learned a great deal from the experience. I suppose if one could see the shows now (they were all 'live' in those days before videotape) they would look fairly rough and ready by today's production standards, but I believe that light entertainment in those days had an atmosphere and a sense of fun and immediacy which we miss today. I have fond memories of my fellow-Producers, George Adams and Chris Palmer and in particular, I was very lucky to have a Production Assistant called Claire Caldwell who was a great help to me.

Television directors seldom forget the shows they worked on; the images become so vivid during the production period that one can almost call up a replay in the mind's eye! Of course some series were more successful than others - how else can it be when the schedule demands such a supply of material. But good or not so good, they will always be in my memory; Tony Martell's 'At the Golden Disc', 'The Bobby Thompson Show', 'The Jimmy James Show',

'Request Time' - these and many more remain in my memor of Tyne Tees Television.

And above all, the friendliness of the Geordies and breathtaking beauty of the Northumberland coast were unforgettable bonus to my two years at City Road.'

Philip was voted 'Producer of the Year' by readers of 'T Viewer' in 1959 and some of the programmes he produced Tyne Tees are featured in this book.

Philip Jones left Tyne Tees Television in 1961 to join A Television in London as Producer/Director. He produce wide range of ABC's variety and comedy shows such as 'I Night Out' and 'Blackpool Night Out' and many TV 'specia featuring Bruce Forsyth, Frankie Howerd, Tommy Coop The Beatles and Peggy Lee. In June 1962 Frank Sina appeared in Concert at the Royal Festival Hall and Philip w the television director. Philip Jones was the originator a producer of ATV's 'Thank Your Lucky Stars', one of t leading pop shows of the sixties.

In 1968 ABC merged with Rediffusion TV to become Than Television and Philip was appointed Head of Lig Entertainment in the new company, a position he held for years with responsibility for Thames' comedy and varie programmes. He retired from Thames in 1988 and joined t independent production company DLT Entertainment Consultant.

He is currently Executive Producer of the long-running BE situation comedy 'As Time Goes By' starring Dame Judi Den and Geoffrey Palmer.

Philip Jones was appointed OBE in the 1977 New Yea Honours.

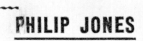

Philip Jones was voted 'Producer of the Year' by readers of 'The Viewer' in 1959.

axwell Deas

fore the war I worked in a Newcastle Quayside shipping ice, days when, on the tide, there was inevitably a collier to seen making its way either to or from the coal staithes at nston.

is was no longer the situation when I was de-mobbed in rch 1946 as the coal trade had yet to re-establish itself, so, me there was a restless period of twelve years in various cupations, all of them interesting but not very creative.

ter a Government Business Training Course, I spent some ne learning rope and cord making in a local ropery before ning North East Trading Estates, then the Federation of itish Industries (now the CBI) followed by a year with its ndon subsidiary, British Overseas Fairs. This took me to lsinki in 1957 where Finland's famous composer, Sibelius, d in the September.

hile in London I was interviewed by George Black who, th his brother Alfred, were to be the principal shareholders d working directors of Tyne Tees Television at that time in urse of being established. Over the decade I had developed enthusiasm for the theatre and show business generally ough membership of the Sunderland Drama Club and the eratic Society. Throughout the summer of 1956 I had played a professional, the lead in Ivor Novello's 'Kings Rhapsody' Scarborough Open Air Theatre.

vas one of the first to join Tyne Tees in its temporary offices Northumberland Street, nine months before the company as due on the air in January 1959. During this time I served salesman for advertising on TV, calling on retailers and anufacturers throughout the North-East.

s the time approached for the station to go on the air I was ade directly responsible to the Managing Director, Anthony lly for the guest list and detailed planning for the Opening ay Banquet in the Old Assembly Rooms as well as an evening nning buffet in the Guildhall. There were over 500 invitees awn from all walks of local, civic, and public life, including e Bishop of Newcastle who said The Grace. My own prayer as that all would be satisfactory. From then on and for the xt few years I was Station Host and Public Relations Officer, th which was coupled responsibility for the Epilogue which as to become a nightly feature for the next thirty years.

part from giving outside talks, one of my responsibilities as to conduct parties (usually of ladies) around the studios ter having watched 'The One O'Clock Show' in production the No 1 studio floor. We were very much the 'in' place to sit and our waiting list ranged from throughout the area, tending for many months ahead. I recall one party of ladies ho came from a mining village so remote that at the outset of y tour, I suggested that, afterwards, in addition to the mplimentary coffee and biscuits, they might like to have nch thereby saving them having to look for somewhere in ewcastle.

Oh! Yes Mr Dee (sic) we'd like to have wor dinners heor, ' as the response. An hour later, having talked about the roduction they'd just watched and having led the 'crocodile' rough the principal production departments, their leader spoke up.
'Well it's aal very interestin' Mr Dee I'm sure but aal we want is wor dinners!"

Though much of my work at this stage was routine, it was enlivened by my other responsibilities, some of which involved meeting well-known and famous people off the plane at Newcastle Airport. In the early years that assembly of wooden huts and sheds still to be seen fulfilling other roles in the distance, at the East end of the main runway served as the terminal!

In the early years there was possibly a preponderance of light entertainment in our output. Later, discussion programmes on political and day-to-day issues were included as well as documentaries and local travel. My spectrum embraced people from all walks of life from Shirley Bassey, Larry Adler and Terry Thomas to Cardinal Heenan, Freddie Trueman, Barbara Castle and John Gilpin. Some introverts, others extroverts, but all very interesting to meet and often very different from their public image!

In those days it was inevitable that I should come in touch with our programme directors and producers. Among these were David Croft and Philip Jones, both of whom were to go on to make programmes and series, acclaimed by viewers throughout the world

In 1962 the pattern of my life changed considerably and very much for the better. I married Joy, a cabaret artiste whom I had met back stage waiting to go on, at the Sunderland Empire. Then too, I was appointed Head of Religious Programmes and Outside Broadcasts Liaison Officer. The latter involved my making the initial approach to the organizers for broadcast facilities for forthcoming events. Some sporting but mostly "one off ' situations such as the opening of the Tyne Tunnel, the first ever to be broadcast Royal Maundy Service from Durham Cathedral, and the last ever Royal Agricultural Show held in the provinces (on the Town Moor, Newcastle) before occupying a permanent show ground at Stoneleigh, Warwickshire.

It was now apparent that religious programming was to be increased and seen as an integral part of the company's overall output. This ranged over Schools programmes, documentaries, discussions and choirs. Many of these were nationally networked, among them, 'Life with Johnny', a six part music/drama series with Cliff Richard and The Settlers; 'Children of the Vicarage,' 12 programmes in which I interviewed prominent nationally known people who were either the sons or the daughters of clergymen. Among them were Mary Wilson (wife of Harold Wilson), Douglas Barder, Virginia Wade, John Snow (England fast bowler of the time), Victor Sylvester (Mr Quick, quick, slow of dance music), Julia McKenzie, Rachel Roberts and David Frost. We took over (and improved) 'The Sunday Quiz' from our neighbours, Yorkshire Television, which elicited a mass of little known aspects of Christianity as well as Other Faiths, audiences ranging between ten and thirteen million.

65

Left to right: Maxwell Deas, Sir Ralph Richardson and Sir John Gielgud outside Tyne Tees Television studios in 1960. Sir Ralph and Sir John were appearing in 'The Last Joke' at Newcastle's Theatre Royal.

In later years, 'Highway' presented by Sir Harry Secombe was to become popular Sunday evening viewing, the series having been conceived by Tyne Tees Television in the first instance. Meanwhile the nightly Epilogue continued but in a varying format, although the spiritual messages remained the cornerstone. The overall assembly of these offerings, was a never ending challenge and the response from contributors, clergy and laity, was always spontaneous. Recruited from various sources, material having a religious content was submitted to one or other of our three Religious Advisors - Anglican, Free Church, and Roman Catholic, prior to recording. It is remarkable that over thirty years I cannot recall any contributor being late for his or her recording session. Contributors were invited regardless of rank or station and ranged from a shepherd from the Durham fells to the Duke of Northumberland in H.M. The Queen's Jubilee Year.

Local choirs and soloists made weekly appearances and among those whom I invited were Seaham Harbour born Thomas Allen, and Ashington born Janice Cairns. They were both in the very early stages of their profession but later to become world famous opera singers. Catherine Cookson recorded several programmes on her philosophy towards life. Interviews were also included in the weekly schedule to which I contributed. My first interview on television was with the former Archbishop of Canterbury, Lord Fisher of Lambeth. After the recording, I was embarrassed to learn that due to a technical fault, we would have to record again. The genial Dr Fisher was quite unconcerned and I was amused to hear completely different answers the second time around!

One Christmas, we broadcast a series of seasonal readings each read by actors. Among them were Bernard Miles, Richard Todd, Barry Sinclair, Dulcie Gray and Michael Denison, Alan Browning and Pat Phoenix, and Linda Thorson.

Poetry readings had already been a regular Epilogue feature and when viewers were invited to submit their own compositions, the response was quite remarkable. I like to think that this contributed to the formation of some writers' groups in the area.

When I had produced 5,000 Epilogues, I was awarded a sabbatical, which took me to Rome for two weeks. I was invited to the Vatican to attend an Audience with Pope Paul VI during which, His Holiness presented me with his personal medal, 'as a symbol of our welcome to Rome and in appreciation of the programmes you are making.'

The unexpected was ever present and one summer, when Queen Elizabeth the Queen Mother had a horse running in the Northumberland Plate, it was announced at short notice that she would be attending the Gosforth Park meeting. In the emergency, I volunteered to do the commentary on her arrival. I assembled as much information on her visit and the history of the race, as time would allow. In the event, the arrival of the motorcade was delayed and I had to 'ad-lib' for ten agonizing minutes.

Then too, for World cup in 1966, I was seconded to run the television Commentators Bureau, established in the Hall of Residence in Sunderland Polytechnic, (now part of the University). I shared the accommodation with Arthur Appleton, acting for BBC Radio. Our duties were to provide the various British and foreign commentators with the updates on team selections, and, most importantly, ensure that each occupied the appropriate commentary box at Roker Park, otherwise, their commentaries would go to the wrong country and, in the wrong language!

1977 was a special year for me, not only because I was awarded the Jubilee Medal 'for services to television', but also because on the same day that H.M. The Queen paid her Jubilee visit to Newcastle, Mohammed Ali was in the city. He was making a series of Youth Club visits and I was successful in getting a twenty minute interview with him on the subject of his Muslim faith; a softly spoken 'Gentle Giant'.

In 1987, I retired from Tyne Tees having produced over 10,000 Epilogues, 150 broadcasts from Cathedrals, churches, chapels, temples and synagogues, and 150 studio programmes of varying descriptions. In addition I played numerous small parts in locally produced drama films, among them, the clergyman in 'Get Carter,' and again in 'Barriers'.

In my retirement, I was for seven years a tour guide in Durham Cathedral and I gave over 200 light-hearted talks to guilds, clubs and associations about my life and times in television.

y schooling was at the Royal Grammar School in Newcastle, t I hadn't done particularly well academically. I remember ying that I wanted a job where I could meet people and not stuck behind a desk all the time. I applied for a job at Tyne es and incredibly, the Programme Controller Bill Lyon-Shaw reed to interview me. This would be 1961 and I was 17. s the sort of thing that doesn't happen any more where the p man agrees to see a very young guy. Bill said,

hat do you want to do?'

eplied, 'I want to work in television.'

hat do you want to do in television?'

want to be a producer.'

ll replied, 'Doesn't everyone?'

ie upshot of a comparatively short meeting, and I still marvel this, was that he offered me a three month trial. He said at he would attach me to the Features Department to be a nd of tea-boy, runner, or gopher and if I was no good after at time, I would be out. Thank goodness, not only did it ork out OK, but at a very early stage I was getting a lot more perience than I could ever have hoped for as just a runner. vas given bits of research to do and after a while was assigned young people's programmes. After the three month's trial I as given my first contract. I still have it at home, it has two ry large paragraphs saying what my duties would be and it vered just about everything: researching, reporting, esenting, writing etc. An amazing contract for a very small nount of money.

ained a tremendous amount of experience on documentaries d current affairs programmes and at the same time I was irown into the deep end' on a number of occasions on iildren's programmes to actually do a little presenting. There as a long-running series called 'The Three Rivers Club' esented by Jim Lloyd on which I occasionally helped out ith the presentation.

emember blushingly to this very day being the scorer on a iildren's quiz programme called 'Who Knows?' with cDonald Hobley.

he reason why it's so clear in my mind is that there were the

5.25   WHO KNOWS?
TYNE TEES TELEVISION
presents
an inter-schools General Knowledge Contest
This week :
NORTH HEATON COUNTY SECONDARY
GIRLS' SCHOOL v BOWBURN COUNTY
SECONDARY GIRLS' SCHOOL
Chairman : McDONALD HOBLEY
Questions prepared and verified by
ENCYCLOPAEDIA BRITANNICA
Directed by LISLE WILLIS
A Tyne Tees Television Production

vo school teams, there was McDonald Hobley known ffectionately throughout the land as 'Mac', and on a sort of nantelpiece between the teams sat myself and a very pretty irl called Pat Pike. We were the scorers and we were the only eople in the whole studio who could not see the scores we ere putting up. We often got it wrong, to the great amusement f the audience! I had an earpiece so I could hear the director,

Lisle Willis. Now Lisle was a great professional but he had a very short fuse and not only was I sat on the mantelpiece putting up the wrong scores, but I was getting Lisle bellowing in my ear telling me what scores to put up.

I was involved with children's programmes at a time when Newcastle exploded with the pop music scene and the Animals. I was heavily into the teenage scene in the city, I was great mates with the Animals, and used to go to the Downbeat and the Go-go night clubs all the time. At the same time I was periodically appearing on children's television. Although I was born in Newcastle's General Hospital and qualify as a genuine Geordie, I don't have a strong Geordie accent, consequently I used to get a lot of stick from the hard lads of town for being 'that kid off the television'. They assumed I was earning a lot of money, and considered me to be a bit of a TV star. Neither of these facts was true, but I still got trouble from them. I suppose if I had wanted to try for a career in presentation, that would have been the time to do it. I remember attending an audition with Adrian Cairns, who was senior announcer then, when there was a vacancy for a continuity announcer. I didn't get it, but it was at that early stage, when I was still a researcher, that I decided I wanted to be a director. That's what I set my sights on.

During my time as a researcher on the programme 'Roundabout 6:15', we had a lot of top names in the pop music business appearing on the show. I remember sitting with Rod Stewart (who was singer with the Small Faces) chatting about where we thought our careers were going. In hindsight, I think it was wonderfully ironic, sitting next to Rod who is now a world megastar, talking about whether one of us was going to make it or not. A lot of the top names passed through the studios because miming was allowed which made it easy for us to produce pop music spots. I remember I was presenting the show 'Roundabout 6:15' one day and we considered it a great 'coup' to get Del Shannon on the show who had a big hit called 'Runaway'. The director was a guy called Pat Johns and I can remember to this day during rehearsals saying,
'Hello and welcome to Roundabout 6:15. Here's Del Shannon.' Pat said, 'Absolutely not. We don't want 'hello and welcome'. This guy has a number one record in the States, he's a megastar. You just come up in vision and say, 'Del Shannon'.'
It was a strange lesson to learn. I was a rookie presenter, and thought I had to be polite to the viewers.

I was a researcher on a programme called 'The Road to Blaydon' along with Andrea Wonfor. The programme was about the knocking down of Scotswood Road and moving people to what was then the showpiece Newbiggin Hall Estate. Andrea and I were tramping around Scotswood in some of the grottiest areas; dreadful places at that time. Andrea was nine months pregnant at the time with her first child and I remember thinking it was an indication of her sense of duty to the job. Much later Andrea was instrumental in setting up 'The 'Tube' programme, was deputy head of Channel 4 for a while and is now an MD at Granada. Geoff Wonfor, her husband, was an assistant film editor in the early days and not only went on to produce some great rock videos with all the

5.25   **IVANHOE**
starring
ROGER MOORE as Ivanhoe
in
THE DOUBLE-EDGED SWORD

Baron Mauray, Prince John's henchman, discovers that King Arthur, before throwing his sword Excalibur into the lake, said that one day the weapon would belong to a King again so he has a replica made

A Tyne Tees Television Presentation

5.55   **NEWS**

6.5   **NORTH-EAST NEWS**

6.15 ROUND ABOUT SIX FIFTEEN

A new extension of *North-East Roundabout*. Strictly for the young at heart

Newscaster : **CHARLES GREENWELL**
Research by TONY KYSH
Written by TOM HUTCHINSON
Produced by PETER GLOVER
A Tyne Tees Television Production

6.45   **JEWEL BOX**

An Advertising Magazine
featuring
PAULINE CLIFFORD and
PHILIP JAMES

A Christmas shopping expedition to one of Britain's most luxurious jewellery centres
Produced by FRED WILBY
An ATV Production

7.0   **TAKE YOUR PICK**
Presented by
MICHAEL MILES

Ten keys . . . ten locked boxes . . . and no one knows what's in any particular box. All we *do* know is that seven contain really magnificent prizes and three contain boobies

Hostess: **ELISABETH KINGDON**
Directed by AUDREY STARRETT
An Associated-Rediffusion Presentation

7.30 EMERGENCY—WARD 10
with
**CHARLES TINGWELL
JILL BROWNE
DESMOND CARRINGTON**
Directed by BILL STEWART
Produced by JOHN COOPER
An ATV Production

8.0   **OUTLAWS**
starring
DON COLLIER as Marshal Will Foreman
BRUCE YARNELL as Chalk Breeson in
NO MORE HORSES
with
RICHARD LONG as Morgan Mayberry
JOHN FIEDLER as Ludlow Pratt

Morgan Mayberry, a con man, coaxes prominent citizens into investing $25,000, then leaves town

A Tyne Tees Television Presentation

8.55   **YOUR WEEKEND
WITH CHANNEL 8**

9.0   **NEWS**

9.15 TELEVISION PLAYHOUSE
presents
WHEN SILVER DRINKS
by FORBES BRAMBLE
starring
**COLIN BLAKELY
DINSDALE LANDEN
DELPHI LAWRENCE
DUDLEY FOSTER**

CAST IN ORDER OF APPEARANCE :

Publican	**Eric Dodson**
Silver	**Colin Blakely**
Michael	**Dinsdale Landen**
1st customer	**Harry Pringle**
2nd customer	**John Barrard**
3rd customer	**Philip Anthony**
Iris	**Delphi Lawrence**
Harry	**Dudley Foster**

Michael, a young student, thinks he knows all the answers. But when he tries to put Silver right, the consequences are far from what he expected

Produced by GORDON FLEMYNG
A Granada Production
(See Page 7)

10.15   **CUE FOR SPORT**

A sports programme for the sportsman and sportswoman of the North-East
Introduced by
MICHAEL NEVILLE

The latest news, views and comments on the North-East sporting scene
Sports co-ordinator: FRANK KILBRIDE
Directed by BERNARD PRESTON
A Tyne Tees Television Production

10.45 HAVE GUN—WILL TRAVEL
starring
RICHARD BOONE as Paladin, in
EPISODE IN LAREDO

CAST ALSO INCLUDES :

Sam Tuttle	**Eugene Lyons**
Tuttle's son	**Johnny Eimen**
Mrs. Sam Tuttle	**Norma Crane**

Paladin is forced into a deadly showdown with a gunman, Sam Tuttle, who feels he must " shoot it out " to preserve his reputation

11.15   **THE NORTH-EAST
IN PARLIAMENT**

They are your watchdogs. They are y spokesmen. And in this new Tyne Tees T vision series local M.P.'s report, through q tion and answer, on the month in Parlian as it affects the North-East

Reporting tonight :
Mr. A. T. BOURNE-ARTON, M.P.,
Conservative Member for Darlington
Mr. E. FERNYHOUGH, M.P.,
Labour Member for Jarrow
In the Chair :
Mr. HAROLD EVANS
Editor of *The Northern Echo*
Directed by DON GOLLAN
A Tyne Tees Television Production
(See Pages 4 and 5)

11.30   **NEWS HEADLINES**

11.32 (approx) THE EPILOGUE
Psalm 19
Read by **MAXWELL DEAS**
A Tyne Tees Television Production

Close down

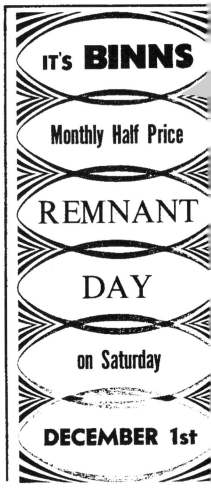

o bands, but actually directed the 'Beatles Anthology'. Geoff
[w]as a fanatical Leazes-end Geordie lad who was a classic
[ca]se of someone from humble beginnings in a small North-
[ea]st station going on to the big time to do probably the biggest
[ro]ck music story ever. Geoff has hardly changed. He's still a
[ch]auvinistic Geordie! I remember at one stage, when he was
[ge]tting into making those big rock videos, meeting him in the
[co]rridor here and he showed me his mobile phone. He was so
[pr]oud of it but it was not simply the phone he wanted to show
[m]e. He pressed a button and the display said, 'Paul and Linda
[wi]ll accept your call.'

[So]me of the directors who were at TTT in the early years
[we]re great characters - Don Gollan, Pat Johns, and Keith
[B]eckett. Keith had been a ballet dancer and was the most
[el]egant and beautifully turned out guy you could ever meet;
[ap]parently ageless. While rehearsing artistes on the studio
[fl]oor he would often go into involuntary ballet movements.
[Li]ght entertainment was his thing, but one day he was directing
[a] horse-racing outside broadcast. He got so carried away with
[th]e excitement of the race that he pulled the top of the
[m]icrophone right off and was prancing around the outside
[b]roadcast van screaming into the top of the microphone which
[w]as no longer plugged into the desk. Another TTT director
[w]ho still is a major figure in the business is Malcolm Morris.
[M]alcolm went on to produce 'This is Your Life'. There was
[al]so a director called Aud Penrose who pioneered TV
[pr]ogrammes for women. She was way ahead of her time.
[T]hey were all hugely experienced directors and great
[ch]aracters.

[S]upergran is probably the high point in my career. It was an
[ex]traordinary success and won an EMMY award. We never
[k]new whether it was going to be
[po]ssible to transform what was in the
[s]cript actually onto the screen. How
[co]uld you get a 70 year old woman
[to] single-handedly wrestle down a

helicopter from the sky? Or the script would say,
'Supergran runs along South Shields pier, climbs a crane, jumps
off into a speedboat, speeds across to Tynemouth, jumps out
and flings the villains to the ground.' We all said, 'How are we
going to do this?' But we did it, along with many other stunts
and effects. 'Supergran' sold in over 60 countries worldwide.
Tyne Tees was one of the first Western companies to sell to
China TV where 'Supergran' was a big success.

One of the first programmes I did as a producer/director at an
incredibly young age was 'Freud on Food'. I was just in my
early twenties and it was so incredible to make the cookery
programmes and to be indulged by Clement in his great passion
for horse-racing. Quite often I'd be whisked off by him to
Gosforth Park to the posh end, with him putting fivers in my
top pocket telling me what to bet on. Over a long period in the
early years I was involved with 'Face the Press' which was a
milestone for this company as it was the first time a Royal
(Prince Philip) had been interviewed on television.

The crews at Tyne Tees are said by many people to be the best
in the world. I remember being assigned by Tyne Tees to
work with the Henson Organisation on a series called 'The
Ghost of Faffner Hall', which involved Muppets, (not the most
well-known Muppets, Kermit, Miss Piggy, etc) but the same
type of puppets. It was marvellous for me; they flew me out
to Canada to learn how to shoot the Muppets and later I went
to LA and New York to shoot the guest inserts. The point of
this story is that the Henson Organisation said that they had
shot Muppets all over the world but the staff at Tyne Tees
were the best they had ever worked with. That's the kind of
feedback we get all the time.'

**The crew of 'Supergran'
performed almost as many 'stunts'
as the star herself in order to film
each episode.**

Heather Ging

'I joined Tyne Tees Television in 1959 after George and Alfred Black and Tony Jelly came to see me in a show which my husband Joe and I had written. That led to us appearing on the 'One O'Clock Show' a couple of times. George felt that I had a comedy talent and that was the direction I was going to go at one point. However, they needed Production people with an enthusiasm for entertainment, so I became a PA (Production Assistant). The Black Brothers era at Tyne Tees was very exciting, colourful and the Blacks themselves were wonderful. I can remember stars like Norman Evans, Jimmy James, and Tony Hancock coming to City Road. Norman was a legend in his own time and to watch stars like him working on the studio floor - I was enraptured. I had been brought up in a family of entertainers, and had always wanted to be in showbusiness, so to see those established artistes working, and to see how thorough and competent they were, made the foundations on which my own professional expertise was built.. All the stars of the era appeared on the 'One O'Clock Show' at some time, and their collective knowledge was there to be absorbed. There's nothing like working with the 'old pros' because they are unselfish, dedicated to their jobs, and are kind to everyone. That's how you get a good production, especially in an atmosphere when everyone was learning about this new medium - staff, artistes, and management. It was a massive learning process and over all of this it was the Blacks, mainly George, who weaved a very beneficent spell. He loved all of his artistes and his staff and would often wander around the canteen and studios chatting to people, and asking about their job and their kids. He was immensely popular and, as a result, drew the best from everyone.

In those days, women were well down the pile, especially secretaries, but there were plenty of powerful personalities. There was 'Big Nan' Coats who worked for Bill Lyon-Shaw, and a lovely lady called Phil, and naturally they wielded an immense amount of power; in terms of access to the management. The PA's were even further below the salt. I joined at the bottom end with PA's like Christine Fuller and Celia Stoker. We became very close and still are. There were seven or eight of us and we were 'sisters' and looked after each other. This was very necessary at Tyne Tees as it was a very dangerous place for anybody who was down in the ranking. Television was new, everyone was twitchy, and the whole place was learning. If anything went wrong, the blame went down the 'ladder'. It always ended up at the PA's door. So the girls were very endangered and of course, as was usual in those days, very denigrated. Tony Sandford was the Head Transmission Controller, scourge of the PA's and he was a powerful personality, to say the least. When something had gone wro on transmission, I remember it often being said,
'Tony Sandford is looking for you.'
And as the junior PA, that was my cue to hide in the ladies Another character was Malcolm Morris whose PA I was one stage. Later he became Producer of 'This Is Your Life'. PA's duties were very demanding. We had to work in t control room with the director, make sure that all t cameramen had their instructions, put a stop-watch on ea item as we went along, and ensure that the programme car off the air on time. That was crucial because time is money Independent Television, and if the programme ran over in the commercial break, there was all hell let loose. In additi to all this, we had to order sets and props, prepare the scrip engage the artistes and give them instructions on what to we Tension was such that Malcolm and I fell out regularly, a on such occasions he would wordlessly slide a Mars bar ov the desk as a way of making up.

Keith Beckett was a favourite with the PA's. Straight fro the world of ballet, his office manners were most unusu Sometimes when the telephone rang, he'd walk over, pick the phone, then stand on one leg and extend the other behi him in a graceful arabesque and give a chirpy, 'Hello'. He w a lovely man and very protective to the PA's.

I also worked on 'Happy Go Lucky' and wrote many of t scripts with my late husband, Joe. The programme was children's drama, and like most programmes then, was liv Jack Haig as Wacky Jacky was the star. Jack was a ve funny man and we all loved his artistry, but he was difficult work with. The person Jack hated the most was the F because she was responsible for the timing of the show and that got in the way of his opportunities to develop his comed he was absolutely furious. In Studio One there was a b glass window in the gallery and about 30 feet down would t

Heather and Joe Ging on the set of Tyne Tees Television's 'Young World' programm

studio set. I remember sitting at the control desk one day, [ter]rified as usual, looking at the monitors, timing everything, [loo]king at the script, listening to the Director Bernice Dorskind [tal]king her head off, and suddenly, in the glass window, 30 [fee]t above the floor, appeared Jack. He'd climbed up one of [the] lighting ladders and was cursing away at me during a live [tra]nsmission. He was absolutely outrageous. However, much [co]uld be learned from him. He was very punctilious, as many [art]istes are, about his work and what his costume had to be. [A]nother problem was his deafness which did nothing for his [te]mper. Jack had many catch phrases such as:

['B]eyond the dreams of Aberystwyth.' (Dreams of avarice.) and ['H]ow *very* dare you,' as he gave a sharp twitch of his bowler [ha]t. Everybody's favourite was: 'Is it bleeding?' as he held his [no]se up to the camera.

[Ka]te Beckley, who was married to Floor Manager John Loukes, [pl]ayed the part of 'Miss Kate' seemingly a 12 year old girl. [On]e day, during rehearsals, Jack was going through Larry [Pa]rker's desk on the set, and pretended to find a card. In a [lo]ud voice, he announced to the whole studio,

['O]h Look! It's Miss Kate's clinic card.'

[Of] course the story went around that 'Miss' Kate was pregnant. [Ja]ck played jokes like that all the time. He was a very funny [m]an but he inspired terror, and I would end up, once again, [cr]ying in the ladies toilet at the end of the show. One fine day, [ho]wever, brought an amazing change. Jack's daughter became [a] PA. Well, that was an interesting turn up for the books. He [sti]ll used to go around shouting,

['W]here's that bloody PA?'

[Bu]t of course it was all in fun then, because it was his daughter. [Fo]rtunately, Sue Haig was a lovely girl and taught us all how [to] cope better with Jack.

[A]fter working as a PA, I became a vision mixer. There was a [ve]ry special lady vision mixer called Anna Moore, who took [m]e under her wing. She was appointed a Director, and while [sh]e was moving over, she trained me to be a vision mixer in [he]r place. Anna had been a Soubrette in many of the Blacks' [sh]ows but had made the transition [fr]om being an artiste to being a [Di]rector. Of course, she understood [th]e artistes and was wonderful with [th]em, always gentle-voiced and [pe]rsuasive.

[W]orking as a vision mixer was even [m]ore of a nightmare for me than [be]ing a PA because I was then [re]sponsible for actually getting the [pi]ctures onto the screen. The [ca]meramen would be yelling over [ta]lkback at rehearsal that they

weren't ready and you were hovering over the buttons ready to 'punch' the picture up. Everything was live so by the time you got to transmission after a hoard of angry rehearsal exchanges, you were in a state of unbearable tension and dire fear of 'finger trouble'.

'What Fettle' was a satisfying part of my career. I felt I was doing something for the region and the audience response was very much there. It was my opportunity as a new Producer, to put my interests in local music and history onto the screen which had been very much part of my upbringing. The people who were involved, say coal miners, with their songs and the stories, made it very cohesive and emotional, and something with which the television audience could identify. We brought the audiences in from the communities in buses so that everyone in the studio knew each other. They all recognised and admired the singers and the comedians, so the atmosphere was fantastic, and the ratings reflected that. The photograph below shows a typical 'What Fettle'. Ed Wilson, the show's presenter, (on the left) played Billy Seaton in 'When the Boat Comes In' and is currently Director of the National Youth Theatre in London. Malcolm Gerrie, who was my researcher, later produced 'The Tube' which was one of Tyne Tees' most successful music productions and was screened on Channel 4. Malcolm is now enjoying international success as a Producer. Norman Dunn is there, a much loved local singer who shared the presenting of 'What Fettle' and Bert Draycott appeared from time to time in the show with his anecdotes of life as a coal miner.

When I became Head of Arts in 1979, we started to make arts programmes mainly because the ITV franchise demanded it. However, it turned out to be very worthwhile and I had a marvellous team who made excellent documentaries resulting in national and international awards. There was a wonderful moment when we won the Top Arts Journalist Award at the Royal Academy of Arts in London. All of the famous arts presenters and arts teams were there, but we won it. The programme was called 'Wild About Liszt' about a Liszt

[T]yne Tees Television's 'What [F]ettle'. (1976) Left to right: Ed [W]ilson, Bobby Pattinson, [H]eather Ging, Bobby Thompson, [M]alcolm Gerrie, Angela Barry, [N]orman Dunn, June Barry, [S]ylvia Scarll (Barry Sister), Bert [D]raycott

weekend at the home of Lord Londonderry - Wynyard where Sir John Hall lives now. Apart from the tremendous music, it was an attractive piece of work by my talented Director Barrie Crosier. We had a most creative researcher Derek Smith, and the three of us drank Champagne all the way back to Newcastle, the corks hitting the ceiling with a resounding smack. How the beautiful glass award survived, I will never know, but as soon as we returned we presented it at the Egypt Cottage p for the admiration of our friends.

However, apart from a number of such satisfying professio achievements, the most important feature of my career w the enduring friendships and close family feelings experienc with so many loveable colleagues. Of course, there w villains too, but I don't talk about them.'

Tony Sandford

Tony Sandford joined Tyne Tees in 1958 and was one of a nucleus of production staff who were seconded from Associated Rediffusion in London. Tony is now retired and I met him at the Imperial Hotel in Jesmond. He told me how it all started.

'I remember coming to the North-East with Ian Westwater in his Austin Roadster, and that night we met the locals at the Egypt Cottage pub who were all starry-eyed at the prospect of television studios next door. We didn't have anywhere to stay that first night so we slept on the floor at Chris Palmer's flat in Whitley Bay. Derek Flanagan, Ian Westwater and I eventually found a lovely place to live called Dene Cottage in Low Fell. There were three bedrooms and all the mod cons, and it was a great place for parties. We were all in our mid twenties and I saw Tyne Tees as a way of getting a bit more experience for a few years and then moving on. I didn't foresee meeting someone here, getting married, and starting a family.

On the opening night; I took the role of Assistant Transmission Controller as I was the most experienced at that time. Donald Hill-Davis was TC. Everybody had opening night nerves but I can only remember one major thing going wrong. There was a forces request programme which went on for a number of years and this was the first one. We had to roll double-headed film from telecine into the programme and the film was upside-down. I can't remember how we got out of it but it was the only obvious technical blunder.

There was nothing glamorous about the control room; it was an untidy place. It was very Heath Robinson as there were wires everywhere; nothing was encased like it is now. A technician called Andy May was always behind the racks pulling wires out. Unlike now, everything was manual; every cue was manual and every button was manual. There were people pressing buttons all the way down the line so the possibility of a cock-up was that much greater. You were relying on Post Office telephone lines switching at the right time, and material coming up from the network at the right time so there was a greater possibility of error. There was a lot of excitement, however, and I suppose we used to look forward in a funny sort of way, to things going wrong so we could get on top of it and sort it out. You had to concentrate very hard, and I think I used to overdo it. If anybody talked or distracted me, I used to snap at them, whoever it was. We used to work very long shifts and it wasn't unusual to come in for the Sunday morning shift straight from an all night party. It was very silly but when you were in your twenties you could get away with it, just about. Sunday mornings were a bit of a doddle in the sense that you didn't have to concentrate very hard. Consequently we had time to lark about. I remember winding-up one of the announcers one morning and blurti over the talk-back,

'The network are going to take us in half an hour. We've to do a live newscast - the Martians have landed on the Ty Bridge.'

He took it for real. The lights came up and he was going actually present the story. It was very naughty of me.

I enjoyed the job as Transmission Controller but my ambiti was to be a programme director. Associated Rediffusion h sent me on a couple of training courses, but in Londo competition for those jobs was quite fierce. By coming to North-East I thought that opportunities for promotion wou come a lot quicker. I was quite young and headstrong, a was convinced I was the answer to everyone's prayers in j terms. I saw a lot of new people coming into Tyne Tees directors who were ex-floor managers and ex-cameramen. couldn't understand why they were getting preference ov me. I went to see George Black and told him my feeling Being the sort of guy he was, George Black, in no uncerta terms, told me that it was he who made the decisions in Ty Tees and nobody like me was going to tell him how to promo people. He said there and then that as long as he was Company Director of Tyne Tees Television, no way woul become a Programme Director. He said it very forcibly; believed him, and it prompted me to start looking for a ne job. A short time later I got a call from Bill Lyon-Shaw secretary, who said, 'Bill want's to see you.' It was all Christi names in those days - it was showbusiness you know. S went in, I had the 'fag on' and he said,

'You can put that bloody thing out. You don't walk into n office with a fag dangling out of your mouth.'

Anyway I was offered the job as his assistant which was tremendous opportunity. Bill was larger than life. He had lot of experience and was very talented. Peter Glover ha been Bill's assistant before me. He was a very talente choreographer and had a tremendous track record in t business. I went to see him the week before I started my ne job. He was clearing out his desk and he invited me into h office. I remember asking him,

'Peter, can you tell me roughly what you do as Bill's assistant He replied,

'No! No f***er told me. Why should I tell you. Just pick up as you go along.'

It wasn't said in a nasty way, but I hadn't a clue what my ne job would entail.

While I was working for Bill, programme planning was ve different from what it is today. We were literally running o own show. We would purchase and schedule all our ow feature films and film series. Networked schedules were n oked upon with the reverence that they are now. On any ening, Tyne Tees Television hour by hour was very different om Rediffusion London, ABC, Granada, or indeed any V franchise. Therefore programme planning, which was e main strand of the job, was very creative and satisfying. I as creating the company's programme schedules, and my ccess or otherwise could be measured by the audience ratings. s the years progressed, films became more and more pensive to buy due to competition from the BBC and the ct that there were fewer films and film series for sale. urchasing became more and more centralised and ITV were aying for the entire network.

ad been at Tyne Tees for about fifteen years and had gained lot of experience in the running of the station and the way ings were organised. I hadn't been directly involved in the ogramme making at Tyne Tees, but, with my four years' xperience as a vision mixer at Rediffusion, and film industry ork, I found the switch, in 1970, to become Deputy ogramme Controller, a welcome change, and was able to t more involved in programme production. It sounds a bit lf-indulgent, but I actually executive produced a number of usic and light entertainment programmes. Tyne Tees became ry famous for its rock music programmes and 'The Tube' is e programme most people remember. It was 'Geordie Scene', owever, which was the first of that type of rock music show at Tyne Tees produced.

e did a programme called 'Those Wonderful TV Times' which as a quiz show where clips of past TV programmes would e shown. No-one had produced a show of that style, and the am and I devised the format which was the first of its type. t first we were worried about the cost of the clips from other V companies, but as it turned out they were very co-operative, nd it cost us a lot less than we thought. Barry Cryer was the resenter for quite a while, and then Norman Vaughan replaced im. There was a different panel each week with big names in how business. As Executive Producer, I had the privilege of entertaining the guest stars before and after the show. It was very free and easy and relaxed; these people were able to be themselves and it was a great thrill to meet them all.

A more serious aspect of my job was when franchise renewal was looming. Most, if not all of my time, was taken up preparing the application for renewal of our contract with the Independent Television Authority. I went through so many of them that I can't remember which one was which, but it used to climax with a visit from whoever was leading the contract renewals. I think it was Lord Pilkington one time who visited Tyne Tees, and all the Executives and Heads of Departments had to meet him for a question and answer session. I will always remember, he asked a question about Dan Smith.
'I understand that Dan Smith was head of Newcastle Council when all the scandal went on. I believe that some time later he was one of the Directors of Tyne Tees Television. Am I right in saying that?'
We had to answer 'yes' to that of course.
'How is it,' he continued, 'that Tyne Tees did not produce a programme on the scandal, and it was left to Granada's 'World in Action'?'
There were a lot of red faces when that question came up.

Later in Tyne Tees' history was a show which holds special memories for me. Heather Ging, who worked in features, had a great love of North-Eastern song, dance, and humour of the folk scene. We decided to put together a show which featured the lighter side of folk entertainment. 'What Fettle' was first transmitted on a Thursday night after News at Ten and quite frankly, we thought it was too late to get decent ratings, but we were amazed by its success. We received more letters, discussion, and the biggest ratings on 'What Fettle' than anything that had gone before. It was like the early years of Tyne Tees again. Heather captured the human interest aspect in the programme, and people could identify with the performers. The show had a rich diversity; if you didn't like a recitation or a song, you would like the dancing or the comedy element, or just the characters that came on the programme from all over the region.'

Tony is now retired from Tyne Tees but is actively involved with local and district council work. He also sits on the board of the Northumberland National Park Authority and also on the board of the Northern Museum Service.

'Supergran' (Gudrun Ure) attempts to teach Tony Sandford the 'secret' magic sign. The photograph was taken at the International TV Market in London which is held every year to allow companies to sell their programmes to buyers from around the world.

Ken Stephinson

'I started at Tyne Tees in November 1958. I was working as a film projectionist at the Plaza Cinema Sunderland when I heard about the vacant post as Film Handler at Tyne Tees. The deadline for applications was the next day, so I didn't have time to write. I caught the train to Newcastle to see the person who was recruiting. When I said I wanted to be a Film Handler he just laughed. They had received over 2000 applications - just about every cinema projectionist in the North-East had applied. They asked me what I was doing and I told them that I was a Chief Projectionist. I didn't tell them there were only four projectionists in our team and on my shift I was Chief over a fifteen year-old boy. They asked me where I had worked and when I mentioned George and Alfred Black's Theatre Royal, I think that did the trick, and they offered me the job. I still didn't know what a Film Handler's job entailed.

On my first day I walked up the steps and was greeted by Fred Johnson who was Head of Personnel. His first words were,

'Welcome to Tyne Tees Television; you are going to be paid weekly in arrears and any overtime you work will be paid a fortnight after that.'

Those first words will always stay in my memory - straight in with the cash. It was the middle of winter, there wasn't any heating, and he gave me some good advice,

'Keep your coat on as it is freezing in here.'

On asking where the film department was, I was told it wasn't built yet, so my first job was for the sales department, who said that we had to spread the word about TTT throughout the North-East. We were split up into teams and had to drive around the region in hire cars telling people about the new television station. When the film department was completed, I discovered that my job was to join together pieces of film for the commercial breaks. Most of the commercials were on film and I remember putting together the very first commercial break which was screened on Tyne Tees Television. The very

first advert was for Welch's toffees. Another part of my j was to assemble feature-films ready for transmission and was responsible for screening the very first film on TTT whi was 'The Adventures of Robin Hood'. Tyne Tees used to sho many second-rate black and white feature-films which we often too long, especially as we had commercial breaks to in as well. I had come from a cinema background where th showed double-features, and quite often the B-movie was too long. Consequently we became quite adept at cutting the down to fit in with the cinema's schedule. When Tyne Te heard about my feature-film editing experience, they though was a boy genius and was soon moved up from joini commercials together, to being in charge of cutting dov feature-films. Editing in those days was limited to news fi editing and documentaries, so they wouldn't class my job editing. The union was very strong at the time and they could call me a film editor. I did the feature-film job for a couple years but would often stay behind after my shift and watch t news film editors at work. Eventually I graduated to fi editor for Tom Coyne's North-East Roundabout, and the moved on to documentaries. Among my duties was carryi out the editing for Adrian Cairn's 'Star Parade' which featur clips from cinema films long before 'Film 97' came along. O week, we were featuring the film 'Wuthering Heights', but v couldn't obtain a print for transmission. Eventually we four a cinema near Stanhope which was showing the film. The said we could borrow it that night at 10:30 after it was screene but they would need it back the next day. I was driving an o Austin 12 at the time and set off to drive up the Wear Valle in the snow to the cinema. By the time the film was over, th village was snowed-in and I couldn't get back. I had to sta the night, and next day had to wait until the snow-plough cleared the roads before I could get back to Tyne Tees transfer the film to tape.

I met my first ever personality whe working for the 'Star Parade' programm A guy came in to the editing room and s on the bench behind me.

'Is it alright if I watch?' he asked, as h swung his legs backwards and forward His face seemed familiar but the penn hadn't dropped. The Head of the Fil Department -Fred Tucker walked in an said,

'Have you been introduced? This Richard Attenborough.' I was gob smacked. He was an actor then of cours

Some time later I worked on Sport Productions. Videotape was being use rather than film to record football matche and we invented a system of diagrams t log the game in a particular way so as t

Left to right: Ray Hole (sound), Fre Thomas (camera), Fred Crone (lights Ken Stephinson (director).

74

e instructions to the video-tape editor. That reminds me of
ay when we were at Roker Park, video-taping a match.
ris Palmer was directing, and I was sitting at the mixing
sk, when suddenly a flash of flames came from the back of
e of the monitors. The engineer jumped out of his seat and
led, 'Fire!' and grabbed the extinguisher just as Sunderland
d been awarded a penalty. Both Chris and I grabbed the
gineer and held him back.

ait a few seconds until the penalty!' we pleaded.

o, I've got to put this fire out,' he screamed.

e flames were rising and the smoke was filling the room.
ang on!' we cried. 'Stand by camera one. Goal! Cut to two
 the reaction. Back to three for the crowd. OK, you can
t the fire out now.'

rtunately we were able to resume taping ten minutes later
er we had put out the fire behind the monitor.

y very good friend Dennis Kirkland worked in the property
re at Tyne Tees. The Prop-men would go to the store for
ops and Dennis would hand them out. He wasn't a 'Prop-
an' but one day a post became available and he applied.
on afterwards, Dennis and I were chatting, and he was most
set. With a lump in his throat he said,

ve been turned down for the Prop-man's job because the Prop-
aster said that he didn't think I had it in me.'

nnis was devastated and left Tyne Tees soon after that to
rk backstage at the Windmill Theatre, and then Covent
arden Opera House. Later, he joined ATV as a Prop- man.
 then became Floor Manager and eventually Producer of
e Benny Hill Show. Benny Hill loved him and wouldn't
rk with anyone else. Dennis didn't have it in him to be a
ne Tees Prop-man, but he had it in him to produce the Benny
ill Show. Dennis is shown in the photograph below.

e used to have football teams at TTT in the early days. As
ell as a league team, we had a charity team in which many
yne Tees' stars used to play. We used to mix and match, that
 to say for the first half we may have had three or four stars
aying with us, and then some different
ersonalities would join us for the
cond half. It was all for charity and
e'd be playing against big names such
 Jacky Milburn and Brian Clough.
ersonalities such as Wacky Jacky, Bob
angley, and Terry O'Neill would play,
d we even had Colin Prince in goal;
 almost filled the goal mouth! We
ould play in some out of the way places
ke Wingate, and typically 4000
pectators would turn up. It was great

**he Tyne Tees Television football
am, c1965.
ack row, left to right: Brian Doyle,
eorge Carter, Jimmy Short, John
onge, Brian Harrison, Sammy
corer. Front Row: Mike Pounder,
en Stephinson, Sam Pearson, Gavin
Iorrison, Dennis Kirkland.**

fun and they were simple times. The locals could walk up and
touch stars like Wacky Jacky and get his autograph.

1969 was a memorable year for me at Tyne Tees as it was the
year that Malcolm Morris and Chris Palmer promoted me to
Producer/Director. The high point for me was producing the
documentary 'Meanwhile, Back in Sunderland' in 1973. Rather
than follow the team to Wembley, we filmed the scenes in the
town and in people's homes as the match progressed. It was a
very novel idea and proved to be a tremendous success.
Sunderland were triumphant of course and I remember as
Producer/Director being carried shoulder-high by the crew at
the end of the game - it was also my last programme for Tyne
Tees so there was more than one reason for the odd tear on the
cheek.'

Ken left Tyne Tees in 1973 to join BBC Nationwide as Producer
where he worked with ex- Tyne Tees Reporters; Bob Langley
and Martin Young, and ex- BBC North East Reporter Luke
Casey. In 1977 he moved to Manchester as Senior Producer
for the newly formed BBC Features Department. There he
produced 'Brass Tacks' and introduced Michael Palin to
Documentary film-making with 'Great Railway Journeys'. Ken
made a 10-part series with Alan Whicker and travelled
extensively to produce a variety of documentary profiles. He
became Head of Light Entertainment-BBC North and
introduced a range of new series with David Essex, Freddie
Starr, and Barbara Dickson. He was producer of the Russell
Harty series which ran for five years, and included specials in
Edinburgh and Hollywood.

In 1990 Ken established Stephinson Television which makes
programmes for all the major broadcasters including another
'Great Railway Journey' with Michael Palin - 'Derry to Kerry':
a ten-part series with Terry Wogan in Ireland and 'Songs of
Praise' from the Arctic Circle and the northern-most church
in the world.

Gavin Taylor

Gavin Taylor is now a self-employed, much sought after director of music productions. I met him at his home in Ponteland and he recalled the early years of his career at Tyne Tees.

'I started at Tyne Tees as a trainee cameraman in May 1960. I worked alongside Ian Westwater and at that time the Head of Cameras was Chris Palmer. As a trainee cameraman I had to assist the cameraman, clear camera cables out of the way, and track the camera dollies. I worked on a variety of productions such as horse racing, football and church services. A regional television company didn't have specialists in those days, you worked on outside broadcasts, studio productions, light entertainment; you did everything. It was an excellent grounding in all aspects of programme production. I used to work on the 'One O'Clock Show', 'Your Kind of Music' and most of the productions which came out of Tyne Tees Television, and if you were very lucky you could even operate a camera. That was a great thrill in those days.

I was a cameraman for about 14 years and then I applied to become a floor manager (studio manager). I managed to get the job and the duties were, if you like, to be the eyes and ears of the Director who was upstairs in the Gallery. You wore headphones so you could hear the Director giving his directions which you had to relay to the artistes on the studio floor. You would tell the presenters when to start, when to finish, and you would talk to the audience with regard to safety etc. With it being commercial television there were lots of instructions regarding timing. Everything had to be timed to the second as the commercials had to run at precise times. The next programme may be coming over the network from a different part of the country and if our programme did not end on time we were taken off the air by the Transmission Controller. I would indicate to the presenter the time remaining by a series of hand signals. That would be 30 seconds to go (he crossed his fingers), that would be wind it up (circle in the air) and you would then count down the last few seconds by the number of fingers. All these signals were done close to the lens so the presenter didn't have to look away from the camera. I worked on various magazine programmes and studio productions but when Tyne Tees started producing drama, one of their first productions was called 'Nobody's House'. I was floor manager on that particular programme and I then worked on 'The Paper Lads' which was a children's drama series. I became Unit Manager on the filming of the series and it was during that period that I learnt a great deal about directing drama and single camera production.

I was Floor Manager for three or four years and eventually became a trainee director. I directed the Magazine Programme, football outside broadcasts, and many other productions. In those days you were a trainee director for nine months and it was during that period that I drifted into music productions. When I was directing the Magazine Programme they used to invite bands and singers into the studio and I used to make a effort to do something very special in the studio to make the band look different. We would dress up the studio with say a

hay-cart and live chickens so there was a 'set' there and n just a plain background with flashing lights. One day Mi Batt, the well-known composer and musician, was coming the studio to be interviewed by Roderick Griffith. T Producer of the Magazine Programme Eric McGuffogh sa that Mike had just written a brand new album call 'Schizophrenia' and one of the tracks was 'Ride to Agadi He had some colour slides which were pictures of horsem riding across the desert and he asked me to do something make the interview look different. So I set up a bunsen burn in the studio and recorded the heat shimmer onto camera a half mixed it with the scenes of the horsemen riding across t desert. I also looked through the National Geograph magazine and found some lovely desert 'scapes which we us in the presentation. Mike Batt was very impressed with t trouble we'd gone to for a simple interview. He felt it illustrat his music very well. Malcolm Gerrie had just joined Ty Tees and had noted what I was doing. One of the ear programmes he produced was called 'Alright Now'. I wa invited to direct 'Alright Now' which featured live music; t programme was not live on air but the music in the studio w live and we had great bands like 'The Police', 'Thin Lizzy', ar 'Dire Straits'. The programme broke new ground in the 7C with music on television.

Tyne Tees then applied to take the children's mid-afternoc network music slot from Granada and were successful. W called the programme 'Razzmatazz' which I directed ar Alister Pirrie was the presenter; it was very successful. Whe Channel 4 started, they said they were looking for a bran

Not used to being in front of the camera, Gavin Taylor is caught by the cameraman quenching his thirst whilst chatting to Herb Cohen, Manager of jazz pianist George Duke.

One of the very first concerts I directed was at Gateshead Stadium. 'The Police' was the headline band. I was on holiday when Tyne Tees asked me to direct the concert so they flew me home in the middle of my holiday in France to do the job. One of the guest bands on the concert was 'U2'. Their manager, Paul McGuinness said that he'd always wanted the band to record a video at Red Rocks in Denver, Colorado and said he would like me to direct it. The video was U2's 'Under a Blood-Red Sky' and it was the very first long-form video I ever directed. After that, the rest is history, because the U2 video was such a massive success selling 500,000 copies in a very short time. After that I directed 'Queen', Eric Clapton, Dire Straits, Hall and Oates, Simple Minds and many more.

It is thanks to Tyne Tees and 'The Tube' that I have achieved what I have. I am now self-employed as I resigned from Tyne Tees in 1996 after 36 years of very happy service.'

...w, innovative, risque, live music show every Friday night. ...ey had seen 'Alright Now', and felt that Tyne Tees had a ...ry good profile in live music shows and they asked us to ...bmit a proposal for a one and a half hour live music ...gramme. That's how 'The Tube' was born. Andrea Wonfor, ...alcolm Gerrie and Tony Sandford were all instrumental in ...nging 'The Tube' to Newcastle. It put Newcastle well and ...ly on the map in terms of music programmes. One of the ...eat appeals of 'The Tube' was that it was transmitted live. ...ople used to watch it in the hope that something would go ...ong and invariably, it did. We were reprimanded on ...merous occasions by the IBA for misdemeanours or 'naughty' ...ngs that happened on 'The Tube' and we were told that if we ...dn't take better control we would have to prerecord it. Rik ...ayall for example appeared on one of the early shows and ...wanted to come out of the Egypt Cottage pub and 'vomit' ...the pavement. We all said, 'No you can't do that on national ...levision at 5:30 in the evening.' The programme was live ...d Rik decided to do it anyway. He took a swig of vegetable ...up and on the opening shot he came staggering out of the ...b and went 'Blugh!' on the pavement. We received a ...mendous number of complaints from people saying, 'How ...re you have this man vomiting in our living room when we ...e having our tea.'

...o once again we received a severe knuckle-bashing from the ...BA. There was a classic scene when we interviewed Jimmy ...ail in the Green Room and the producers thought it was a ...ood idea to give him some fish and chips to eat while he was ...eing interviewed. He came out with the line.

...ish and chips? It's like being in the f-ing BBC canteen.' ...here was that horrendous clanger when Jools Holland did a ...ve promotion spot at about 4:30 in the afternoon on Children's ...elevision and said,

...et down you groovy f- ers, and watch 'The Tube'.' ...e were horrified and couldn't believe it. To this day Jools ...n't remember saying it but we always recorded the ...ogramme just in case of things like that. We played it back ...d he had definitely said it. He was suspended from the ...ogramme for several weeks. 'The Tube' was constantly ...shing the boundaries right to the edge and we walked the ...ghtrope' every Friday night.

John Reay

'In 1962 I applied to Tyne Tees Television for a job but received a letter back saying the usual 'thank you, but no thank you'. However, they said they would keep my name on their books. I never thought any more about it until, three months later, completely out of the blue I received a letter saying that there was a job available in the film library as a vaults boy and was I interested? My immediate reaction was: 'what's a vaults boy?'. So I asked around and found that it went back to the film industry with the film vaults when the vaults boys were responsible for looking after and delivering film stock. When I arrived for the interview I was amazed to find that it was such an important person as the Programme Controller, Bill Lyon-Shaw, who saw me and thankfully offered me the job.

The first three or four years were spent in the film library along with Mike Pounder and Barry Crosier. It was the library's responsibility to look after not only programme material, which was mainly on film, but also commercials. New black and white 35mm commercials arrived every week and a daily routine sheet was issued by the presentation department showing all the programmes and commercials to be transmitted that day. Our job was to make sure that the commercials were passed on to the film assemblers to be joined together in the correct order for transmission.

It was also the library's responsibility to collect news film shot by 'stringers' from around the region and which were sent to Newcastle Central Station by train from where the film department transported the film back to City Road using a little scooter and sidecar. Trying to find a little box of 16mm film on the great long platform was quite often a nightmare - the News Department always wanted the film 'yesterday' and it was never on the train it was meant to be on. It then had to be brought back for processing and editing.

Sometime in the mid-sixties an opportunity to work in the Camera Department came up and I became a trainee cameraman, working on a combination of OB (Outside Broadcasts) and studio programmes for a total of twelve years. One memorable series of programmes TTT made in the 60s was called 'Say it in Russian' which was the first language programme an ITV company had produced. The Director and Producer was Lisle Willis and, if he got half way through the programme and there was one word wrong, he would stop and start all over again from the beginning. There was many an occasion when we did five or six takes on this half-hour programme; in those days we didn't edit, and, by the end of the day, we were all fed up. The programmes were made on a Thursday and it became affectionately known as 'Black Thursday'. All the artistes came from the Russian Embassy in London and we got on quite well with them. When the series finished they threw a party for the crew at the Gibraltar Rock pub in Tynemouth where they laid on caviar and vodka and other Russian delicacies, including an excellent Russian brandy. When I asked one of the Russians if you could buy it anywhere he said he would send me a bottle from London and I gave him the money. A week later the bottle arrived by post but nobody was at home, so the postman threw the package in the coal-shed. When I went to get some coal later that nig[ht] I found the parcel, but the bottle had broken – for wee[ks] afterwards we had the sweetest-smelling coals in Newcas[tle] and had no bother lighting the fire!

Towards the end of the 70s I joined the Presentation Departm[ent] and became a Transmission Controller. This department w[as] responsible for the daily transmission of all the station's outp[ut] of programmes and commercials and the TCs, as we w[ere] known, had to make it run smoothly and to time from [the] moment we went on the air in the morning to close down [at] night. I initially found it a very lonely job after being used [to] the hustle and bustle of studios and outside broadcasts.

One of the biggest mistakes a TC could make would be to [get] involved in a movie, forget that a commercial break was comi[ng] up and find that the film had run out on air. You always h[ad] to give the operator a minute's warning so he would have t[he] commercials ready, acknowledge your cue and be ready [to] press the button at the appropriate moment. If none of th[is] happened, you couldn't quickly cut to put the announcer [on] screen as he/she would probably have their feet up on the des[k]. By the time you got everything sorted out, you'd lost [30] seconds; OK, you could restart the film 30 seconds late b[ut] when the film ended and you were probably joining the netwo[rk] again, you had to try and figure out how to lose 30 second[s].

Vacancies for Trainee Directors came along in 1982 an[d I] applied for and got the OB Director's job. Since then I ha[ve] been involved in many types of outside broadcast; I worke[d a] lot with Maxwell Deas on Morning Worship, directed a lot [of] Football, Horse Racing, Snooker and Athletics and, of cour[se] these are frequently 'live' which can cause many pan[ic] situations. One such situation occurred when I was directi[ng] indoor bowls from Darlington one day with David Burton [as] the presenter. We were going live in the afternoon so we we[re] all taking a lunch-break, due to go on air (I thought) at 1.[4?] pm. Everyone was finishing their lunch ready to make the[ir] way back to cameras etc. when I thought I'd go to the OB v[an] a little earlier to check that everything was all right. Whe[n I] entered the van I glanced at what is called the 'off air monito[r]' which, in effect, is 'transmission'. I noticed a badly-fram[ed] shot of the carpet bowls trophy on this monitor and asked t[he] engineer why there was that shot on 'transmission'. He looke[d] at his desk and said: 'John, that is transmission'. My reacti[on] was unprintable, we were 'on the air'. I got straight on to th[e] Transmission Controller at Newcastle and said 'what are y[ou] doing?' to which he replied 'we're on you – we changed th[e] transmission time and brought it forward by seven minute[s]'. From that point there was just sheer panic and my heart w[as] pounding. David Burton was running to his camera positio[n] script in one hand, sandwich in the other, trying to comb h[is] hair at the same time. Titles rolled, followed by David in visio[n] looking would you believe it, cool, calm and collected.

Another memory is of when Roker Park football ground w[as] the venue for a special morning worship programme. Evangeli[st] Billy Graham was visiting the UK, and ITV had the televisio[n]

hts to broadcast a special service which I got the job of
ecting and which had to be pre-recorded midweek in the
ening prior to editing and transmission the following Sunday.
axwell Deas wanted the service to be that little bit different,
it was decided to shoot an opening sequence from the air,
e idea being a journey from Holy Island to Roker, taking in
igious sites on the way, and this particular sequence was
ot in brilliant weather conditions. However, the last part of
e sequence had to be shot on the evening of the service,
oking down on a Roker Park full of worshippers, in
ticipation of the service itself. As the day of the service
proached, it rained and rained continuously; we realised
at this might give us continuity problems with the already
ot opening sequence, but on the day itself the weather cleared
time for the recording so that our continuity worries
appeared. The following day - back came the rain! This
ppened to Maxwell on so many occasions that he was always
ing accused of having a direct line to the Almighty when we
eded fine weather!

e early 80s saw a new Sunday night religious programme
lled 'Highway' with Sir Harry Secombe. The programme
s controlled for the ITV network by Tyne Tees TV and co-
dinated from our London office. The Executive Producer
s Bill Ward who has been part of British Television from
e early days of Alexandra Palace and he's still going strong
w – someone from whom I have learnt a lot.

y first 'Highway' programme was shot in Hexham and
er that I directed many of them and also took over the role
Producer. It was very enjoyable to work on these
ogrammes and Sir Harry was a pleasure to work with. There
e many stories to tell and this is just a couple of them. Firstly,
les from a shoot in Gibraltar. It had been arranged with the
itish Forces to use a private single track Military Road which
ns along the very top of the rock and gives wonderful views
the Mediterranean. We had set up all the equipment and
hts etc. to shoot a musical item,
en a rather flustered forces liaison
ficer arrived who had forgotten to
ll us about the Upper Rock Road
ace which happens once a year and,
ould you believe it, was happening
at very day. The race had by then
ready started and the race
arshal's car arrived - only to find
e road blocked by our trucks and
uipment;. however, we managed to
ear everything away in time for the
st runner, but left the marshal and
e liaison officer to have a rather
ated discussion as to who was to
ame. Also on this shoot, it was

arranged to film the band of the Gibraltar Regiment on one of
the highest points at the top of the Rock which is where the big
wartime guns are situated - a bit like the guns of Navarone. It
is such a high, dangerous position that there is a safety rail all
around the gun placement platform. To enable me to film the
band, I asked the regiment's engineers if they could temporarily
remove part of the safety rail. This they agreed to do but,
when we arrived at the top of the rock, there was such a heavy
mist that we couldn't see the gun platform. However, once
the mist cleared, I realised to my shock and horror that they
had removed the rail from the wrong part of the gun placement,
leaving a sheer drop from the platform down thousands of feet
into the Mediterranean - without any safety rail. It made
shooting a little more difficult – and certainly more dangerous
– but we got it 'in the can'. Nowadays no director would dare
shoot it with all the safety rules and regulations in force.

Christmas 1989 and Durham Cathedral was the location for a
one-hour Christmas Special Highway featuring the American
opera singer Jessye Norman. Although we had recorded a
backing track with the 'Highway' orchestra in London for a
number specially written for her called 'Christmas-tide', Jessye
Norman said on the day that she would prefer to sing 'live',
using the Cathedral's magnificent organ to back her. Despite
the fact that we knew she was only available to record on one
evening between 6.30 and 8.30 pm, we were also aware that
the Cathedral is a place of worship and would only be available
to us after it had closed to the public. Four items had to be
shot during the 2-hour period and Jessye Norman had to be on
the 8.30 pm train to London. Nevertheless, although the
recordings went well, we had problems with her 'Christmas-
tide' song. The first 'take' hadn't been right but the second
appeared to be going perfectly until the very last word of her
song when one of the rigger drivers from the OB unit slammed
the Cathedral door after going outside to the loo! She held the
note beautifully until the camera's red light went out, then she

ir Harry Secombe with the crew
f the very last 'Highway'
rogramme.

turned to look at the culprit and, if looks could have killed, he would have been done for! Although we went for a third 'take' it was not a good one and we only had time then to whisk her off to the station to catch the London train. During the subsequent editing and sound post-production we fortunately managed to remove the slamming door and no-one 'spotted the join'.

I'm often asked about my job and whether I enjoy it. M answer has always been that I have considered myse extremely lucky in life to have had the opportunity to do a j which I have enjoyed so much, and to work with such a gre variety of talented and enthusiastic people.'

Howard Thompson

In the mid 1950's I was Telecine Supervisor at ATV working in the main network control room alongside the presentation people there. I got very interested in the work they were doing. It was Raymond Joss, then TTT's Head of Presentation, who rang me at ATV and asked if I would like to be Transmission Controller at City Road. I accepted the offer and was due to start work on 22 January 1959. I hadn't done the job of TC before so I arrived on 17th to find out what the job entailed. There was a flu epidemic in Newcastle at the time and many of the staff were off ill. George Black collared me in the corridor and said,
'Oh Howard, you're the new man. They need you urgently tomorrow. Go and see Raymond Joss now.'
I didn't receive any training or anything. When Raymond heard that I hadn't done a TC's job before he said,
'Well, you'll be doing it tomorrow.'
Fortunately I had a very good assistant, John Dightam who helped me through the difficult bits.

In those days, the reliability of the equipment feeding the programmes from all around the country was dire. There were breakdowns on the lines quite often, so the breakdown procedure was commonplace. We often had to ask the announcer to fill in for many minutes while we sorted out the problems. Quite often you'd be looking at a monitor which showed a network feed, and it would suddenly go dead. I remember asking Tom Coyne to 'fill' for five minutes and he did it no bother. We just had to get on with it. Nobody telephoned you from the network or anything. If there was a long delay, you had to tell the Telecine Operator to find a short film and show that. Five minute films of singers such as Mahalia Jackson were tremendous 'fill-ins'. It was wonderfully exciting.

I didn't actually drink in those days, but it was a fact that the station in general was

fuelled on copious quantities of alcohol and nicotine. I us to smoke cigars at ATV, and if everything was ticking alo nicely in Telecine, I would treat myself once a week to a cig on Sunday evenings. When I came to Tyne Tees I brought r stock of cigars with me and with the pressure of the new stati and a new job, I smoked my entire stock in one week. I chang to cigarettes after that.

The Telecine people were tremendous. You could ask for film at short notice and they would find it and have it loaded about a minute. Val Parnell used to visit Tyne Tees qu frequently and he would always go to the Telecine departme because he knew they would give him a seat and he cou watch television in peace and quiet without being disturbe He came to Tyne Tees one Sunday afternoon to see an episo of Robin Hood which had just been edited and TTT were t first to receive a print. The film was on one telecine machi and the soundtrack was on the other. We sat Val in betwe the machines and I remember we were short of time and had load the film quite quickly. About a minute into the film, v realised it hadn't located in the take-up spool. We could stop the film, so I told the operator to open up the doors of t take-up spool. Hundreds of feet of film came flying out a

Head of Presentation - Howard Thompson (right) checks the evening programme schedule with announcer, Paul Honeyman.

rted to snake all around the floor. We had to shout to Val ask him to put his cigar out as mountains of film started to ther in the telecine room. Val was slowly submerged in ovie film and it wasn't until the commercial break that we re able to stop the machine , cut the film, and re-thread it.

hen a day's television was being planned, the resulting cument was called a Routine Sheet which detailed second second what was to be transmitted. Production of the utine Sheet was a very complex process. There weren't mputers; everything had to be done by hand. Things were anging all the time and you had to use correcting fluid on Routine Sheet if alterations were needed at the last minute. tworked programmes would suddenly change their times, the schedule of adverts would change. For the first three onths of transmission we were working until 8 or 9 o'clock ery night to complete the Routine Sheet for the next day. ter the day's programmes, a document called a Transmission g was produced which was a record of what actually ppened. The charts below show part of the Transmission g for the day that TTT first went on the air, 15 January 59. Most of the adverts were on film and they had to be ned end to end using glue. We had three commercial semblers in Telecine who did nothing else but join together m of adverts. You didn't 'lose' a commercial in those days.

Sunday Night at the London Palladium, may have been showing, and when the commercial break came up, if the Telecine machine jammed for a few seconds, the operator would correct the fault and then run all of the commercials. We would then rejoin the Palladium Show late, rather than lose any of the commercials. The viewers didn't mind - they assumed that was the way of things.

I'll never forget Bill Lyon-Shaw; he was a terrific man. He owned a huge house in Wylam and threw some super parties. He had a butler called Bennett who was wonderful. Bennett would be everywhere doing job after job. Bill would be sat there giving out orders.
'Bennett, there's someone at the door.'
'Bennett, get me another whisky.'
This chap would just swan around and do one thing at a time and never got flustered. He was a terrific butler.

I became Head of Presentation at TTT but much later I took over the programme planning function from Tony Sandford. My final post, when I retired four years ago, was Controller of Programme Planning and Presentation. It was a wonderful life being in television considering I started at the BBC in 1952 as Technical Assistant Grade 2 (which was the lowest of the low) and ended up in a top position at Tyne Tees.

e lists below show part of the transmission log for the first day's programmes on Tyne Tees Television. The log details cond by second what was actually transmitted and shows the first ever advertisement on TTT was for Welch's Toffee

TYNE TEES TELEVISION LIMITED TRANSMISSION LOG. Thursday, 15th January, 1959.

Logging Clerk: Nan Coats   No.1

TIME	PROGRAMME or ADVT.	FILM REFCE.	ORIGIN-ATOR	DURATION	REMARKS
16.55.00	SIGN ON ROUTINE			05.00	
17.00.00	STATION OPENING PROGRAMME		No.1	16.20	
17.16.20	WELCH'S TOFFEE		AMP	01.00+3	
17.17.23	THE ADVENTURES OF ROBIN HOOD 1 The Coming of Robin Hood	FILM		14.50	
17.32.13	Cap.			00.04	
7.32.17	PRIMULA CHEESE	PRIM/8/1A		00.30+1	
17.32.48	LAWSONS SWEETS	ASFP/15/145		00.15+1	
17.33.04	NUTTEX BREAD	1866/15/3		00.15	
17.33.19	Cap			00.04	
17.33.23	THE ADVENTURES OF ROBIN HOOD The Coming of Robin Hood	PART 11 FILM		09.52	
17.43.15	"TTT Presentation"			00.05	
17.43.20	Annt.			00.23	
17.43.48	POPEYE "Blow Me Down" "Bride and Gloom"	FILM		03.38	
17.52.26	MARS BOUNTY	BOUNTY No.10		00.30+1	
17.52.57	PETFOODS	PALMEET No.6 (FXS)		00.30+1	
17.53.28	LOXENE	NSW/T.292 (FXS)		00.15+1	
17.53.44	BERO FLOUR	50/10		00.15+1	
17.54.00	Annt.			00.40+1	
17.54.41	S.I.			00.09	
17.54.50	T.S.MAX FACTOR	MS CP/7/61		00.08	
17.54.58	Clock			00.03	
17.55.01	T.S. HOVIS	Schoolboy		00.08	
17.55.09	NEWS		ITN	09.51	
18.05.00	NORTH EAST NEWS		No.3	10.02	
18.15.02	THE PRIME MINISTER		No.2	06.58	
18.22.00	Annt.			00.20	No Sound
18.22.20	STRANGE EXPERIENCES "Grandpa's Portrait"	FILM		03.12	
18.25.32	"TTT Presentation"			00.08	
18.25.40	KLEENEX	KX/TV/8		01.00+1	

(Cannot 4.30)

No.2   Thursday, 15th January, 1959.

TIME	PROGRAMME or ADVT.	FILM REFCE.	ORIGIN-ATOR	DURATION	REMARKS
18.26.41	Annt.			03.00	
18.29.41	S.I.			00.09	
18.29.50	T.S. MAX FACTOR	MS CP/7/62		00.08	
18.29.58	Clock			00.03	
18.30.01	T.S. HOVIS	Paco Boy		00.10	
18.30.11	HIGHWAY PATROL 1 No.124A	FILM		15.16	
18.45.27	VILLA LEMONADE	TC/FEN/1		00.15+2	
18.45.44	JOPLINGS STORE	J.I.		00.15	
18.45.59	BISTO	AP/1/58 No.6		00.15+1	
18.46.15	TUDOR CRISPS	TV 976		00.15+3	
18.46.33	HIGHWAY PATROL 11 No.124A	FILM		09.42	
18.56.15	"TTT Presentation"			00.06	
18.56.21	BINNS STORE	BINNS 1		00.30+2	No Sound Considered Lost
18.56.53	FARLEYS INFANT FOOD	3402/8/1B		00.15+1	No Sound Considered Lost
18.57.09	MARKET PLACE including BISTO REGENT FROZEN FOOD PRINCES CANNED SALMON HCE'S SAUCE & CHUTNEY NEWCASTLE CO-OP TRAVEL BUREAU SUN VALLEY TOBACCO BMK CARPETS	ATV/MP/710 ATV/MP/711 ATV/MP/751 TTT/MP/26 TTT/MP/32 ATV/MP/540 STV/MP/270		00.49+15	No SOF but grams radiat Considered Lost
18.58.13	ISAAC WALTON	TTT 3,1 & 2		00.15+1	
18.58.29	NORTHERN GOLDSMITHS	TTT 18		00.05+4	
18.58.38	Annt.			01.03	
18.59.41	S.I.			00.09	
18.59.50	T.S. MAX FACTOR	MS CP/7/63		00.08	
18.59.58	Clock			00.03	
19.00.01	T.S. HOVIS	Knife Thrower		00.08	
19.00.09	THE BIG SHOW 1		No.1	26.35	
19.26.44	LUXOL PAINT	No.1 "KICK"		00.30+1	
19.27.15	SUMMER COUNTY MARG.	SCTV/30/114		00.30+1	
19.27.46	SURF	SUR 202		00.15	
19.28.01	NORTHERN GOLDSMITHS	TV1428B		00.15+1	
19.28.17	MOORLANDS INDIGESTION TABLETS	RP161/6322		00.15+1	
19.28.33	THREE RIVERS PRESS	SFP/15/155		00.15+1	

(Cannot 4.54)

Christine Williams

'I started my career at Tyne Tees as a Production Assistant in 1960. I applied for the position of secretary to Walter Williamson, Head of Sales, but he thought I would be better suited to Production, and two weeks later I joined the Company as a Production Assistant. The training period was nine months, and the first three months you were supervised by an experienced PA. The work was hard, the hours were long, but it was exciting and I loved it. Nowadays the emphasis is on retraining staff to be multi-skilled. In the 60s we *were* multi-skilled. Directors not only directed, they produced as well. There were no researchers or production secretaries; that work was done by the PA. Researchers were only engaged on certain documentaries, or programmes like 'Farming Outlook' where specialist knowledge of a particular subject was required.

The PA was responsible for ordering all the technical requirements e.g, the studio, number of cameras, and special lens requirements, sound microphones, studio set requirements, props, wardrobe, make-up, dressing rooms for the artistes, camera script, and camera cards. The camera cards had to contain all the relevant information the cameraman needed to know - the shot number, the type of shot, ie whether it was a close-up, wide-shot, mid-shot, or long-shot. Each description was abbreviated, and accompanied by a concise camera movement instruction. The cards were the bane of a PA's life, for if she made a mistake, or missed off a camera shot, there was trouble!

I remember when I was writing a manual for PAs and standardising script and camera card layout, one of our cameramen, Arthur Best, who was rehearsing a musical number in Studio One, and always particular about his camera cards, came up to me and said,

'You're supposed to be sorting these cards out aren't you?' I nodded. 'Well, here's a little problem for you to solve - take a look at this.'

I looked at the card, which contained the briefest of details. 'You see this,' he pointed, 'it says 'CU (close up) peanuts' - well, I looked all over the ruddy set for a bowl of peanuts, or a bag of peanuts, or a pile of them on the studio floor - nothing, not a single peanut in sight. Would you like to know what the actual shot was?' he demanded. I nodded again. 'Would you believe, a close up of June (a vocalist) when she sang the word 'peanuts'? I operate a camera,' he reminded me, 'not a bloody crystal ball!'

Once in the production gallery, the PA is responsible for calling all the camera shots and timing the programme. As most of our programmes were 'live' in those days, this was the most exciting part of the job. Every programme had a specific running time and it was the PA's responsibility to count it out to the exact second. If she made a mistake and the programme over or under-ran its allocated time, the Transmission Controller, who was putting the programme out on air, would flick down a switch and say 'Would the PA please come and see me.'

Those words struck terror in a PA's heart I can tell you!

There was a wide range of entertainment programmes in those days, and a week's schedule for a director and PA could include say four 45 minute 'One O'Clock Shows' and a 'Happy Go

Christine Fuller (as she was called before marryi[ng] camerman Lewis Williams) timing a programme item .

Lucky'. The latter was a live children's programme with Ja[ck] Haig as Wacky Jacky. Jack was a great favourite with you[ng] viewers but not sometimes with PA's! He was an absolu[te] professional and expected PA's to read his mind when it cam[e] to the unusual props he wanted for each show. If the p[lot] demanded that he be hit by a chimney pot for instance, it ha[d] to be made of balsa wood. To the experienced PA this w[as] obvious, but not sometimes to the trainee! Many a sharp wo[rd] (most of them unrepeatable) was fired by Jack in the PA['s] direction on the Wednesday afternoon studio rehearsal, if t[he] prop wasn't exactly what he wanted!

My favourite programmes were music productions and the[re] were two which I was lucky enough to work on. One w[as] 'Request Time', a weekly programme with a ten pie[ce] orchestra, with resident singers Chris Langford and Lar[ry] Mason. The other was a monthly hour-long live programm[e] called 'Your Kind of Music'. Bill Lyon-Shaw was t[he] Executive Producer and Peter Glover was the Director a[nd] co-Choreographer. It was a prestigious show for Tyne Te[es] and Bill Lyon-Shaw engaged some of the top names in t[he] world of ballet, stage and music to take part. The orchest[ra] was the newly formed Northern Sinfonia Orchestra, conduct[ed] by Arthur Wilkinson. Band call was held in St. Anne's Ha[ll] just down the road from the studios. My job was to time a[ll] the pieces as they were rehearsed. This was easier said tha[n] done, for Arthur would often stop the orchestra midway throug[h] a piece to run over a particular passage. Once satisfied, h[e] would then say, 'Let's take it from Letter C,' which was nev[er] where we had previously stopped, so my timing was total[ly]

t. How I longed to say, 'No Arthur, from the top please,' but
I could hope for was that he would run through it again
fore the rehearsal ended! On the day of transmission, the
chestra would be playing in Studio 2 while the artistes
rformed on the set in Studio 1. With a complicated lighting
; in both studios, nine cameras and every available sound
annel in use, it was a big show to mount each month for a
all regional station, but it was certainly one of the most
citing and everyone loved working on it.

ay It in Russian' was the first language learning programme
ITV and it was produced by Tyne Tees. It was the brainchild
Producer/Director Lisle Willis who was previously a
riptwriter for The 'One O'Clock Show'. The series took
arly two years to develop and produce and was a nightmare
work on! In each programme, four Russian actors would
act the different 'situations' and at specific points in the
alogue, captions with the English subtitle had to be in place
r the cameras . This was the responsibility of the Props boys
no would be at their wit's end, trying to match each subtitle
a language that sounded like English run backwards on a
pe machine. As an ex-schoolteacher, Lisle was in his element.
e whole studio was his classroom and he loved it, but he
as the only one who did!

January 1964 I was working with Malcolm Morris on
dless 'One O'Clock Shows', when we received word that
ur next programme would be a documentary on air versus
a travel across the Atlantic. At the time, Swan Hunter was
dding for the contract to build the new QE2 and there were
gh hopes that the contract would come to the Tyne. The
ogramme was called 'The Multi-Million Promise' and the
an was to film the passengers and crew of the Queen Elizabeth
the outward crossing and do the same on one of the new
peing 707 airliners on the return journey. For Eric Coop the
meraman, Gerry Barnes the sound recordist, Tom
utchinson the writer, Malcolm and I, it was a great
perience, but filming on deck in force eight gales in near

Producer Malcolm Morris with Christine Williams filming on board the Queen Elizabeth for the Tyne Tees production 'The Multi-Million Promise' which was screened on Monday 16 March 1964

freezing conditions wasn't much fun! There was a certain
protocol with regard to dress on board the QE. When we
were filming in the restaurant at night, Malcolm and the boys
had to wear dinner-jackets and I had to wear a cocktail dress.
Also on board, filming for the programme 'This Week', was
Desmond Wilcox and a film crew from Associated Rediffusion
(later to become LWT) With such a captive set of interviewees,
we often found each other setting up to interview the same
people.'

7.0 THE MULTI-MILLION PROMISE

" North-East shipyards tender for the job
of building the new Cunard luxury
liner . . ."
A Tyne Tees Television film unit journeyed
to America on the *Queen Elizabeth* and
returned on a Boeing 707 jet. Their pur-
pose: to show what present-day sea and
air travel are like. What lessons can be
gained for our shipyards? What would
the new liner mean to the North-East?
These are questions probed tonight in THE
MULTI-MILLION PROMISE
Commentator:
ANTHONY BROWN
Cameraman:
ERIC COOP
Sound recordist:
GERRY BARNES
Film editor:
PETER DUNBAR
Writer:
TOM HUTCHINSON
Directed by MALCOLM MORRIS
A Tyne Tees Television Production

Christine Williams was until 1998, Head of Entertainment at
Tyne Tees, producing 'Cross Wits' and 'Chain Letters' and
many other entertainment programmes for the ITV Network.
In 1997 Tyne Tees produced the 12th series of 'Cross Wits'
with Tom O'Connor, and the 7th series of 'Chain Letters', both
of which have been very successful for the company.

Tom O'Connor, Presenter of Tyne Tees' quiz programme 'Cross Wits', with Producer Christine Williams.

Doug and Marj Collender

Marj Collender (Connor in those days) was recruited as Tyne Tees' first ever Autocue Operator. She recalled the early years.

'I was given basic training for the job in London before being 'thrown in the deep end' at City Road. I remember the smell of paint, damp plaster, and water running down the corridors when I first arrived, as the builders were still converting the old warehouses into the studios. The Autocue system in those days was perforated paper on sprocketed rollers which turned slowly under motor control. I was given a script and had to type up the paper rolls with a huge typewriter which had half-inch high letters. If there were any alterations to make, we had to use sticky tape and write on it. The paper had to be kept at a certain temperature otherwise it would crackle on air as it was being pulled around on the sprocket holes. That created no end of problems for the sound department. I had to rig all three cameras with the Autocue and run all the cables around the camera cable. The cameramen hated the Autocue because of the extra weight on the front. There had to be a counter-balance weight on the back to offset it. I then sat in the corner of the studio and operated the Autocue at the speed the artiste spoke. We worked very late at night typing the Autocue scripts for the next day. The programmes I remember the most from the early days are the Ad-Mags like 'Ned's Shed', 'Trader Horne', with the late Kenneth Horne, and 'Mary Goes to Market'. The Ad-Mags purported to be 'programmes' with a story line but they were just out and out selling. In 'Ned's Shed' Lisle Willis played the part of Ned and he would be sat in his shed talking to his mate Knocker - played by Dan Douglas, and would say,

'What have you got in your sandwiches Knocker?'

Marj Collender at the vision mixing desk getting some dodg advice from Norman Vaughan.

'Well I've got this Primula cheese spread Ned. It's really cann One of the products they used to mention quite regularly w H J Indestructible Socks.

Some time later they decided that they didn't want young gir like me working on the studio floor because of all the b language from the men. So they made the Autocue Operat a male post and I then went to the script writing departme typing scripts for the 'One O'Clock Show'. I actually m Doug (now my husband) at Tyne Tees as I used to go into t Telecine/Ampex Department every day to allocate the stud facilities. Young girls like me were terrified of going in the because of a lovely man called Bert Powell. In Telecine the were large fibre film bins which stood about three feet high. the film snapped in the middle of a reel, they would grab t loose end and feed it into a film bin which was lined wi calico so as not to scratch the film. If I went into Telecir when Bert was around, he used to pick me up and drop n into an empty film bin. We wore pencil-slim skirts in tho days and it was impossible to cock your leg up to climb out the bin, consequently you were trapped. You had to wait un someone felt sorry for you and lifted you out. The Managir Director, Tony Jelly came in one day and found me standir in a film bin. If you think about it, these days it would b classed as sexual harassment but then it was just 'good clea fun'.

Later I became a Vision Mixer and worked on programme like 'The Tube' and other Tyne Tees music productions. remember one particular group coming in to do a show. took them hours to set their equipment up during rehearsal They had an enormous drum kit which took ages to set u Eventually we got 'round to 'Band Call' and the lead sing arrived and he was drugged up to the eyeballs. It was qui frightening to see the state he was in. We went for a rehears and he was dancing around with a can of Coke in his hand ar it was spilling all around the studio and all over the crew. H lost his balance and fell headlong into the drum kit and sent

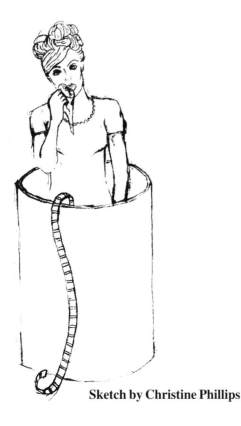

Sketch by Christine Phillips

ying. In a few seconds he had undone hours of work
ent setting up the kit. When it came to transmission,
e were all worried whether he'd make it or not, but
erything was great and no-one knew the problems we'd
d during rehearsals. On another occasion I was vision
ixing for a particular Director who was very excitable.
e was sat next to me and on that particular day I was
earing a lovely baby-pink dress. The Director was
anding up and getting quite wound-up as the programme
ogressed. He just happened to be holding a fountain
en and started to direct with it as if he was conducting
 orchestra. All of a sudden he said, 'Zoom in! zoom
!' as he jabbed the air with his pen. I ended up with my
vely pink dress covered with dots of ink. On another
casion he actually jabbed me on the hand with his pen.
was sat at the desk with this pen sticking out of the
ack of my hand.

ventually I became a News Director and was
sponsible for the day to day direction of local news
ogrammes. I also produced and directed the 'Newsweek'
ogramme for the deaf. I was the first Director to use a deaf
gner' on the weekly news summary on a Sunday. Normally
e 'signer' was a hearing person but when the usual person
as off ill, I made contact with a lovely deaf lady called
aureen Reed who could read the Autocue and 'sign' directly
om that. It 'opened the window' for the employment of deaf
ople on TV. I retired in 1997, having spent 38 years working
r Tyne Tees Television and I loved every minute of it. It has
ft me with some wonderful memories.'

oug Collender was working in the Research Department at
A Parsons in Heaton when Tyne Tees came to town.
My first job was in the Telecine Department where we ran
lms and commercials for transmission. Most of the
ommercials were on 35mm film and it was our job to load
em onto the machines and the Transmission Controller would
de them up on cue. Some of the advertisements were actually
one 'live' by the Continuity Announcer on duty at the time.
hey would read a short script over a slide. I'll never forget
e commercial for Strongarm beer. It was a seven and-a-half
cond advert which was read 'live' by the Announcer. The
ide was faded up and the Announcer would say,
trongarm - a good beer, a mighty good beer.'
was quite plausible when Tom Coyne or Adrian Cairns read
, but sometimes the ad would be in our schedule when Sally
orton was on duty. It just didn't seem right for the ad to be
ad by a woman. The client never complained.

yne Tees was always like a 'Village' where you had the 'Elders'
r experienced staff and then you'd come down through the
enerations. Nobody used surnames - you referred to people
y their first name followed by the job they did. For example
ere was Ian Cameras, Jack Lighting and Jim Sound. There
as a guy I worked with called Joe Cassidy and for many
ears he was known as Joe Ampex because he worked on the
mpex video recording machines.
s a 'relic' from the film industry, demarkation was the name
f the game. If there was a table on a studio set, that was the
esponsibility of 'Stage'. If there was a cup on the table, that

TELECINE DEPARTMENT

Shift Leader, Fred Smith (left) with Doug Collender (right) monitoring a Vidicon machine in Tyne Tees' Telecine Department in 1959.

was 'Props'. If you wanted the table moving, 'Props' had to move the cup first before 'Stage' could move the table. If there was a towel on the table as well, that involved 'Wardrobe'.

Whenever a new Managing Director was appointed, they used to like to make a 'splash' to say they'd 'arrived'. I remember when Peter Paine came he had all the corridors decked out with beautiful photographs of the region. There was a Director's dining room in the canteen and they usually had wine with their meal. A new MD thought it would be nice if the staff could enjoy a drink also. The Canteen Manager pointed out that Tyne Tees did not have a licence so they couldn't sell alcohol. They could give it away, however, so the MD introduced free wine in the canteen. When you'd got your meal at the counter, next to the till were dozens of bottles of white wine and you were invited to pour yourself a glass. Well, like anything else, it was grossly abused by a small minority. Some people would grab a bottle and take it to their table. You could hear the sound level in the canteen get louder and louder as the level in the bottles got lower and lower. It eventually got completely out of hand and was stopped.

I was a Vision Controller for a while, responsible for the exposure and picture matching on the studio cameras. Later I became a Lighting Director which was a very demanding position. I was Lighting Director on the 'Highway' programmes for quite a while and on a show like that there was no room for error. I had to attend a survey with the Director before the 'shoot' to determine what would be needed in the way of lights, and what the power requirements were. When it came to the 'shoot' on the day, you just hoped the Director hadn't changed things. The schedule was tight and usually, so was your stomach on the worst sequences - a time of stress! But I wouldn't change a thing and would willingly do it all over again. Sir Harry Secombe was a lovely guy and I have many happy memories of the series.'

David Petrie

David was one of the youngest employees at Tyne Tees when the station started transmitting in January 1959. He was attending Middlesbrough College of Art with the aim of eventually entering the television industry in the production design field. He was very interested in photography and had applied to Tyne Tees when they first advertised for staff. It was as well that the letter was written in a fairly legible chancery cursive style of handwriting, for it prompted Directors George and Alfred Black to offer him an interview.

David was offered a position as a Trainee Cameraman and was asked to start work in December 1958, just six weeks before the station went on air. It was during that late autumn, in Linthorpe Road in Middlesbrough, when he saw the Tyne Tees Outside Broadcast unit doing a promotional closed circuit demonstration and was able to persuade the crew to let him acquire some initial experience with a TV camera. I met David at his home in the Tyne valley and we talked at length about the early years.

'I remember thinking how professional all those people around me were. Most of them had quite a few years experience in television with companies like Associated Rediffusion, Granada and of course the BBC. It was quite daunting, since I was expected to learn at least the basics of the job in less than a month to enable me to control the wheeled dolly used for the main camera in Studio 1.

I remember on the opening night, I thought that my career was about to be the shortest on record. During the live walk-about showing the viewers the studios and talking to some of the people, Sally Morton was to talk to a cameraman and then the camera had to quickly track past her and out of shot. Most of

the crew were very experienced, so in the somewhat chaoᵗⁱ atmosphere that evening the fact that we hadn't rehearsed aᵖ of the moves should not have been a problem. Unfortunateᵖ when Sally was about to finish the interview with tʰᵉ cameraman, I noticed her microphone lead had snaked arouᵖ the camera dolly, no-one was paying the slightest attentionᵖ my frantic signals and if we had moved it would have cut tʰᵉ cable and resulted in a loss of sound. Not to be recommendᵉᵈ on a night when the station was trying to impress.

Fortunately I managed to free the cable to allow Sally tᵒ continue walking and was only slightly late moving the cameʳᵃ but I well remember the agonising dilemma and seeing imagᵉˢ of employment cards and money floating before my eyes. Laᵗᵉʳ in that same sequence there was an item about the technicᵃˡ aspects of the new service with some film of the transmitterᵖ Burnhope. The camera panned down from the top of the maˢᵗ as the commentary progressed. We were all watching tʰᵉ monitors and when the camera shot reached the base of tʰᵉ mast we were surprised to see a covering of snow on the grouᵖᵈ It wasn't until the film cut to the next shot of the transmitteʳ buildings that we realised the film was being shown in negatiᵛᵉ On the telecine machine there was a positive/negative switcʰ used when transmitting unprinted news film footage, this haᵈ been inadvertently set to the wrong position. The teleciᵖᵉ operator did not live *that* down for some months!

When the programme schedules started, I was working on tᵉᵖ shows a week. The 'One O'Clock Show' would finish at 1:ᵃᵖ pm. The studio would then be reset between 2 and 3pm reaᵈʸ for rehearsals for the next programme. We were starting ᵃᵗ 8.30am and finishing at nine or ten at night, five days a weeᵏ

Ted Ray making a guest appearance on the Joan Turner Show. David Petrie is on camera

y weekly wage was about £6 but this went up to £9 with all e overtime. We worked in teams or crews and quite often I s working with Ian Westwater and Arthur Best. There is truth in the story that we were referred to as West, Best and st!

ter about nine months as a trainee cameraman, they casionally allowed me to operate a camera for the Epilogues. ten we'd do musical Epilogues but as there was no budget provide a film crew, they'd send a stills photographer to ke ten or twelve shots of the church. The script may have quired that the camera shot start at the cross on the top of e church, tilt down and after eight bars of music track out d pan right. We were trying to produce what looked like e pictures from a 20' x 16' photograph with a heavy TV mera, using fairly narrow-angle lenses with a small depth field. We were simulating tracking up and down the church sles and the focus pulls were substantial. Those are the rly memories I have, straining to do things which today would her be done electronically or with a lightweight video camera location.

chnology has moved enormously since those days, the uipment, although 'state of the art' was not as reliable as it today. If a camera began to display picture faults, you lost e use of it and had to continue with only two. All the cameras ed thermionic valves which sometimes failed and that meant camera could be out of action for ten minutes or even the hole show. They would occasionally change parts of the assis to get a camera back in action, but then there would a arm-up time for the valves.

e cameras used large tubes, called image orthicons, in which e picture was created, but the imaging elements of these could ck up burn marks if you accidentally pointed the camera at e of the studio lamps. A cameraman was not popular if he

burnt a camera tube, since the company had to rent them from the manufacturer, and a damaged tube would have to be returned for repair - at considerable cost. Sometimes an image would be retained or 'stick' on the tube and you had to burn it off by actually pointing the camera at a lamp, but with the lens set out of focus. You would often see a cameraman with a 'sticky' tube, 'shooting' a light for a minute or so, while the camera wasn't required.

The cameras themselves weighed over 150 lbs; to carry one safely you often needed four men. If a camera was required on a scaffolding tower perhaps for a race meeting, a pulley and a rope sling were used to hoist the equipment. You were putting 25% of the camera capability of the Outside Broadcast unit on one rope sling. The cameras cost about £2000, an equivalent camera today would cost perhaps £50,000; beware whoever tied the knot on the sling! On one particular occasion, two of us had gone to the top a 60 ft tower and were waiting for the camera to be hoisted with a Land Rover mounted winch. When the sling was two-thirds of the way up, the tower gave way. The scaffolding ties at one corner had failed. We both raced for the ladder, I have never come down a tower as fast since that moment; we thought the whole assembly was going to collapse.

In the middle of the 1960s, Tyne Tees was innovative in designing a novel outside broadcast unit. It used the conventional heavy cameras but towed a large generator and this allowed the equipment, including a video tape recorder, to be powered up whilst on the move. It was decided to make a test run to the coast at Whitley Bay and I was posted with the camera on the top of the van. We were making steady progress until we started to cross Jesmond Dene towards the Corner House, which was then a trolley bus route. There was some clearance between me and the high-voltage trolley wires but

OB3, the first mobile videotape facilty in the UK capable of recording on the move.

as we crossed the centre of the Dene, I could see up ahead the trolley wires were sagging more than they should have been and I was convinced I was heading straight for death by electrocution. This was definitely not in my job description and I made the point rather forcibly to those inside the van, via the talkback system, and I lived to tell the tale!

Early video tape recordings were very difficult to edit. The tape had to be physically cut with a razor blade and joined together. The tape had to be cut at a specific point otherwise the picture would jump when it was replayed. It was a very crude system and once a tape was edited you couldn't really use it again. In order to avoid editing after recording a programme, it was treated as if it was live, and the method was to return to the start and repeat the whole programme if serious mistakes occurred.

I remember one day someone in the vision control room had accidentally left camera 2 plugged directly into the video recording machine instead of using the output of the vision mixer. The Director set the programme away and after about 2 minutes the video tape operator came over the intercom and asked, 'Is this how you want it?' the Director's reply gave one to understand that he thought the show was going ever so well and how dare anyone interrupt!

We ended up with a 15 minute recording of one camera only, doing all its moves, including lens changes and just holding a shot for perhaps 5 seconds at a time, during what was a very busy edition of the advertising magazine programme 'Mary Goes To Market'. There was quite a panic to re-record before the studio was required for a live programme.

I remember working as an assistant cameraman with David Croft on a situation comedy long before he became renowned

for 'Dad's Army' and the other shows that he subsequen[...] produced for the BBC. David wrote and produced the Ty[...] Tees 'Under New Management' comedy series which w[...] very much the forerunner of his future style being based o[...] 'group situation', in this case drawn together to run a pub

An ever so slightly set-up picture just to prove that Ty[...] Tees could compete with network companies in equipme[...] The line-up of cameras used to produce the very success[...] 'Geordie Scene' pop show in 1975. From the top: Jo[...] Reay, Dave Leeder, and David Petrie.

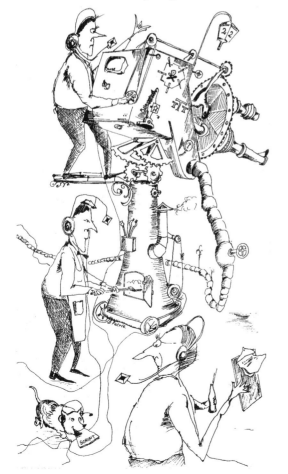

Good Wishes for Christmas

Every Christmas, t[...] 'Gentlemen of the Camera[...] as they called themselve[...] would put together [...] departmental Christmas ca[...] which would be sent [...] camera departments in oth[...] Independent Televisio[...] companies as part of t[...] friendly rivalry whic[...] existed. David Petrie dre[...] this cartoon, and sends h[...] apologies to Ronald Searle

...n Westwater

...ldom seen by the viewing public, yet key personnel in any ...evision company are the cameramen. Ian, who was Head ... Cameras at TTT from 1968 until his retirement in 1988, ...still working as a freelance cameraman for the major TV ...mpanies. He told me of his life at Tyne Tees from 1958. ...was George Adams, then Head of Cameras, who employed ...e at Tyne Tees. I had worked on his crew at Associated ...ediffusion on many live dramas and light entertainment ...ows. When Tyne Tees first started, there were six ...meramen: George, Arthur Best, Derek Flanagan, Roy ...omas, Chris Palmer and me. We also had a young trainee ...lled David Petrie. There was a great team spirit in the ...rly days, the 'One O'Clock Show' was a springboard of ...novation and was the show in which to experiment with ...w ideas. The crews would vie with each other to do ...mething different. I remember, with the use of videotape ...e arranged for Shirley Wilson to walk away from herself ...d sing her song in the foreground while her other image ...nced around a park bench in the background.

...1959 most programmes were transmitted live. All cameras ...ad a complement of four lenses (no zooms) and during ...hearsal we would mark down on a 'crib-card' which lens ...as used for which shot and then mark the floor for the position ...f your camera. Floor space was quite scarce; in addition to ...e cameras there were two microphone booms, monitors, a ...oor Manager with a headset and a cable which seemed to ...ail everywhere. You had to be on the ball because if someone ...issed a shot it would cause chaos in the following sequences. ...remember a sketch on the 'One O'Clock Show' where the ...ameras had moved from a musical number. The three cameras ...ad moved before the two booms because they were easier to ...ove and the next item had a visual introduction. When the ...ketch was coming to the end, the Director called to clear ...amera one (move to the next item) only to find that it couldn't ...ove. The Director shouted for any camera to move, but it ...asn't possible because the two booms had locked the three ...ameras in. Fortunately we had a quick thinking vision mixer ...ho faded to black. The next item was the closing song of the ...how and a stick microphone was being used. The sound was ...aded up and pictures followed moments later.

...t was standard practice when 'shooting' presenters to leave ...5 to 20% of the frame height at the top of the picture as ...eadroom. This was because cathode ray tubes in television ...ets were manufactured with a round screen and some of the ...icture was obscured by the frame around the screen. If we ...idn't leave this headroom, there was a chance that some ...iewers' television sets would not show all of the head of the ...resenter. Occasionally viewers would ring up and complain ...hat Tyne Tees cameramen were chopping off the heads of the ...resenters. One particular viewer was a real pest and kept on ...omplaining. We knew it was his television set but Bill Lyon-...haw heard about the complaint and was furious. He sent ...Maxwell Deas and Head of Cameras Chris Palmer to ...nvestigate. Studio cameras are mounted on a pan-tilt head ...which is supported on a variable height pedestal. When not in ...se, the camera is anchored with two safety chains attached to

Ian Westwater operating camera 1 as Tom Coyne interviews Eva Gabor.

the head, front and rear. On the day that Maxwell and Chris visited the viewer there was a live audience discussion programme in progress. A 'fledgling' cameraman was 'on' a speaker in the audience and the Director asked him to 'track-in' to make the speaker bigger in the camera frame. He immediately complied but he could not pan up as he had left the front anchor chain on the camera. At that very second Maxwell and Chris were at the viewer's house looking at the programme on his set and the speaker's head was well and truly chopped off.

'There, I told you so!' bellowed the viewer.'

Ian recalled a story about a quiz show at Tyne Tees.

'I was on camera 2 and there was a memory man appearing every week. There was a big carousel with hundreds and hundreds of postcards with questions on sport written on them. They'd spin the carousel and pick out a question for the memory man to answer. After a few weeks, I noticed that the carousel stopped at the same place every time. So one day, when they'd all gone for tea, I swapped some of the postcards around. Come Dress Rehearsal, the memory man couldn't answer any of the questions. They had to stop the rehearsal and there was hell on. The memory man said that someone had been meddling with the cards. I remember thinking that it was not a joke any more. They had to stop and put new cards in. They didn't call it cheating; they called it vetting, as they didn't want the man to appear foolish. Nobody knew that it had been me who swapped the cards, but years later, John Brown said to me, 'Can you remember the memory man on that quiz show? Well I was in the control room and I saw you switch the cards!'

Much later I was doing racing from Ayr for ITV Sport. When the Director is planning a race meeting 'shoot', he decides on cut points where he is going to switch from one camera to the

Rigger Frank Murray (left) and cameraman Arthur Best on top of the crane gantry prior to the launch of the Empress of Canada.

next as the horses gallop around the track. It was quite common to use something like a house or a distinctive landmark as the cut point. As soon as that came into camera, the Director cut to the next camera. On this particular day the Director had chosen some washing hanging on a line as the cut point. Tom Young was on camera 1 and was following the horses as they were coming 'round the bend. I picked them up in my view-finder but the director was still on camera 1. Tom was hanging right over the safety rail on the tower trying to keep the horses in view. Eventually Tom switched on his talkback microphone and shouted to the Director, 'CUT!' Some inconsiderate housewife had taken in the washing and there was no cut point for the Director. Tom was dangling over the side of the tower when we heard the Director's voice bellowing in our headphones,

'Where's the bloody washing? Where's the bloody washing?'

Some time later, at another race meeting at Ayr, the same Director was looking for a cut point on the back straight, when he saw a caravan parked in someone's back garden. A cameraman on talkback suggested that the Director should enquire whether the caravan owner was going away that weekend!

'Shield and Deter' was a programme recorded at RAF Middleton St George to show how fast the defence forces could move if a military 'strike' was reported through NATO. There was a camera in the control tower and several others around the airfield. The programme was to be recorded

Ian Westwater 39 years later, working part-time at TTTV operating a camera on 'North-East Tonight with Mike Neville'

on the first mobile video recorder in Britain. Because of t communications that day, it was decided that the signal for squadron of Vampires to take off would be an Aldis lamp the control tower. The Programme Director gave the instructi to 'stand by' and a lamp was switched on to illuminate the traffic controller. The pilots thought the camera lamp was t Aldis lamp signal and they took off in quick succession. T Director screamed at his Floor Manager to bring them bac he hadn't cued them or rolled the videotape!! The planes h to fly around for what seemed like hours, burning off the fu before they could land and give the Director a second chan to videotape the event.

Another big event we covered live was the launching of t Empress of Canada. We mounted one of the cameras on t gantry of the biggest crane in the shipyard to give a supe shot of the launch. We had many other shots planned for t launch, but during live transmission, the Director took clos ups of dignitaries, the ship, seagulls, babies in prams, wavi children, cheering workers, but he missed the planned shot the drag chains and then the actual launch! The Senior 'Racl Operator Les Rowarth and I were the only two people to s this magnificent ship take to the Tyne live on Commerci Television.

I tried to make the Camera Department a happy and relaxe area to work in, where creativity wasn't stifled. Here are son random memories I have of the times.

In the mid 60's control of cameras was taken out of t Production Department and transferred to the Engineerir Department. As Colin Reeve, a Senior Cameraman, remarke at a meeting,

'When I came here I couldn't spell Engineer - now I are one

Lewis Williams, when asked by another young blade Vic Slar how he cleaned his winkle-picker shoes, gave the instant repl 'With a pencil sharpener.'

The blacking-up of the camera view-finder visor with boo

...ish just before transmission was popular, got loads of laughs ...m the audience and the crew, but nothing from the recipient ...ho couldn't <u>see</u> the joke!

...hen we were shooting football in mid-winter, many ...meramen took to wearing their wives' tights to keep warm. ...ey would have had some explaining to do if they had been ...volved in a traffic accident.

...mera parties were legendary - only held when we had enough ...ney in the kitty. Camermen would travel the length of Britain to be there. The last party (1984) was the company's 25th anniversary and was attended by more than 40 cameramen with wives/partners, and was hosted by Derek Flanagan who besides being a cameraman, is a first class chef.

I am grateful to George and Alfred Black and Bill Lyon Shaw who created the original happy family atmosphere we all enjoyed, and to all the talented people who made the Camera Department such a success. It has been a great life at Tyne Tees Television; if only there was time to do it all again.

..superb Saturday night's viewing on Tyne Tees in 1962 which generated a tremendous feeling of well-being.

SATURDAY
TT CHANNEL 8 — SEPT 29

.50 THANK YOUR LUCKY STARS

Introduced by **BRIAN MATTHEW**
Tonight's all-star hit parade :
BILLY FURY
THE KARL DENVER TRIO
MIKE SARNE with **BILLIE DAVIS**
CHRIS BARBER'S JAZZ BAND
America's fabulous **DION**
...nd guest appearance of **PETULA CLARK**
panel of teenagers and disc jockey
...AN FREEMAN comment on the latest
...nerican releases in *Spin-a-Disc*
Directed by PHILIP JONES
An ABC Production
(See Page 11)

.30 BONANZA

THE MOUNTAIN GIRL
...dying old man asks Little Joe to take his ...anddaughter Trudy to meet her paternal ...andfather
A Tyne Tees Television Presentation

.25 MAN OF THE WORLD

CRAIG STEVENS
as Michael Strait
in
DEATH OF A CONFERENCE
with
TRACY REED
as Maggie Warren
WARREN MITCHELL
as Alex
JOHN PHILLIPS
as General Montreux
PATRICK TROUGHTON
as Thiboeuf
...hen an Algerian revolutionary leader is ...und dead, Michael Strait, sent on an assign-
...ent to cover the story, plunges into a mystery ...ll of unexpected twists and turns
(See Pages 8/9)

8.25 BRUCE FORSYTH

invites you to
BRUCE'S SHOW
The first of six programmes in which Bruce appears with stars, personalities and celebrities from all walks of life
His special guests tonight include
HARRY SECOMBE
DAI REES
Music supplied by
ALYN AINSWORTH AND HIS ORCHESTRA
Script by S. C. GREENE, R. M. HILLS *and* RICHARD WARING
Presented by Bernard Delfont
An ATV Production
(See Page 13)

9.0 NEWS

9.10 HAWAIIAN EYE

starring
ANTHONY EISLEY
ROBERT CONRAD
CONNIE STEVENS
in
MALIHINI HOLIDAY
CAST INCLUDES :
Tracy Steele .... **Anthony Eisley**
Tom Lopaka .... **Robert Conrad**
Cricket Blake .... **Connie Stevens**
Kim .... **Poncie Ponce**
Mavis Purcell .... **Patricia Driscoll**
Holidaying in Hawaii beautiful Mavis Purcell nearly loses her life in two unusual accidents. But Detective Tracy Steele discovers that the " accidents " were planned

The perfect combination . . . Tyne Tees TV for tip-top viewing. THE VIEWER for tip-top TV reading

10.5 THE AVENGERS

starring
PATRICK MACNEE
in
MR. TEDDY BEAR
also starring
HONOR BLACKMAN
The greatest assassin in the world is a worthy opponent for Steed, but he and Cathy find that " Mr. Teddy Bear " knows many tricks, all of them deadly . . .
Teleplay by MARTIN WOODHOUSE
Produced by LEONARD WHITE
An ABC Production

11.0 NEWS REVIEW

The week's North East news in retrospect including a film report of one of today's major events
A Tyne Tees Television Production

11.15 SHOOT

Tyne Tees Television Film Cameras bring you the highlights of the week-end's big soccer games
Today's programme features a full report on
Sunderland v Scunthorpe
A Tyne Tees Television Production

11.45 (approx) THE EPILOGUE

The Rev. Arthur Chetwynd, St. Oswald's, Walkergate, Newcastle-upon-Tyne
Close down

Frank Wappat

One of my readers asked me if I ever fancied working for television. Well, to tell the truth, I have the distinction of being the only man to be sacked from Tyne Tees Television's epilogue after my first 'show'. The Producer asked me to do a series called 'Christian Comment'. The problem was, they gave you the subject, the angle they wanted, then I had to write the script and submit it for approval. Not unnaturally, it was altered. On the night of transmission, I was a bit bored and on-edge, so, forgetting the script, I thought I'd make the viewers laugh.

'Good evening - now normally there is a deafening sound, all over the north, of clicking as millions of TVs are switched off as the Epilogue starts.'

Then I noticed the red angry face of the Producer. Ah well, in for a penny, I thought, and ad-libbed for the rest of the five minutes. I had barely finished saying 'Goodnight and God bless', when the Producer strode angrily towards me and said, 'You'll never do that again - you're fired!'

The following week the BBC offered me full-time employment. Since my initial brief encounter with Tyne Tees Television's Religious Broadcasting Department, I have done a lot of work for them. One Christmas I was asked to provide the choral backing, arrangements, and conducting for Janie Marden, Larry Mason, and George Romaine. The first number was 'Away in a Manger', the story of the baby Jesus sleeping in the hay, and each singer took a verse. Janie loved the arrangement, Larry was so easy to produce - but when we got to George's verse, he shouted, 'Stop! Frank, can I have a bit more allegro vivace in mine.'

'Don't be daft George,' I replied, 'you'll wake the bairn up.' '

The Programmes and the Performers

In Tyne Tees 'Black Brothers Era', 1959 to mid-sixties, light entertainment was 'King' and the City Road Studios buzzed with music, singing, dancing and comedy. Every weekday the 'One O'Clock Show' gave North-East viewers their first taste of daytime television light entertainment. Tyne Tees' talent show, 'At the Golden Disc' attracted the highest viewing figures for a local programme in 1959. The children's comedy programme 'Happy-Go-Lucky' with Wacky Jacky and Larry Parker became a big favourite with older viewers as well as children and ran for five years. 'The Boy's Request' featured tape-recorded messages from soldiers stationed abroad to the folks back home, and requested songs dedicated to their loved ones to be sung on the show. 'Your Kind of Music' was Tyne Tees' monthly classical music programme which featured the Northern Sinfonia Orchestra and many stars from the world of opera, modern jazz, and ballet. To the viewers' surprise and delight, Spike Milligan appeared on the programme in November 1961 playing 'Moonlight in Vermont' and also giving a recitation of prose by T S Elliot.

The photograph below shows Dame Vera Lynn who was a star guest on the Tyne Tees programme, 'Ten O'Clock Special' which was screened on 2 February 1962. The TTT Personality of the Year Awards for 1961 were presented during the programme. Shirley Wilson received the award for Female Personality of the Year, David Hamilton won the Male Personality Award, and Keith Beckett was voted Producer of the Year. Left to right are Larry Mason, Shirley Wilson, V Lynn and George Romaine. In the background is the Con Citizens Choir said to be the most romantic choir in the a as its members comprised almost entirely of married or court couples.

The Black Brothers and Bill Lyon-Shaw had many conta in the world of entertainment and invited big stars of the c to appear on Tyne Tees programmes. Among the stars w appeared in Tyne Tees' productions were Shirley Bassey, M Torme, and Bruce Forsyth.

Before a production, artistes would have to visit the Make- and Wardbrobe Departments. Wardbrobe was run by a la called Irma May who was very experienced in her professi Television made special demands or restrictions on t costumes which could be used. Stripes were not allowed they caused a stroboscopic effect with the cameras. Sequ were generally not allowed as the light reflections from th could cause the camera tubes to be 'burnt'. White was t bright for the cameras and men's white shirts had to be dy blue. Chain-smoking Irma could boast that her stock includ 750 dresses, 300 blouses, 200 blue shirts, a policema uniform and a jockey's outfit. Costumes weren't made on t premises but dresses were sometimes altered by one of Irm two seamstresses.

scene from 'Young at Heart' ich was hosted by Sir Jimmy vile and transmitted live from e City Road studios in May 60. It is thought that the ger is Ray Coussins.

Dennis Ringrowe rehearsing his augmented orchestra for a special New Year's Eve show in 1959. There are signs that the rehearsal may have lasted several hours. There are very few photographs of the pianist/arranger Billy Hutchinson, however, Billy may be seen in this photograph just to left of the conductor at floor level.

One O'Clock Show

George and Alfred Black kept their word and sought out local entertainers and artistes to participate in light entertainment programmes to be produced at Tyne Tees studios. Vocalists such as George Romaine, Shirley Wilson and the Barry Sisters made regular appearances on TTT. The programme most people remember from the early years of Tyne Tees is the 'One O'Clock Show'. At the beginning it went out live for 40 minutes, five days a week. The programme caused a domestic revolution in the North-East as housewives changed their routine so as to have time free to watch the Show. Shopping was done earlier or later than usual and the washing-up had to wait. It had the highest viewing ratings in the country for a lunchtime show and boasted over 150,000 viewers each day.

It was Tyne Tees' first Programme Controller Bill Lyon-Shaw, who was the driving force behind the 'One O'Clock Show' when the station first went on the air. This is what Bill had to say about the show.

'For me the great success was the 'One O'Clock Show' and I'll tell you why. First of all everyone was against it when we started, but I'd been responsible for the 'Lunchbox Show' at ATV in Birmingham. That is where we got the idea for the 'One O'Clock Show'. George Black and I decided we would produce this show because Peter Paine, then Head of Sales, said he could sell air time at that time of the day. We found out that in the Tyneside area many of the children went home for lunch (sorry, their dinners) and after the food was cooked it was the mother's relax time. I had brought from London a nucleus of top people, musicians, cameramen, Central Controller Raymond Joss, and Peter Glover, my No1. With

THE VIEWER, February 28, 1959
THE TYNE TEES ITV PROGRAMME JOURNAL
MARCH 1 TO 7 4
'THE VIEWER'
No. 7 c   The Daily News Ltd., 1959

THE ONE O'CLOCK SHOW
What makes it tick?
READ BOB STOKER'S EXCLUSIVE FEATURE ON PAGES 6-7

Chris Langford and Terry O'Neill star in TTT's "One O'Clock Show"

Have fun with our new TV Puzzles feature PAGE 33

this nucleus of top staff we were able to train people so t 'One O'Clock Show' was a great training medium because the were never long bits of it. David Croft came up from Lond with me and I knew him as a writer. He said that he wanted train at Tyne Tees as a television Director. Malcolm Mor and Bob Reed also wanted to train to be Directors so we ga them all a chance on the 'One O'Clock Show'. The Show h everything; music, dialogue, drama, movement, and sometim dance. It was a great way of giving those people a chance a of course there was a show every weekday. I was there not 'rollock' them but to advise on how things may have been do better.'

Terry O'Neill was born in Ireland as Terry Norris. He w the Show's 'Front Man' and was an experienced 'all-roun entertainer. His first professional engagement had been at t age of 12 when he appeared at London's Windmill Theatr He later met Peggy Haig who was Jack Haig's sister, formec double act with her and eventually they married. She al became one of the Show's regular artistes in August 195 Many people will remember Terry's novelty act with Cinder the singing dachshund. Terry's 'sidekick' was Austin Stee who was born in Jarrow and had made a name for himself a straight actor, scriptwriter, and playwright. He had writt the production 'Friends and Neighbours' which was staged k George and Alfred Black at a theatre in Blackpool in 1958. 1959 the show played at the Victoria Palace in Londo Nineteen year-old Chris Langford was the Show's first reside girl singer and captured the hearts of many viewers. Shildo born George Romaine, son of the famous Durham Coun

MONDAY

JAN 19 | **TT CHANNEL 8**

12.55 Opening Announcement

1.0 **NEWS FLASH !**
followed by

THE ONE O'CLOCK SHOW
Light-hearted lunch-time entertainment
with
TERRY O'NEILL
GEORGE ROMAINE
CHRISTINE LANGFORD
AUSTIN STEELE
and
THE DENNIS RINGROWE QUARTET
Settings by ERIC BRIERS
Script by LISLE WILLIS *and* DAN DOUGLAS
Produced by DAVID CROFT
Produced by PHILIP JONES
Today's audience is from Ashington
A Tyne Tees TV Production

The very first 'One O'Clock Show' was transmitted on Monday 19 January 1959.

ofessional cricketer, Billy Romaines, was resident singer
ring the Show's five year run. George's enchanting voice
d personality won him countless thousands of fans in the
rth-East. It is said that throughout the Show's five year
n, George only missed two editions. Ethna Campbell had
en working in a cigarette factory in Belfast when she was
couraged to enter a singing contest in London. That was
e start of her showbusiness career which took a major 'step-
ward' when she was invited to join Tyne Tees as one of
ir resident vocalists.

e original scriptwriters for the show were Lisle Willis and
n Douglas who wrote for many of Tyne Tees' other
oductions. Lisle, who was born in Sunderland, had been an
glish teacher, and Dan, who came from Newcastle, had
died for an Arts degree at Durham University. Len Marten,
ad of Scripts at Tyne Tees, was also one of the Show's
iptwriters and was a well respected comedian in his own
ht. Len had been scriptwriter for Charlie Chester's radio
w 'Stand Easy' and had also done all the character voices.
n wrote the little jingle 'Down in the Jungle...' which was
yed at the beginning of Charlie's Sunday BBC radio show.
was also heard on 'Housewives' Choice' and 'Family
vourites' in the 1950's. For many years he was Hughie
een's right hand man acting as talent scout. On joining
ne Tees, Len had the unenviable task of having to write a
w script for the 'One O'Clock Show' every weekday. He
en said that many of his ideas for jokes came to him when
was in the bath consequently people joked that he was the
eanest comic in showbusiness. Len would appear in the
ow from time to time as one of a number of characters he
d created including: Ivor Giggle the strongman, Professor
ggins, Marlene, and the Soccer Manager. After leaving

**Irish-born Ethna Campbell was one of Tyne Tees'
resident singers in the early 1960's.**

Tyne Tees, Len went on to assist Hughie Green on
'Opportunity Knocks'.

Shirley Wilson came from Leeds and sang on many of
TTT's productions such as 'The Boy's Request' and the
'Bill Maynard Show'. In May 1959, she took over from
Chris Langford for the Monday 'One O'Clock Shows'
only and used to travel from Leeds on Sundays and stay
with her grandmother who lived in Washington. In
March 1960, Chris Langford left the Show to join
Granada Television. Among the shows she appeared in
there was 'People and Places'. She returned to Tyne
Tees from time to time, however, as a guest artiste.
Vocalist Barbara Law joined the Show in August 1960
and became very popular with the viewers. She won
'The Viewer Female Personality of the Year Award' later
that same year.

In September, 1959, TTT decided to reduce the Show's
schedule to four days a week, the Monday edition being
replaced by the 'Eve Arden Show', an American film
import. There were many complaints from the viewers
throughout the North-East.

**Shirley Wilson appeared regularly throughout the
five year run of the 'One O'Clock Show'.**

Jack Haig joined the Show in May 1959. Bill Lyon-Shaw remembered offering him the job and told the story.

'I had known Jack for many years but he had given up the entertainment business due to his hearing problem. He had gone as deaf as a post and couldn't hear his cues on stage. When I found him, he was working in a post office for £10 a week. I asked him to join us at TTT and he told me of his problem. I said we'd buy him a hearing aid which were very expensive at the time; that's why he hadn't bought one. It was a revelation for Jack. It was as if he had been given a new lease of life. He worked wonders for the 'One O'Clock Show' and became a household name as Wacky Jacky. The sound men used to play tricks on Jack and tune the sound equipment to a particular frequency so that when George Romaine sang a certain song, Jack's hearing aid would squeal. Every time George sang the song, Jack's hearing aid would whistle. Sometimes David Croft used to tease Jack by writing scripts with him as a particular character. Jack would read through the new script each day and sometimes would throw the script onto the studio floor in a rage. He'd storm off the set and mumble,

'David has written me as a bloody postman again.'

Much later, when Jack was working with David Croft on BBC's 'Allo Allo', it was discovered that his hearing problem could be cured by an operation. He went ahead with the operation and it was a success. He didn't need a hearing aid after that.'

The stage crew also used to play tricks on Jack Haig from time to time. One particular show had a sketch about Jack going on holiday. The props were quite crude with a set of lighting ladders as the aircraft steps and whatever the props men could find for the air terminal furniture. At the end of the sketch, he was to grab his suitcase, and wave goodbye to everyone as he walked off the set. Unknown to Jack, the crew had packed the case full of stage weights. At the end of the sketch, he went for the case and couldn't lift it. He played along with the joke and dragged the case along the floor as he cursed the stage crew under his breath. If the script was not too demanding, occasionally Jack would not show up for

Jack Haig was with the 'One O'Clock Show' for most of the 1098 editions.

rehearsals until the last minute. This used to upset many the Producers who would complain to Bill Lyon-Shaw. O day Bill asked to see Jack, and said,

'Come in, close the door, and sit down. What would you lik a cup of tea or a gin and tonic?'

Jack opted for a G and T.

'Now Jack,' continued Bill, 'I'm getting complaints from n Producers that you are not turning up for rehearsals until 11:3 What's the problem?'

'Have a look at the script,' Jack explained, 'I could do th sketch standing on my head. I don't need a rehearsal.'

Bill understood, and sympathised, but said to Jack,

'I'm going to have to give you a rollocking. You'd better op the door now so that everyone will hear .' So Bill proceeded dish out a severe reprimand which echoed down the corrid of the offices. As far as the staff at City Road were concerne Jack had received the rollocking of his life. Jack understo Bill's viewpoint and they remained be of friends.

At some point in the Show, usual during a comedy sketch, Jack wou receive a thump on the nose. He wou walk right up to the camera, cock h head back so the cameraman cou focus on his nasal passages and then would deliver his famous catch-phras 'Is it bleeding?'

There is no doubt that Jack Haig w one of the funniest production comi on television, and Wacky Jacky wi remain in the hearts of many viewe who remember the early years of Ty Tees Television.

...e O'Clock Show ' Trivia'

...ry and Austin invented two stone-age characters called Ug ...d Og. They would do a little sketch where one would say, ...'otcha makin' ?'

...e other would say, 'I'm makin' money.'

...ris Langford would be dragged along by her hair at the end ...the sketch.

...e Show featured a housewives' painting competition which ...s judged by Professor Kenneth Rowntree of Newcastle ...iversity.

...e 'One O'Clock Show' introduced one of the first TV chefs, ...nest Bates, who gave cooking demonstrations. Some time ...er he bought the Cock of the North Hotel in Durham.

...1960 a regular feature called 'Anniversary Day Spot' was ...roduced where viewers were asked to write in to tell them ...out an anniversary of something out of the ordinary.

...e show occasionally 'dabbled' in adult education such as ...e time a feature called 'Baby Growing Up' was introduced.

A 15 month-old baby, who had to remain anonymous, appeared on the show regularly, accompanied by a doctor and a nurse who gave advice to viewers about childcare.

The 'One O'Clock Show' was 'exported' twice a week to Border Television in 1961.

George Romaine performed a sketch dressed as an Ancient Briton, but forgot to remove his wristwatch. One observant viewer spotted the watch and wrote to 'The Viewer' magazine pointing out the error and was awarded two guineas for the 'letter of the week'.

In the first 100 editions the following guest artistes had appeared on the 'Show':
Diana Dors, Margaret Lockwood, Alma Cogan, Eve Boswell, Barbara Kelly, Bernard Braden, Toni Dalli, David Whitfield, Ronnie Hilton, Kenneth McKellar, the Gaunt Brothers, and Jewel and Warriss.
Terry O'Neill's closing catch-phrase was, 'See you tomorrow and don't forget your fruit!'

...he 100th edition of the 'One O'Clock Show'. **Back Row left to right: Bob Reed, Joe Ferris, David Croft, Austin ...teele, Terry O'Neill, Bob Hughes, Rees Hughes.**
...Iiddle row: George Romaine, Len Marten, Jack Haig, Dennis Ringrowe, Peggy Haig, Philip Jones.
...eated at piano, Colin 'Tiny' Prince. Sat on piano, Chris Langford.

Terry O'Neill and sons of Cinders?

George Romaine's career up in smoke?

Which frilly, fetching, frock do you fancy?

Chris Langford crushed by cameras?

Terry O'Neill in the 'Spot Margaret Lockwood in the audience' Competition

Guest Stars Pearl Carr and Teddy Johnson

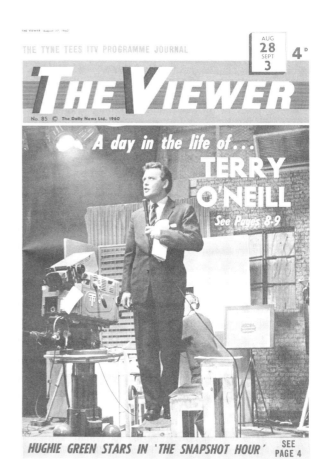

Shirley Wilson and Valerie Pitts

Guest Star Alma Cogan with George Black

The musical accompaniment was provided by the Dennis Ringrowe Quartet with Dennis on piano, Joe Ferris on drums, Rees Hughes on reeds, and Colin (Tiny) Prince on bass. Dennis had been Bill Lyon-Shaw's rehearsal pianist at the BBC and then ATV. He had been in charge of music at two other ITV companies when they started up. Colin Prince (real name Proctor) was a local guy and a keen sportsman. He was 6ft 7in tall and weighed over 19 stones hence the nickname 'Tiny'. Colin could play piano as well as bass and had a good singing voice. Joe Ferris had been working in Blackpool before accepting an offer to join Tyne Tees. He met and married Patti Boyd whilst with TTT. Rees Hughes also came from Blackpool where he ran a boarding house with his wife Dorothy. The Musicians' Union rate for a TV 'session' in those days was £9 but the key members of the band received £12 a 'session' which was a very respectable fee. Rehearsals started at 8:40 am and continued until transmission time. George Romaine was the station's resident male vocalist and he remembers that every day was a new and exciting experience. George recalled a time when he was rehearsing a song one morning and was feeling thirsty. He noticed one of the lads of the band had a bottle of Tizer. He asked for a drink and took a large swig only to find that it was laced with whisky. The band kept the Egypt Cottage in business for many years.

The band became very popular with the viewers and were often 'roped in' by Producers to participate in some of the comedy sketches on the Shows. Bill Lyon-Shaw remembers that the musicians were always willing to try new ideas and they rarely refused to 'have a go' at something in spite of trades union rules. 'They never complained like musicians in London or the other big cities,' Bill recalled.

The brilliant local pianist Billy Hutchinson joined Tyne Tees later in 1959 and was soon hailed as the station's musical genius. Billy was a very modest man despite his enormous talent, and preferred home life to post-transmission socialising. In July 1962, after 782 performances, the whole of the 'One O'Clock Show' cast and musicians took their first significant holiday. For four whole weeks the lunchtime slot was filled

Dennis Ringrowe Quartet.
Top to bottom, Colin (Tiny) Prince, Joe Ferris, Rees Hughes, Dennis Ringrowe.

by the 'One O'Clock Gang' which was a show relayed from Scottish ITV. The band decided on a working holiday at a top hotel in Majorca, but the problem was Billy Hutchinson. He wanted to stay at home. Billy was the band's star musician and they couldn't do the gig without him. Bill Lyon-Shaw sent for Billy and tried to talk him 'round. When Billy told him that he didn't have anything to wear for Majorca, Bill sent for the wardrobe mistress, Irma May and asked her to kit him out. Eventually Bill Lyon-Shaw had to 'order' Billy to go. Some time later the famous singer and actor Howard Keel was appearing at a theatre in Newcastle. Whenever 'stars' were in Newcastle, TTT would usually invite them to appear on the 'One O'Clock Show'. Howard agreed to appear, was very impressed with Billy Hutchinson's playing, and approached Bill Lyon-Shaw with a proposal. Howard was looking for a pianist/ arranger to be his new Musical Director

...ck in Hollywood and wanted to meet Billy Hutchinson. Bill ...as not one to stand in the way of anyone's career advancement ...d sent for Billy to come and meet Howard. There and then ...oward asked Billy to go back to Hollywood with him for a ...lary which no-one at Tyne Tees could have ever imagined. ...was a chance in a lifetime. Billy turned the offer down and ...s words were something like,

...n sorry, my wife wouldn't like leaving Newcastle. She doesn't ...ow anyone in Hollywood. Anyway I can't accept, as I've ...omised the folks at Lemington Workingman's Club to play ...r them next month.'

...ennis Ringrowe and Billy Hutchinson shared the enormous ...sk of writing the musical arrangements for the shows at Tyne ...es. Billy would often be seen in ...e canteen with piles of manuscript, ...ting a breakfast of scrambled eggs ...ith one hand and writing musical ...ores with the other. It is said that ...ere were many filing cabinets full ... musical arrangements which had ...en written for the Tyne Tees shows ...uring the 'Black Brothers Era'. ...nfortunately they were all ...estroyed.

...ennis Ringrowe, his wife Peggy, and ...is daughter Georgina all died ...agically in a car accident in the ...ummer of 1963. Dennis's son George ...rvived the crash.

...erry O'Neill (second left) ...troducing a sketch which is to be ...erformed by Lisle Willis (man ...ith hat) and Peggy O'Neill (to the ...ight of Lisle). Anne May from ...Vardrobe is in the foreground next ...o camera 2. The cameraman is ...erek Flanagan. Len Marten ...Iressed in a policeman's uniform) ...s seen on the far right and above ...im is Denver Thornton.

1.0 NEWS FLASH
and then
THE ONE O'CLOCK SHOW
with
**AUSTIN STEELE   GEORGE ROMAINE
JACK HAIG   PAT BECKETT
THE DENNIS RINGROWE QUARTET**
Today's Guests :
DIANE TODD   JANIE MARDEN
The show features *Who? What? Where?* and the studio audience includes members of the Berwick Hills Community Centre, Middlesbrough, Yorks

Script by HERBIE BUTCHERT
Edited by LEN MARTEN
Designed by BARRIE DOBBINS
Produced by BERNARD PRESTON
A Tyne Tees Television Network Production

had to work very quickly during rehearsals. Consequent many of the floor staff would come up with solutions problems. The atmosphere was such that quite often th Programme Directors were happy to accept ideas from sta on the studio floor to help improve the programme.'

If something went wrong in the Show (which was quite oft because it was live) Bill Lyon-Shaw was always ready advise the artistes or the Production staff how it could ha' been done better. Bill's voice would be heard booming the unfortunate person who was responsible. The sho lasted 40 minutes, but the camera crew used to joke, 'If you wanted a little more light entertainment after the sho you'd keep your headphones on and listen to Bill giving verb encouragement to the Production people in the gallery.'

Every Christmas Day a special edition of the show wa produced for underprivileged children. Great care was take to invite those children who were most in need. Th production staff and artistes weren't compelled to work Christmas Day but most of them volunteered. The childre arrived in buses at about 10:30am, they were taken to th canteen for a glass of milk and a piece of cake, and then eac child was given a goodies bag containing, sweets, crisps and small toy. By the time the show started, Studio One wa buzzing with atmosphere as over 100 excited children joine in with the festivities on the 'One O'Clock Show' Christma party. Key members of staff took it in turn each year to pla Santa Claus.

David Petrie, who was Trainee Cameraman in the early years remembered working five days a week on the 'One O'Clock Show'. He recalled some of his memories of the show.
'The Show featured five or sometimes six musical numbers from the singers and the resident band and there would be four sketches and items which would involve the audience, such as 'Take it From Terry' and the 'Fruit Spot'. Studio audiences were often parties from organisations such as WI's and social clubs, who would come in on a bus and bring fruit for distribution to local hospitals. The fruit was displayed on a table at the front of the audience and Terry would go into the audience and chat with some of them. It was a buffer which helped to compensate for an overrun or underrun in the programme's running time as we never knew to any degree of accuracy how long the show was going to be. All of a sudden the director would say,
'We're underrunning by seven minutes.'
And we would all groan and mutter to ourselves,
'Oh No! Not seven minutes on the 'Fruit'.'

Many of the people I was working with had come from the BBC and other major television companies and they had brought with them a high standard of production expertise. We were always on a very tight schedule on the 'One O'Clock Show' and

A Christmas edition of the 'One O'Clock Show' when underprivileged children were invited to the studios. Each child was given a bag of 'goodies'. The cameraman is Ian Westwater. His colleagues used to jokingly refer to his jumper as the 'Grey-scale sweater'.

special 50 minute edition of the show was screened when it
reached the 1000th edition on Wednesday, 9 October, 1963.
As well as the usual cast, the show featured past cast members
and guest artistes including Norman Vaughan who had
compered 'Sunday Night at the London Palladium'. Norman's
catch phrases were, 'swingin' and 'dodgy'.

The regular cast remembered times during the 1000 editions
that they would rather forget. George Romaine forgot all of
the words of a song one day and had to whistle all the way
through. Terry O'Neill recalled the time he was knocked out
cold when Peggy swung a fish at him and thumped him on the
side of his head. The Producer of the show, Malcolm Morris
(who left Tyne Tees to eventually produce 'This is Your Life')
remembered a time when a local singer, (a bus driver), was
booked to appear on the show. He sang his song at rehearsals
and then put his coat on and went home. He thought the
rehearsal was the actual show.

Since the 'One O'Clock Show' started in 1959, 250,000 people
had attended the show as members of the audience. Nearly
eight tons of fruit had been collected and distributed to local
hospitals.

★★★★★ **1000**TH EDITION ★★★★★★★★
THE
OF THE ONE O'CLOCK SHOW
with

TERRY O'NEILL	AUSTIN STEELE
JACK HAIG	SHIRLEY WILSON
GEORGE ROMAINE	LARRY MASON
PAT BECKETT	LEN MARTEN
CHARLIE SMITH	BILL SELBY

THE ONE O'CLOCK QUARTET
and special guest stars
NORMAN VAUGHAN
DAVID MACBETH
VALERIE MASTERS
CHRIS LANGFORD
ETHNA CAMPBELL

Today's show includes *Spinning Tops* and *With Us Today*. The studio audience is from all over the Tyne Tees area, including Yorkshire, Durham, Newcastle upon Tyne, Northumberland, Cumberland and Berwick

Script by LEN MARTEN, BOB HEDLEY *and* HERBIE BUTCHERT
Designed by BARRIE DOBBINS
Produced by MALCOLM MORRIS
A Tyne Tees Television Production
(See Pages 10-11)

The 1000th edition of 'The One O'Clock Show'. Left to right: Norman Vaughan, Valerie Masters, Pat Beckett, George Romaine, Austin Steele, Chris Langford, Larry Mason, Shirley Wilson, David McBeth, Ethna Campbell, Len Marten, Herbie Butchert (scripts), Bob Hedley (scripts).

The last edition of the 'One O'Clock Show' was transmitted on Friday, 27 March, 1964. The programme had run for over five years and had clocked up 1098 editions. Soon after the Show's demise, an eight week series called 'Best From One O'Clock' was screened on Tuesday nights and featured the best videotape clips of the series. Unfortunately, not one foot of videotape of the shows remains today.

The last 'One O'Clock Show' was screened on Friday 27 March, 1964. George Romaine remembers that he sang 'For All We Know (We May Never Meet Again)'

1.2 THE ONE O'CLOCK SHOW
with
GEORGE ROMAINE
AUSTIN STEELE
SHIRLEY WILSON
LEN MARTEN
BOB HEDLEY
JOHNNIE LEA
HERBIE BUTCHERT
The One O'Clock Show Band

Today's guests:
DIANA DORS
THE POLKA DOTS
LARRY MASON

Today's audience includes members of the Reliant Owners' Club, Annfield Plain, County Durham
Script by LEN MARTEN
Designed by BARRIE DOBBINS
Produced by KEITH BECKETT
A Tyne Tees Television Production

Artistes and production staff of the 1000th edition of 'The One O'Clock Show'.
Left to right: front row, Bill Sykes (Floor Manager), Celia Stoker (P.A.), Don Gollan (TV. Director).
Second Row, Fred Crone, Bill Hughes, Dave Dowson, Jack Archer (Lighting), Bill Padgett, George Romaine, Bill Hutchinson, Colin Prince, Vic Slark, Shirley Wilson, Clarry Sampson (Music), Ethna Campbell, Len Marten (Scripts), Irma May (Wardrobe), Jim Lascelles, Herbie Butchert (Scripts), Anne May (Wardbrobe), Sam Scorer, Pam Luke (Make-up), Albert Massarano (Props), Wanda Lyon-Shaw (Make-up).
It was difficult to identify some people in the back row however those who have been recognised are: (man with pipe) Jim Goldby (Sound), Don Atkinson, Brian Jackson, Bob Stoker (Sound), Roy Lomas, Bob Rhodes, Derek Nicholson (Camera), Lewis Williams (Camera), Geoff Mott, Bill Slark, Malcolm Dickinson, Chris Palmer, xxx, George Savory, George McKenzie (Props), Trevor Smith, Bob Dial, Brian Bell, xxx, George Carter (Props), Bill Davies, Tom Sandford (Production), John Kemp, Derek Ensor (House Manager), Ted Davenport, John Dinsdale (Head of Design). Apologies for any errors or omissions.

THURSDAY
T T CHANNEL 8
SEPT 21

● ●

15 NORTH-EAST ROUNDABOUT
THURSDAY EDITION

nightly magazine that features people in North-East and takes a lively look at nts serious, humorous and curious

Introduced by **TOM COYNE**

Interviewers :
**VALERIE DENNIS   JACK CLARKE
PHILIP McDONNELL**

Edited by LESLIE BARRETT
Designed by JOHN DINSDALE
Directed by BERNARD PRESTON
A Tyne Tees Television Production

30 LOOK NOW
A five-minute Advertising Magazine
Presented by **DAVID REES**
Assisted by **BRENDA RALSTON**
Script by DENNIS NACMANSON
Directed by LISLE WILLIS
A Tyne Tees Television Production

35 THE COUNT OF MONTE CRISTO
starring
**GEORGE DOLENZ
ROBERT CAWDRON**
in
THE TALLEYRAND AFFAIR

e Count and his friends have an important ssage to deliver

A Tyne Tees Television Presentation

0 STAR PARADE

United Artists Story : 3
this evening's programme you will be seeing cerpts from the following :
*The Alamo
Goodbye Again
West Side Story
Judgment at Nuremburg*
Also interviews with
**INGRID BERGMAN
BING CROSBY
BOB HOPE**
Introduced by **ADRIAN CAIRNS**
Edited by FRED TUCKER
Directed by GEORGE ADAMS
(See Page 5)

30 DOUBLE YOUR MONEY
starring
HUGHIE GREEN
the seventh series of the popular quiz game th the £1,000 Treasure Trail
Directed by ERIC CROALL
An Associated-Rediffusion Production

0 OUR KIND OF GIRL
starring
**ALMA COGAN
GARY MILLER
MIKE and BERNIE WINTERS
THE DALLAS BOYS**
YN AINSWORTH and his ORCHESTRA
Produced by JO DOUGLAS
(Alma Cogan appears by permission of Harold Fielding)
An ATV Production

30 FAMILY SOLICITOR
starring
ROBERT FLEMYNG
**J. BROWN   BERNARD HORSFALL
ARY KENTON   GEOFFREY PALMER**
in
WAGE SNATCH
with
LIA ARNALL FREDERICK BARTMAN
ALAN McLELLAND
Produced by JACK WILLIAMS

girl is attacked on her way from the bank th a Holton firm's wages. A man who goes the girl's aid is badly hurt in the struggle. strange clue to the attack is found
A Granada Production

9.25 NEWS
World events from ITN

9.35 TELEVISION PLAYHOUSE
presents
LEE MONTAGUE   MAXWELL SHAW
in
TAKE A FELLOW LIKE ME
by RONALD HARWOOD
with
**RUTH GORING
CATHERINE LANCASTER**
CAST INCLUDES :

The Man	**Lee Montague**
Riza	**Catherine Lancaster**
Ribnik	**John Bennett**
Halfa	**Maxwell Shaw**
Sammy	**Ronald Harwood**
Esther	**Ruth Goring**

A stranger suddenly appears in an East End tailor's shop and throws the lives of five people into a state of confusion. But who is he ? What does he really want ? Is he as sinister as they think, or is he just a stranger ? Only Esther seems unafraid
Directed by CASPER WREDE
An Associated Television Production by
H. M. Tennent
(See Page 7)

10.35 CRISIS ON THE SLIPWAY

In the past three years British shipyards have lost £140,000,000 of orders to foreign yards. Why ? How does it affect the North-East ? And what can be done about it ? Tonight Tyne Tees Television seeks the answers to those questions
Taking part :
Mr. E. J. HUNTER, CBS
Chairman, Swan Hunter and Wigham Richardson Limited

(Continued in next column)

Mr. **TED HILL**,
General Secretary of The Boilermakers' Society
Mr. **PAUL WILLIAMS, MP**
Mr. **FRED WILLEY, MP**
Chairman :
BRIAN INGLIS
Investigation by TOM HUTCHINSON
Designed by JOHN DINSDALE
Produced by LESLIE BARRETT
Directed by AUD PENROSE
A Tyne Tees Television Features Production
(See Pages 4 and 5)

11.6 NEWS HEADLINES
including a report from the Liberal Party Conference in Edinburgh

11.15 WHIPLASH
starring
PETER GRAVES as Christopher Cobb
in
CANOOMBA INCIDENT
Chris Cobb and Dan Ledward come to Canoomba to set up a branch office for the Cobb stageline
A Tyne Tees Television Presentation

11.40 (approx) THE EPILOGUE
by the **Rev. Leslie Forster**, Christ Church. Dunston on Tyne

Close down

Chris Langford

Chris was one of the first resident vocalists at Tyne Tees when transmission began in January 1959. She had been studying to be a barrister in Manchester and used to socialise quite often at the Northern Sporting Club. One evening there was a talent competition and she was talked into entering by her student friends. To her surprise she won. A chap called Len Marten was sitting in the audience and he approached her to say he was a talent scout for Tyne Tees Television. He asked her if she would like to attend an audition in Newcastle. She said, 'Where's Newcastle?' Chris recalled her parents' reaction.

'My father wasn't too keen as he didn't like showbusiness. My mother talked him 'round and said that she would go with me to the audition. Len met me at the railway station but didn't know my mother had tagged along. She was still sorting out the cases in the carriage when Len saw me on the platform, came running up and apologised that he could not find me a hotel. He suggested that I stayed in his flat and marched ahead with my hand-luggage. He hadn't seen my mother until she caught up and announced, 'Hello Mr Marten. I'm Chris's mum.' I remember much later at his flat, he offered my mother and I drinks and I think he was trying to get us drunk with vodka.

There was a large plant next to the sofa where my mother and I were sitting and every time Len looked away we were pouring some of our drinks into the plant pot. After a while Len said,
'Are you getting tired Mrs Herring 'cause I would like to do a little rehearsal with Chris?'
She was a wise Lancashire lady my mum and she stayed until the end. Unfortunately for Len he didn't get his wicked way. Len ended up paralytic and I think the plant died a few days later. Many years later of course I was able to talk to Len about that experience and laugh about the whole thing.

We went into the studio the next day and there were sixty girls who were also auditioning for the same job. Anyway I got the job and they asked me to sign a ten year contract. I wasn't as daft as they thought I was and thought that maybe I couldn't stick that sort of life for ten years. I said I would 'have a go' for six months. I stayed in a flat in Scotswood Road with two make-up artists Yvonne Coppard and Heather Jackson. They had promised my mum that they would look after me and by golly they did. One of Tyne Tees producer/ directors Bernice Dorskind was in the flat with us too.

As a 19 year old 'lass' I was expected to learn all the words of the songs by heart. George Romaine was allowed 'idiot boards' because he was a mature singer, but I had to stay up until the early hours of the morning learning all t[...] words. I remember being very nervous as there was a li[...] audience every day on the 'One O'Clock Show'. It didn't con[...] home to me at first that we were being seen by hundreds [...] thousands of viewers. One day George and I were singing t[...] 'Drinking Song' from the 'Student Prince'. We were getti[...] carried away with the song swinging our glasses aroun[...] George had his glass up to his lips and I swung 'round quick[...] with mine and crashed into George. His glass shattered a[...] cut his nose which started to pour with blood. It was a li[...] transmission and we had to keep going. The cameras had [...] keep on me as George was being mopped down by the mak[...] up artists. The commercial break came up and George w[...] rushed off to hospital. He had to have three stitches in h[...] nose and still has a small scar even to this day.

One day I remember my song was 'Baubles Bangles and Bead[...] I was dressed in veils and a little bra and panties. Half w[...] through the song my bra snapped and I had to finish the sor[...] with my hand across keeping my bra in place. My picture a[...] the story appeared in the Daily Mirror. On another show v[...] did a spoof on the Black and White Minstrels and were ma[...]

with red make-up. You couldn't use black make-up on
television, so we used heavy red greasepaint. After the show,
the make-up wouldn't come off. For the rest of the week we
were all walking around with red faces as if we had been
sunburnt.

One of the things I enjoyed while working at Tyne Tees was
being able to wear so many wonderful dresses and costumes.
Can you imagine how I felt? I was just 19 going on 20 and I
was taken to Fenwick's store in Newcastle with TTT's wardrobe
mistress Irma May to select some dresses. I used to feel like
the Queen. We would be ushered into a private fitting room
and shown dozens of wonderful gowns. Irma was very bossy
but she knew her business. She would say you can't wear
that, it's got stripes. You couldn't wear stripes on TV as it
flashed with the cameras. I would spend a whole day trying
on frocks and then get a taxi back to the studios with the dresses
we'd selected. Irma trained me to hang up my dresses correctly
after every show and then I had to remove every scrap of make-
up before going outside. The hairdressers were wonderful too.
I would have a different hair style almost every day. Fans
would write in and give their opinions on my hairdo. I answered
all my fan mail personally with the help of a secretary.

The Producers were very strict. One winter I was late because
of the snow and when I arrived at the studio I was told that I
couldn't appear that day as rehearsals had already started.
Those people were our 'mums and dads' in those days and you
had to do what you were told. When I came in for rehearsals,
all the lyrics for my songs were buzzing around in my head
ready for when I went onto the floor. The Director's PA would
be there with the script and even if you got an 'and' or a 'so'
wrong, you would be checked. And then there'd be 'coming
down time' when it was leading up to transmission. We'd be
doing the dress rehearsal and the PA would say,
'Chris! you sang 'everybody' when you should have sung
'somebody'.' You'd have to get it all correct before transmission.
I had a long mirror in my dressing room and I thought it was

just for me to have a look at myself in, but Bill Lyon-Shaw
put me right. He came down to see me and said,
'Have you seen what you're doing with your hands? You're
making the same gesture every 5 seconds. Have a look at
yourself in the mirror.'

We all volunteered to work on Christmas Day and we used to
bring underprivileged children into the studios and treat them
to a party on the show. I remember one little lad who sat on
my knee during a song. He sat on George's knee for his song
and he wouldn't let George go. He followed him all around
the studio. George and I sang a duet and the little lad was sat
on my knee. Now today people would say that it was contrived
but it actually happened this way. I asked the lad what he'd
got for Christmas and he said,
'I got a pair of football boots, and they are nearly new!'
And that was it. We were all in tears; the camera crew, the
audience and all the cast.
When the 'One O'Clock Show' came to an end, there were
floods of mail saying, 'We don't want to lose you. Bring the
show back.' It was the end of a wonderful part of my career.'

Chris now lives in a little village just outside Oldham with her
husband Richard Guinea who is retired from Granada
Television where one of his experiences was to direct
'Coronation Street'. Up until fairly recently Chris sang with
the Northern Dance Orchestra and is currently putting together
a jazz ensemble to entertain at a local hotel.

**Chris Langford, now Chris Guinea, with her husband
Richard.**

George Romaine

George Romaine is remembered as one of the star vocalists who regularly appeared on many productions from Tyne Tees Studios. I met George and Ian Westwater, (one of the original cameramen) at the Egypt Cottage, a public house next door to the Studios on City Road.

'How did you get the job at Tyne Tees Television?' I asked. George recalled,

'I was appearing in a show at Scarborough and in the audience was a TV producer called Fred Wilby who evidently was impressed with my work and from this meeting I did spasmodic radio work in London and later in Manchester with the Northern Dance Orchestra with Alan Ainsworth, produced by Geoff Lawrence. Things were beginning to move. A few weeks later I was appearing at the Aston ATV studios in Birmingham with the Northern Dance Orchestra, and at the end of the shows, the floor manager, who was a chap called Bob Hope, (who could forget a name like that) said there was a telephone call for me. With my make-up still on, I went to main reception and was about to pick up the 'phone when I spotted someone, waiting next to me, whom I had the greatest respect for.

It was the ex-Middleweight World Champion Randolph Turpin. I asked the lady on reception to hold the call for a moment while I asked Randolph for his autograph. I was, and still am a great boxing fan. When I picked up the 'phone a voice said, 'I have just seen your spot on Television and I am impressed. You may not know me, my name is Joe Collins, and I am a showbiz agent. You may have heard of my two daughters, Joan and Jackie.' He asked me if I had an agent and when I answered 'No', he asked if I would employ him as my agent. I agreed and as I left the studios *it was raining and it was Friday!*

More radio work came my way with the Big Bands via Joe Collins and one day, he rang to inform me that he had sent some of my recordings to George Black. A few weeks later it was revealed in the press that Tyne Tees Television would be opening some months in the future. Weeks passed before a letter arrived asking me to attend an interview at TTT's offices, which at that time were in Northumberland Street, Newcastle upon Tyne. On arrival, I was welcomed by the receptionist Jill Atkinson and sat down alongside twenty other chaps who were there for 'the singers job'. Jill asked if I would like a cup of tea. I declined (as it makes me sweat and the future interview had me sweating already without steaming tea to add to the problem). I had barely sat for ten minutes when I was told I could go into the office to meet Mr George Black and the Programme Controller, Mr Bill Lyon-Shaw.

I entered the office and leaning against an Adams fire mantelpiece was a very distinguished grey-haired gentleman, smoking a cigarette and flicking the ash over himself! Next to him was a dark-haired gentleman, rattling the change in his pocket. I naturally went over to the silver-haired man with the cigarette, extended my hand and said, 'Mr Black, how do you do?'

He said, 'You've cocked it up already. I'm not Mr Black.'

This was my very first meeting with Bill Lyon-Shaw. So I said that I'd go out and start again. As I left the office *it was raining and it was Friday!*

THE VIEWER, January 30, 1960

THE TYNE TEES ITV PROGRAMME JOURNAL

JAN 31 FEB 6

THE VIEWER

No. 55 © The Daily News Ltd., 1960

GEORGE ROMAINE

'Singing keeps me young,' he says (see page 5)

GRAND FINAL FOR 'GOLDEN DISC' • SEE PAGES 8-9

I got a contract with Tyne Tees Television for a period of fi weeks as a singer featuring in the 'One O'Clock Show' fi live shows each week. (Incidentally, that five week contra extended to almost 27 years, not a bad contract was it?) thought, 'That sounds alright; I had some experience of wh was required so I wasn't coming into television work absolute cold.' The team consisted of Austin Steele, Terry O'Nei Ethna Campbell, Shirley Wilson, Chris Langford and myse (And what a great team it turned out to be.) However, I done three weeks work, 15 shows and I'd sung 45 songs! T Musical Director, Dennis Ringrowe, came to see me and sa 'How many songs have you got left in your briefcase?'

I boasted that I had quite a few.

He said, 'You'll need more than quite a few, because this 'O O'Clock Show' is really taking off.'

The following week my contract was extended, and who wou have thought it would last for over 1200 shows. And that when the hard graft really began. We had to find rehears pianists who were really up to the job and after a few fals starts, we had in place, the very best of all who had playe with the big bands. Accompanists of the very highest standar such as Alan Blomerley, Malcolm Saul, Ken Maddison, Alla Robson, and of course the great Billy Hutchinson. Colin 'Tin Prince also played piano and often helped with key-settir and routines. Our 'enemy' regarding the shows was th CLOCK on the wall as there was never sufficient time to real get things as you wanted them. Not only were you rehearsir

s week's shows, but another director would be planning xt week's programmes, and the week following that. levision directors would approach you with their ideas, so any time you would have three weeks' songs buzzing inside ur head and you had to find time to set keys, routines etc. It sn't always easy to find a vacant rehearsal space or a pianist. ets complicated things even more and we had to plan tween ourselves to enable us to rehearse at the same time. get around this problem I persuaded Colin Prince to assist e at 8:30am on many, many occasions. (He was paid of urse). Have you ever tried singing at 8.30 in the morning? t easy. I'll tell you the easy part and that was doing the tual performance. The hard work was achieving the right ndard... if you can sing, singing is the easy bit. Studio 1 as the 'One O'Clock Show' workshop where many called it e 'Fun Factory' and others referred to it more like a bullring here at any time you could be gored with your blood dripping the sand. It was a very dramatic place.'

orge remembered the Egypt Cottage pub,
im and Jessie Edwards were the tenants and had been there any years when Tyne Tees opened. Naturally the pub became tremely busy, so much so that I can recall a Sales Director om Newcastle Breweries telling us that the Egypt Cottage ld more bottles of Champagne than they did at the Royal ation Hotel. And literally thousands of people came to the gypt to rub shoulders with so-called television stars. It was right in the early days, and generally people were kind, but entually it became too much. Before the pub was altered, e used the upstairs room for rehearsals. It cost £1 a day if e used the gas fire, and ten shillings if we didn't use the fire. e had to sweep up after use for the lower fee!'
n Westwater recalled, 'This room downstairs was called the ug. I used to chase Claire in here for my eggs on toast.'
s that another name for it?' joked George who continued his ory.
Vhen they changed upstairs from the rehearsal room to the lmeda Bar, Newcastle Breweries hung two large signed ussell Flint prints on the wall. It was a stage in Flint's career

when he concentrated on painting Spanish ladies and it contributed to the overall ambience of the room. (Both prints mysteriously disappeared when the bar was re-decorated some time later, never to return). When the new bar was about to open (Jack Haig and I were asked to officially open it) Len Marten, Head of Scripts at TTT, asked the landlord, Jim Edwards,
'Who is going to look after this new cocktail bar?'
'I am,' replied Jim.
'What do you know about cocktails?' laughed Len.
Jim was a bit put out. 'I have a book here and all the cocktails are listed. If someone asks for a Manhattan or whatever, I just look in the book and put 'all the gear in'. No problem.'
That week, a chap came in with two ladies and asked Jim for two Pink Gins.
'Sorry! we've only got white gin,' said Jim.... Well done Jim!

Jack Haig didn't join the 'One O'Clock Show' until the latter part of 1959. The show needed an injection of special comedy and Bill Lyon-Shaw quite rightly said,
'We've got to get someone to liven up the show; we need a good comic.'
And Terry O'Neill suggested his brother-in-law.......
Bill Lyon-Shaw knew the quality of Jack Haig's work and he was right. Jack was a brilliant production comic. For many years Jack, Austin Steele and myself shared dressing room No 2 and shared thousands of laughs. I must tell you this story. It was the evening of a Big Show and in our dressing room there was Jack, Ted Ray, Austin, Dennis Spicer, a brilliant ventriloquist, and myself. Dennis was late, having been delayed in traffic, and we had already done one rehearsal. We had 'broken' on the floor and were in the dressing room when the door burst open and in came Dennis Spicer. He was carrying his vent's case, which was like a large cricket case. Throwing his case on to the table, he opened it and took out his dummy which he hung on a peg, facing into the centre of the dressing room. Dennis closed the case, asked if he had time for a cup of tea in the restaurant, and off he went.
Ted Ray said to me, 'George, have you ever had a look in Dennis's case?'
I replied, 'No I haven't.'
Ted said, 'Let's do it.'
So we opened up the case, and inside were yellow frogs, pink caterpillars, green spiders, and all sorts of things. We closed the case, and a few minutes later Dennis came bursting in and the dummy hanging on the peg said,
'They've had a look in your case Dennis.'
We all fell about and asked Dennis how he knew we'd had a look in his case. He said that everyone had a look in his case when he was out of the room. We'd been set up. During that show, while Dennis was doing his spot I remember John Brown was on the boom microphone and Dennis had the large pink frog on his knee.
Dennis said to the Frog, 'Well, what have you been up to today?'
And as the frog answered, John moved the boom mike over to the frog, moving the mike back to cover Dennis when he spoke and then moving it back to the frog when the frog 'spoke'.
John never lived that down.'

professionals and you've done it all before without V[something]
machines, and furthermore, every time a VTR machine
stopped, it costs £100.'

Whether this was true or not I never enquired nor did I ev[er]
stop a VTR machine whilst doing my spot! I can't ever rec[all]
saying, 'Forget it - we'll do it again.'

After a quick change from a sketch at the side of the stud[io]
floor, it was Pat Johns, TV Director of Perry Como fan[e]
who suggested that we hire a chimpanzee, dress it in lit[tle]
girl's clothes, and suggested that I sing 'You Must Have Be[en]
a Beautiful Baby' to the chimp! And sure enough, the chi[mp]
arrived on the studio floor with its keeper, ready to go!

Pat said, 'We'll keep the chimp out of shot, sitting with you [on]
a park bench, and then, on the last eight bars of the song, we[']
pull back so you'll be seen singing the song to the chimp.'

I asked the chimp's keeper, 'Is the chimp safe?'
'Of course she's safe,' he replied.

REHEARSAL
'You must have been a beautiful baby....'
'Is the chimp safe?'
'Don't worry,' replied the keeper.

DRESS
'You must have been a beautiful baby....'

I gently put my hand on the chimp's shoulder and it attack[ed]
me. I stood my ground even as it took a chunk out of my ha[nd]
and there was blood running down the microphone lead a[s I]
wrestled with this mad chimp still singing, *'You must ha[ve]
been a beautiful baby'.*

I returned to the studios after receiving jabs at the Gene[ral]
Hospital, but sadly, the chimp died of some curious blo[od]
infection!!!

Sitting on an easy chair, and halfway through a song on a li[ve]
show, out of the corner of my eye I saw someone walki[ng]

George continued his story. 'David Croft (of 'Dad's Army',
and 'Allo Allo' fame etc etc) produced many One O'Clock
Shows and incidentally wrote a song for me which I sang on
one of his shows. However, one day we were rehearsing and
one of my songs was 'Sitting on Top of the World'.

David asked, 'What can we do with this song?'
I said, 'I don't really know.'

'I know,' he said, 'see that lighting ladder there (a very high
set of stepladders) you can sing the song on top of the ladder
and we'll put some mattresses on the studio floor. When you
get near to the end of the song, start rocking the ladder
backwards and forwards, and right at the end of the song, you
fly off and land on the mattresses out of camera.

I said, 'You're joking.'
He replied quite seriously, 'No, give it a try.'
So, during the break we gave it a try.
'I'm sitting on top of the world......'
I started to rock the ladder and then whoosh! I landed dead
centre on the mattresses.. Great!

DRESS REHEARSAL
'I'm sitting on top of the world...' top and tail, the item.
I started to rock the ladder and then Whoosh. I landed smack
in the middle of the mattresses.

LIVE TRANSMISSION.
'I'm sitting on top of the world............'
I started to rock the ladder and it began to walk across the
studio floor. I came flying off, missing a camera by inches,
and landed on the hard studio floor.

'Great' said David as I lay there checking for broken bones.

I don't remember the exact time when the first Ampex video
tape recorders arrived at TTT, but I do recall thinking,
'Great, if something goes wrong when we are recording, we
can stop the tape and do it again.' Wrong.... Mr Lyon-
Shaw got us together in Studio 1 and made this
announcement.

'I just want to tell you this. Forget about stopping the VTR
machine as it is not there for you to stop. You are all

Len Marten (left) with Chris Langford and George Romaine
appearing in a New Year's Eve Special in 1959

wards me from the audience area. I looked across, and saw
was a little girl maybe four or five years old, dressed in a
etty frock. Bob Hughes was on the move to stop her when
caught my eye when I nodded to let her come to me. She
t out her arms for me to pick her up and I sat her on my knee
d continued singing (she didn't bite me). When I finished
e song, the audience applauded quite a long time and then I
ok her back to her mother. She was a delightful little girl.
any years later I was attending a fashion show at the Grand
otel in Tynemouth, when one of the models, a tall very
ractive young lady, came up to me and said,
ello Mr Romaine. Do you remember that little girl who sat
your knee while you sang?.......'

was the 500th One O'Clock Show, and there in the studio,
s a huge Birthday Cake.
rry O'Neill said, 'What are we going to do at the end of the
ow? We can't just cut the cake.'
ck suggested that we got a prop cake and pack it with a
arge. As someone puts in the knife, the cake explodes. Props
ovided the cake and the electricians wired it up.
s it safe?' I asked.
h yes,' assured the electricians.
I took the knife and said, 'Someone cue me'.
UE!'
tuck the knife into the prop cake and there was the most
afening explosion with bits of cake flying everywhere; the
ilding rocked! We had pieces of cake in our hair, over our
stumes, and plastered all over the camera. It took ages to
an up... and still the show to do.
VE
ming to the end of the show, there in front of me was THE
AKE. I said to Jack as I handed him the knife, 'You cut the
ke Jack.' Jack's face dropped ... a live show and the audience
d no idea what had transpired previously. Jack approached
e cake while everyone turned away. Jack plunged the knife
to the shivering cake and there was an almost inaudible 'plop'
und and nothing else. And that was the end of the 500th
ow. Only another 700 to go!

ming out of the studios one evening there was an elderly
dy with her two grandsons.
an I have a word, George?' she asked. 'I've brought my
andsons along to have a look at the horses.'
Vhat do you mean?' I asked.
Vell,' she said, 'you know all those cowboy programmes,
ell you must keep all the horses here. Do you think these
ds could see them?'
hat was the power of television in those pioneering days and
e were a vital part of the whole experience. The lady thought
Vagon Train' and other cowboy films were actually made at
ity Road, Newcastle upon Tyne.

ne Tees Television was an instant success and we became
mous overnight, whether we liked it or not! The photograph
ove shows Terry and I opening a new Cat and Dog Shelter
Gateshead. I remember that particular day very well. We
d just finished a 'One O'Clock Show' and during one of the
etches, I had played a drunk. After we had performed the

**George Romaine (left) with Terry O'Neill, opening a new
cat and dog shelter in Gateshead.**

opening ceremony, a little old lady came up to me and said,
'George, I want a word with you. Never, ever, come on the
show again when you're drunk!'
I told her that it was just a comedy sketch.
'I don't care,' she said, 'it's no good making excuses.'

Naturally we were recognised wherever we went in those days,
as today's personalities are. However, today's viewers have
seen it all before.... 40 years ago it was brand new and very
different and I am quite sure fame or whatever you wish to
call it, never ever went to my head.

One of my recordings prior to the TTT days was called
'Someplace to go', and the B-side was 'Unspoken'. My
recording manager at Fontana, Jack Baverstock said,
'Great song this George. There's only one problem - Sammy
Davis Junior has also recorded it.'
I think I only sold seven records, all in Ashington. (I'm joking
as it didn't do too badly really). However, sometime later I
was asked to do an LP of songs from the shows. I preferred
the Sinatra, Haymes, and Como style standards, however, I
could sing the songs from the shows if I was asked. David
Croft told me to go to London and show them what I could do.
I did the audition in a Bond Street studio and as I left, *it was
raining and it was Friday* . Three weeks later I sang Curly's
part on the Oklahoma LP. When it came to signing the contract
I was told,
'You have two options. You can either take a percentage of
every LP we sell, or you can take a fee.'
The seven records in Ashington loomed before my eyes, so I
opted for the fee. The LP went to the top of the hit parade in
Australia!! Well done George!

When the One O'Clock Show series finished, I was asked to front a new series called 'Glamour Trail' which turned out to be an enormous success for TTT. 'Glamour Trail' was an Outside Broadcast, which made it an event every time the OB Unit was on the road. Billy Hutchinson was Musical Director of a sixteen piece Big Band and I was in my element with this great backing and superb arrangements. In each show there was a beauty contest featuring local girls (not chosen by me, I hasten to add). The panel of judges usually included a local dignitary such as the Lord Mayor and two other local personalities from the region. The panel was chaired by Walter Williamson (who was later to become my boss at TTT). He was introduced as the Personal Assistant to the Managing Director, Tony Jelly. Walter, an ex-Squadron Leader- DFC, had a magnificent, large handlebar moustache. He was a very distinguished looking Yorkshireman and very correct in his dress when at work at TTT. However, the moment he 'acquired' the job of Chairman of the Panel, he turned up at the first show in a red sequined jacket, and wore it throughout the series. I had great fun with him and called it his 'Juggler's Jacket'. Walter took it all in fun ... I think! But I never missed a chance to refer to his 'Jugglers Jacket' in the show. 'Glamour Trail' also included a dancing competition and featured a local singer or a group (they're called bands now and I can't see how groups of four players can be called bands). I remember that they were always of a very high standard. The show ran for an hour every Thursday night and attracted staggering viewing figures; it was like the early days once again. 'Glamour Trail' was top of the North-East television ratings 12 weeks out of 13 beating 'Coronation Street' into second place over three months. I understand the Sales Department had known nothing like it. The final show of the first series of 'Glamour Trail' was staged at the Mayfair Ballroom in Newcastle upon Tyne and included singer/songwriter Jackie Trent. I believe everyone who worked on this first series enjoyed it tremendously, however, I realised it was time for big changes. I had received an offer to join the Ted Heath Band and I had this in my mind, when the Managing Director's secretary informed me that Tony Jelly would like to see me. Mr Jelly wanted to know what were my plans. I explained the Heath

offer, however, Mr Jelly said th he would like me to join the Pub Relations Department at TTT. looked out of the window, gue what? *It was raining and it w FRIDAY.* It was a tremendo opportunity and I decided accept this generous offer. probably had the fine professional teachers and frien one could possibly have. T journalists who had impressi credentials from Fleet Street Hannan Swaffer Award Winne Tyne Tees' Press Officer Dav Dawson helped me enormous and we still remain great frienc I call David 'my posh friend'. retired from Tyne Tees Televisi as Public Relations Executive in 1985 and as I left the buildi *it was raining and it was FRIDAY.* Geoff, I'm sure you knc during the time we've been talking, that it was great fun a hard work at TTT. I started with a five week contract a stayed 27 years (I must have been doing something righ From the day I started at Tyne Tees until the day I retire every morning of my life, whether it was raining, snowin thundering, or a lovely sunny day, I said 'Lets get to work. How many can say that?'

George Romaine in 1998
President of the Bishop Auckland Cricket Club

55 NEWS

8 NORTH-EAST NEWS

15 WILD BILL HICKOK
starring
GUY MADISON
as Wild Bill Hickok
and
ANDY DEVINE
as Jingles
nother episode of fun and excitement with
Wild Bill and Jingles

45 MARY GOES TO MARKET
An Advertising Magazine
introduced by
MARY MALCOLM
and
MICHAEL RATHBORNE
Script by LISLE WILLIS
Produced by DON GOLLAN
A Tyne Tees Production

.2 HIGHWAY PATROL
starring
BRODERICK CRAWFORD
as Patrol Chief Dan Mathews
masked gunman holds up several super-
arkets and makes a clean getaway. Patrol
ief Dan Mathews ferrets out the bandit's
ysterious method of operation and sets an
usual trap to catch him

.30 DOTTO
fast and fascinating game which turns dots
to pictures and pictures into pounds. Count-
g the dots and looking after the pounds is:
SHAW TAYLOR
Music by
JERRY ALLEN and his QUARTET
Directed by DINAH THETFORD
An ATV Production

8.0 GUN LAW
starring
JAMES ARNESS
in
BOOTS
Zeno, a famous gunman, has lost his nerve,
and lives in Dodge, drinking away his dis-
appointment and shame. But when Hank
Fergus arrives, Zeno is faced with a difficult
decision

**8.30 S.M.S.
(SOMERSET MAUGHAM STORIES)**
presents
**NAUNTON WAYNE   ELIZABETH WELCH
JOHN LE MESURIER   JULIA ARNALL
DERRICK SHERWIN
HELEN SHINGLER**
in
THE FACTS OF LIFE
The short story by W. SOMERSET MAUGHAM
Dramatised by STANLEY MILLER
Introduced by
DANIEL FARSON
CAST INCLUDES:
Mawson .... **Noel Dryden**
Henry Garnet .... **Naunton Wayne**
Mackenzie .... **Robert Sansom**
Teesdale .... **Harold Siddons**
Nicky Garnet .... **Derrick Sherwin**
Tim Mortimer .... **Donald Oliver**
Colonel Brabazon .... **John Le Mesurier**
Muriel Garnet ....**Helen Shingler**
The Girl .... **Julia Arnall**
Night Club Star .... **Elizabeth Welch**
Directed by MICHAEL WESTMORE
Worldly experience, as Henry Garnet never
tires of impressing on his son, Nicky, is con-
fined to one's elders and betters. It is all the
more unfair, therefore, to appear a bumbling
old innocent to one's progeny and a figure of
fun to one's friends
An Associated-Rediffusion Production
(See Page 7)

9.25 NEWS

9.42 YOUR KIND OF MUSIC
A programme of popular music
with
LUCILLE GRAHAM
Soprano
LARRY MASON
Baritone
JAMES REAVEY
Accordion
THOMAS BAPTISTE
Bass
CLIVE LYTHGOE
Piano
EILEEN BRENNAN
Contralto
**KEITH BECKETT
PATRICIA KIRSHNER
JOHN MASSEY
GROUP 99**
Woodwind sextet
A MODERN JAZZ GROUP
featuring
COLIN PRINCE
Double Bass
JOSEPH FERRIS
Vibroharp
REES HUGHES
Clarinet and Flute
WILLIAM HUTCHINSON
Pianoforte
**THE GEORGE MITCHELL SINGERS
THE CONSETT CITIZENS CHOIR**
(Conductor, W. Westgarth, M.B.E.)
THE
NORTHERN SINFONIA ORCHESTRA
conducted by
ARTHUR WILKINSON
and
MICHAEL HALL
Music co-ordinated by DENNIS RINGROWE
Choreography by PATRICIA KIRSHNER
Executive producer: W. LYON-SHAW
Directed by PETER GLOVER
A Tyne Tees Production

10.42 SABER OF LONDON
starring
DONALD GRAY
in
THE MAN WHO WAS TWICE
CAST:
Mark Saber .... **Donald Gray**
Wells .... **Robert Raikes**
Larry Nelson .... **Gordon Tanner**
Mr. Rodney .... **Ian Fleming**
A young man, accused of embezzlement,
decides to make a run for it—under the name
of a person he knows to be dead. But imper-
sonation can be dangerous, as he discovers

11.9 WHAT THE PAPERS SAY
In this review of the week's events **BRIAN
INGLIS** compares the ways in which the
different Sunday and daily newspapers re-
ported the same news
Directed by MIKE WOOLLER
A Granada Production

11.23 NEWS HEADLINES
followed by
THE EPILOGUE
Close down

At The Golden Disc

'At The Golden Disc' was a talent show which was hosted at first by Tony Martell and Eric Nicholson. It was first transmitted on Wednesday 21 January 1959 and proved to be the most popular locally produced show on TTT that year. George and Alfred Black said that the programme was to give a chance to youngsters of promise. They wanted to give young folk a break and it was their aim to find local artistes who, after grooming, would appear the next year in shows built around them. Critics of the show said it was simply entertainment on the cheap.

Tony Martell was born in Dundee and had tried a variety of jobs before opening a hairdressing salon in Heaton, Newcastle. He was looking for a gimmick to help his salon along and came up with the idea of recording local artistes on his tape recorder and playing the tapes in the salon. A local recording company took an interest in his tapes and so did TTT and the 'Golden Disc' talent show was born. The show was playing at theatres before Tyne Tees adapted it to the television studio. Perhaps the most well known contestant of the TTT version is David Macbeth who appeared regularly on Tyne Tees in productions such as 'Request Time' and 'Sunshine Street'. His record 'Mister Blue' (flip side - 'Here's a Heart') reached No18 in the Hit Parade.

The Black Brothers came up with the idea of staging the TV version of the show in a coffee-bar set. The audience were sat around tables drinking coffee and it was thought that it would put the contestants at ease. At the beginning of each show, Tony would invite the viewers into the bar as the camera tracked through an arched entrance. Tony and Eric would take turns in making announcements as the other 'tut-tutted'. The first series was planned to run for 16 weeks and every fifth week was a quarter final where winners of the last four weeks would compete. Tony auditioned over 100 acts every week; no-one was ever refused an audition. In the first year of the show, over 6000 acts had been auditioned.

Among the contenders for the first series were pop singers - The Walker Twins; Geoffrey and Albert who were apprentice surveyors. Don Crockett, a comedian from Middlesbrough won his heat in the show and later was given a contract by the Black Brothers to appear in their variety shows.

Another series of the show started in September 1959 and included contestants, Timothy Malone, Del Perry Four vocal group, Freddie Miller a comedian from Sunderland, singers John Moran, and Brenda Ibbotson, and George Carter, a comedian from Darlington. All quarter final winners appeared on the One O'Clock Show the following week and some went on to appear in

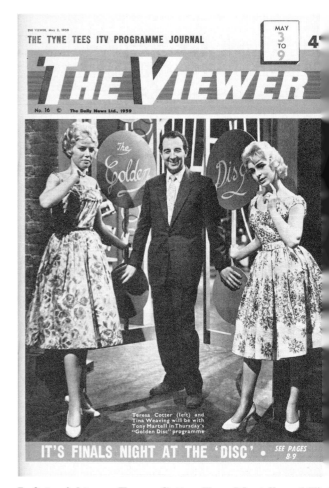

THE VIEWER, May 2, 1959

THE TYNE TEES ITV PROGRAMME JOURNAL

MAY 3 TO 9

4'

THE VIEWER

No. 16 © The Daily News Ltd., 1959

The Golden Disc

Teresa Cotter (left) and Tina Weaving will be with Tony Martell in Thursday's "Golden Disc" programme

IT'S FINALS NIGHT AT THE 'DISC' • SEE PAGES 8.9

Left to right are: Teresa Cotter, Tony Martell, and Tina Weaving; hosts of Tyne Tees Television's talent show, 'At the Golden Disc' in May 1959.

The photograph below shows an interlude in the show when the audience danced to the music of Dennis Ringrow and his band. The show's host, Tony Martell is dancing with the dark-haired girl. 'One O'Clock Show' star, Terry O'Neill is dancing with his daughter Coral (centre).

114

7.30 £350 ALL WINNERS NIGHT AT THE GOLDEN DISC

introduced by

TONY MARTELL and **ERIC NICHOLSON**

Two winners from last week's semi-final join

**THE PANAMA JAZZMEN
THE BURTON BOYS
HAZEL DAY**

and

THE JOE BOSTON TRIO

for prizes of £250 and £100

Chairman of the judging panel

Mr. JACK PAYNE

Prizes awarded by TTT's Programme Director

Mr. GEORGE BLACK

with

DENNIS RINGROWE and his ORCHESTRA

Setting by ERIC BRIERS

Produced by PHILIP JONES

A Tyne Tees Production

(See Page 8)

The Joe Boston Trio, who were winners of the first series. The final was screened on Thursday 26 March 1959.

...her TTT productions. The Dent Brothers got their big TV ...eak from the 'Golden Disc'. They appeared on TTT's Bill ...aynard Show and were also engaged to sing Hymns on many ...the Epilogues. The Joe Boston Trio from Teesside won the ...al of the first series on Thursday 7 May 1959.

...e first series topped the audience ratings in the North-East. ...e second series featured established guest artistes such as ...arl Carr and Teddy Johnson to give the show an extra appeal. ...e Grand Final of the second series was screened on Friday ...February, 1960. The finalists included Harold Hall, a tenor ...om Hetton-le-Hole, The Gamblers pop group, and Larry ...ason, a singer from Horden. The judges included Marion

Ryan, a popular singer of the day (mother of Paul and Barry Ryan, who had hit songs in the charts in the late 60's Barry Ryan had a No2 hit in 1968 with the song 'Eloise'.) Joe 'Mr Piano' Henderson was also on the panel of judges along with Jimmy Henney and Alan Freeman. Larry Mason won the second series of the contest and went on to appear regularly in TTT productions such as the 'One O'Clock Show', and 'Request Time'.

On the strength of the success of the show, Tony Martell launched his 'Television Training Academy' at No1 Pink Lane in Newcastle. They gave training in modelling, social etiquette and dancing.

BOBBY THOMPSON SHOW

" Off to bed with you ! " Bobby has to act the stern father when son Michael and Keith show signs of becoming tele-addicts.

By BOB STOKER

PHYLLIS was peeling the potatoes, carefully taking their eyes out, when Maureen, who helps with the household chores, gave her the idea for the latest Bobby Thompson gag.

Said Maureen, back from a shopping expedition : " Sixteen shillings I had to pay for that fish you wanted, Mrs. Thompson. We could have got a few fish-cakes for that."

Phyllis dropped her knife, wiped her hands on her apron and dashed off into the dining-room to make a note. It was only the germ of an idea so far, but she would work on it later. A gag was born.

There was great excitement at Tyne Tees when Bobby Thompson was signed up for a 16 week run of 'The Bobby Thompson Show'. The first show was transmitted on Monday 16 March 1959 from 9:30 till 10pm. It was screened straight after 'Wagon Train' which was the number one programme at the time.

The first show was a hit with rating figures even beating 'Wagon Train' and 'Take Your Pick'. The euphoria among TTT's directors was short-lived, however. The next week's ratings placed Bobby at No6 and the show never figured again in the top-ten ratings after that. Jack Haig was brought in to try and boost the ratings and top acts such as Lita Roza, Teddy Johnson and Pearl Carr made guest appearances but to no avail. Bobby was a very funny stand-up comedian with a unique act which has never been emulated, but he was not an actor and was not 'at home' in the comedy sketches that were written for him. Consequently the sketches did not flow and viewers switched off. Sadly, it was one of Tyne Tees mistakes. The shows almost finished Bobby's career because of the age-old stage maxim, 'You are only as good as your last gig.'

Phyllis Thompson (centre) takes charge of the situation as the German rent collector 'Caal Back' is looking a bit fed up.

.0 THE ARTHUR HAYNES SHOW

starring
ARTHUR HAYNES
with
AILEEN COCHRANE
and
NICHOLAS PARSONS
FREDDIE FRINTON
GEORGE CARDEN DANCERS
JACK PARNELL and his ORCHESTRA
Scriptwriters JOHNNY SPEIGHT,
JOHNNY JOHNSON *and* MALCOLM KEEN
Designer RICHARD LAKE
Produced by STEPHEN WADE
An ATV Production

.30 WAGON TRAIN

starring
ANNE BAXTER
WARD BOND   **ROBERT HORTON**
in
THE KITTY ANGEL STORY
with

Henry Hull	Frank McGrath
Terry Wilson	Viv Janiss
Kathleen Freeman	David Leland

Written by LEONARD PRASKINS
Directed by JAMES NEILSON
Produced by HOWARD CHRISTIE

A beautiful dance-hall hostess joins the wagon train and gets a cold welcome from the other women. They fear she will be a bad influence on their husbands and children, and appeal to Major Adams to send her packing. Adams seems to have no choice, until an orphan Indian baby brings a solution—and trouble

9.30 THE BOBBY THOMPSON SHOW

with
LEN MARTEN
HAROLD BERENS
and
PHYLLIS THOMPSON
The lodger brings his work home with him and persuades Phyllis to insure Bobby.
with
the Tyneside singing stars
THE BARRY SISTERS
and
THE DENNIS RINGROWE ORCHESTRA
Script by LISLE WILLIS *and* DAN DOUGLAS
Settings by ERIC BRIERS
Produced by PHILIP JONES
A Tyne Tees Production

10.0 NEWS

World news of the minute from ITN

10.15 MYSTERY IS MY BUSINESS

HUGH MARLOWE
as Ellery Queen
in
CUSTOM MADE
CAST INCLUDES :

Ellery Queen	**Hugh Marlowe**
Inspector Queen	**Florenz Ames**
Dorothy Smith	**Jalma Lewis**
Larry Hacket	**Joey Pay**
Jason Beckworth	**Melville Cooper**

Because his date's dress was switched, Ellery gallantly offers to go for the right one, and finds, instead, a dead man on the floor

10.45 RAINBOW ROOM

JEAN MORTON

invites viewers to meet her guests for the evening

Music by
Jerry Allen and his TV Trio
Settings by ELIZABETH DORRITY
Devised by REG WATSON
Produced by JACK BARTON
An ATV Production

THE EPILOGUE
by **Canon Charles Crowson**

Close down

'Little Bobby' waiting in the 'wings' at the right as the comedy sketch in the Co-op store unfolds.

Sometimes Bobby's show would be pre-recorded on the Ampex video machine. Bobby would say, 'Aa can gan home early today 'cause they've Tampaxed me show.'

Bobby's last show was transmitted on Monday 29 June 1959.

WOR BOBBY TOPS THE LOT !

BOBBY THOMPSON, Tyneside's own comedian, has set up a record. His Monday-night "Bobby Thompson Show" on the TTT channel is the first local programme to get to the top of the hit parade.

It did this, in the week ended March 21, with a TAM (Television Audience Measurement) rating of 77—which means that the show was watched in an estimated 291,000 homes.

Bobby topped such well-liked and established successes as *Wagon Train, Take Your Pick, Double Your Money* and *Emergency—Ward 10.*

In this winning Thompson week, only two programmes had higher

ratings anywhere in the country— *Take Your Pick* and *The Army Game* — two nationally-networked productions, which scored 82 and 80 respectively in the Southern region.

Only once before has a locally-produced show been at the top of regional ratings.

This (after many months of building up) was the sports magazine of Scottish TV.

" So we have reason to feel both pleased and proud about our success," says Bobby.

" Notice I speak in the plural. The credit has to be shared out among such people as the producer, Philip Jones, Len Marten, Harold Berens, Peggy Patterson, Vic Gilling, the Barry Sisters, Dennis Ringrowe —and Phyllis."

The full " Top Ten " list reads:

PLACE	PROGRAMME	RATING
1	*The Bobby Thompson Show*	77
2	*Wagon Train*	76
3	*Take Your Pick*	75
4	*Double Your Money*	74
5	*Emergency—Ward 10*	71
6	*Shadow Squad*	70
	Spot The Tune	70
8	*Assignment Foreign Legion*	67
	Criss Cross Quiz	67
10	Seat in the Stalls: *The Ghost Goes West*	66

The Barry Sisters

The original Barrys were genuine sisters: June, Anne and Angela. I met June Barry at her home in Darras Hall where she lives with her husband Harry Green who is retired after an equally impressive career in radio and television - he directed 'Look North' for BBC North-East. June confessed she was the self-appointed 'boss' of the Barry Sisters and, as well as being the eldest, was the most ambitious. She told me about the early years of the Barrys.

'Richard Kelly, a BBC Producer, was the man who gave us our 'break' in the North-East. We were singing 'pops' of the day and we attended an audition at the BBC studios in Croft Street and Richard said that he couldn't use us as the songs we were singing were not suitable for 'Wot Cheor Geordie'. He gave us a music copy of 'Dance ti thi Daddy' and told us to rehearse it and come back later. Well, we took the song home and couldn't even understand it at first as it was all in 'phonetic Geordie'. My husband, then Allan Robson, wrote some fabulous harmonies for the song, and when we presented it to Richard we got the job and sang many times in the radio show 'Wot Cheor Geordie'. Our agent, Forrester George got us pantomime and similar theatre work. We engaged a new recording manager and signed recording contracts with Decca and then Columbia. Our first record was 'Italian Theme'. Our most successful record, however, was 'Little Boy Blue' written by Lionel Bart. It was also released in America and did quite well there too. One of our records was called 'Tall Paul' which also did quite well and led to a season on BBC's 'Drumbeat'.

George and Alfred Black had seen us working on stage and asked us to attend an audition at Tyne Tees. Tyne Tees Television *was* George and Alfred Black in those days. I think it was the Bobby Thompson Show which was our first television engagement. We had to learn completely new techniques when working for television. On stage you had to be larger than life and exaggerate your movements. On TV however, you had to be much 'smaller'. When they switched from one camera to another you had to gradually move your eyes from one to the other and not make a sudden change. And our eyes had to move exactly together. We were all different heights but the hems of our dresses had to be in line and our toes always had to point towards the camera.

I remember we sang on 'Request Time' with David McBeth and the song was 'I'm an Indian Too'. The words included all the names of the Red Indian tribes, so it was a difficult song to sing. We were all dressed up in Red Indian costumes and while we sang the song with David, we had to tie him to a totem pole. We were dancing around the totem pole with coloured ribbons and after the third take I asked the Producer Philip Jones if we could pre-record the song. When he asked why, I explained that because we were dancing around, we were out of breath and couldn't sing properly.
He said, 'Is that a problem?'
Usually he was very sympathetic, but he must have been having a bad day.

On another edition of 'Request Time' we were dressed in cute little nighties for the song 'Don't Tell Me Anymore Bedtime Stories'. We got a lot of laughs from the cameramen. 'What time did you get up?' they joked. Why anyone would request

The Barrys in 1960 during a photo-session which was held for the front cover of the Christmas edition of the Viewer.

The Barrys in the early 1960's singing 'Don't Tell Me Anymore Bedtime Stories' on the Tyne Tees Television programme 'Request Time'.

...at number surprises me but there we were. ...ost of the time we sang in our own outfits ...t when we were asked to sing a production ...mber such as 'Bedtime Stories', we had to ... to the Wardrobe Department to see Irma ...ay. Irma was a stickler for detail - you ...dn't dare argue with Irma. In general, ...owever, there was a lovely atmosphere at ...yne Tees. Everyone was just 'starting out' ...d so keen.

...remember working with the ventriloquist, ...ennis Spicer. He was married to a Geordie ...ss. He had a wonderful act. He used to ...ake all his own dummies and whenever he ...ade a new one he would take it to show ...veryone he knew, to get their approval ...efore using it on stage. He was tragically ...lled in a car accident and when the police ...und a small shoe, they thought a child must ...ave been involved in the accident and ...arched for hours for a body. The shoe ...ctually belonged to one of Dennis's ...ummies.

When we were working away we'd usually rent a house so we could be together all the time. Sometimes we'd argue and end up screaming at each other - nose to nose. Then we'd have to go on stage and smile and be nice. By the time the show was over we'd forgotten what the argument was about and we'd be friends again.

To our surprise, one day Angela eloped. She simply left a note on the mantelpiece, 'Gone to get married'. Once the story hit the press, the 'phone never stopped. I remember saying 'Angela has left. What are we going to do?' Our agent said that all the bookings were for three Barry sisters so we had to find a girl singer. Harry, who was sound balancer at the BBC at the time, told us about a girl singer called Sylvia Scarll. He said that she had a very good voice, was very attractive, and was resident singer at the Rex Hotel in Whitley Bay. She had a nice low voice which was what we wanted, so we asked her to join us and she only had three days to learn all

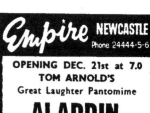

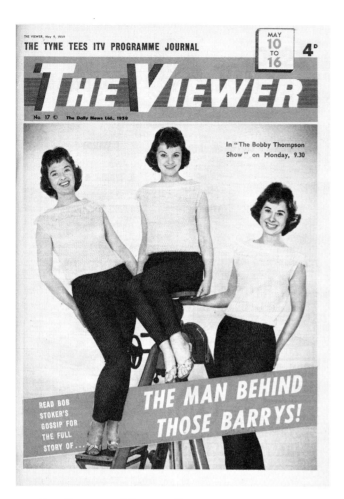

THE VIEWER, May 9, 1959

THE TYNE TEES ITV PROGRAMME JOURNAL

MAY
10
TO
16

4ᴰ

THE VIEWER

No. 17 © The Daily News Ltd., 1959

In "The Bobby Thompson Show" on Monday, 9.30

READ BOB STOKER'S GOSSIP FOR THE FULL STORY OF ...

THE MAN BEHIND THOSE BARRYS!

our Geordie songs. When we first sang together, she put her hand half closing her ear so she could hear herself more than Anne and me. She was terrified but the show went well, and when it was over, Harry came 'round and said that he couldn't tell any difference from the original sound. If Sylvia hadn't joined us, it could have been the end of the Barrys. Angela rejoined the act some time later and for a while we worked as a foursome. In 1965 we had one more year's contracts to honour and as both Anne and Sylvia had left the act, we had to get another girl in. It just didn't work, so Angela and I decided that we would rather just call it a day.

Harry was working for 'Look North' at the time and he asked me if I would like to audition for a job as presenter while Mike Neville was on holiday. Instead of having one presenter they were going to try a man and a woman co-presenting. It was something completely new for me and I was a nervous wreck every night of the three week stint. When they asked me to interview someone, I didn't have questions carefully planned like who? what? or where? - I just sat them down and we had a good old natter. I enjoyed it very much and after the three weeks, they offered me a full-time job to co-present with Mike Neville. I was thrilled. Angela was very upset at the time because she had just been divorced. Anne, who had been out of the act, said that she would come back for a year so the three of us could fulfil the contracts we had. So that's what we did, but, looking back, I wish I had taken the job with Mike Neville. I might have been a Sue Lawley of the North!

In 1978, my husband Harry, who was Director of 'Look North', said that lots of people were asking, 'What happened to the

Barry Sisters?' He asked us how we felt about doing Christmas show on BBC with Mike Neville. We agreed, a one of our songs was to be 'Where did my Snowman Go?' a Harry thought it would be nice if we could wear similar cloa to the ones we wore for the front cover of the Christmas 'View in 1960. He asked Tyne Tees if they still had the Christm cloaks from 1960, and to our amazement they still had the in their wardrobe department!

I've done some acting work since the Barrys stopped singir I did four episodes of 'Byker Grove' last year. My agent ra and asked me to do an audition for the programme which enjc 'cult' status down south. He said that the part was abou lady who was desperate to get her daughter on the stage. related to the part so I agreed, and they sent me the script. the audition I started to read and they interrupted and said. 'Oh you have the wrong script. We have you down as t granny with Alzheimer's.'

I got the part! In the programme, I got mugged and spe what seemed like hours lying on my back in the middle Byker Grove car park.

Some time later I appeared in one the 'Spender' episodes wi Jimmy Nail. I played a Conservative Agent assisting Aman Redman who played a Conservative Candidate who w canvassing for a seat in Sunderland. Spender was giving poli protection to the candidate who had received death threats. June continues to do occasional television work, Angela liv in Essex and only sings once in a while. Sylvia lives Glasgow. Anne died in 1983.

June Barry (right) with her sister and former singin partner Angela, enjoying some 1990's Spanish sunshine

.0 REQUEST TIME
introduced by
NORMA EVANS
and starring
**THE BARRY SISTERS
DAVID MACBETH
SHIRLEY WILSON**
and
ENNIS RINGROWE and his ORCHESTRA
Settings by ERIC BRIERS
Produced by PHILIP JONES
A Tyne Tees Production

.30 SKYPORT
starring
**GEORGE MOON
MANNING WILSON**
Written by JAN REED
Directed by ADRIAN BROWN
Monsieur Plessey, a couturier, is to hold an important fashion show in London. But when e arrives at Skyport with his mannequins, he finds that his collection has disappeared
A Granada Production

.0 SPOT THE TUNE
with
ACKIE RAE   MARION RYAN
Contestants with a knowledge of pop music re given the chance to win cash prizes in this uneful quiz. There is also a Jackpot which ncreases by £100 weekly until won
PETER KNIGHT and his ORCHESTRA
A Granada Production

.30 NO HIDING PLACE
starring
RAYMOND FRANCIS
as Detective Chief Superintendent Lockhart
ERIC LANDER
as Detective Sergeant Baxter
in
THE GOLDEN CLOWN
By PETER BAKER
Sets designed by BERNARD GOODWIN
Film directed by BILL MORTON
Directed by IAN FORDYCE
Produced by RAY DICKS
Every clown wears a mask; but when the mask is torn away, Lockhart decides it's time to investigate
An Associated-Rediffusion Production

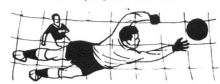

une remarked. 'It's amazing how many people emember us. As well as the lovely 'double takes' sometimes get in town, people come up to me nd say, 'I know you. I've seen you somewhere efore.'

never say, 'I used to be one of the Barry Sisters.' am a Barry Sister. I just can't think how people emember us after so many years, but they do, nd it's wonderful.'

This schedule shows the Barrys on 'Request Time' in January 1960, but all four Barry Sisters appeared on the last edition of 'Request Time' on Thursday 23 March 1961.

June   Angela
Sylvia   Anne

9.25 NEWS
ITN's spotlight on world news

9.36 SATURDAY FEVER
A study of facts, figures, symptoms, causes and effects, confessions and case histories relating to that widespread national ailment—**FOOTBALL FANATICISM**
Film Unit :
BRUCE ALLAN   BILL SCOTT
VARICK EASTON   JOHN FLETCHER
RON WILKINS
Produced by JOHN WILSON
A Scottish Television Production
(See Page 13)

10.5 SPORTS DESK
introduced by
GEORGE TAYLOR
of the *News Chronicle*
Tyne Tees Television brings you the latest news, views and personalities from North-East sport
Directed by BERNARD PRESTON
A Tyne Tees Production

10.20 OVER THE COUNTER
A Five Minute Advertising Magazine
Presented by DAVID REES
A Tyne Tees Production

10.25 SEAT IN THE STALLS
presents
NO HAUNT FOR A GENTLEMAN
CAST :
John	**Anthony Pendrell**
Miriam	**Sally Newton**
Rassobake	**Jack McNaughton**
Madame Onskiya	**Joan Hickson**
Sir Roger de Clancy	**Bill Shine**
Mrs. Mallett	**Dorothy Summers**
Miriam's mother	**Patience Rentoul**

Produced by LEONARD REENE
Directed by CHARLES REYNOLDS
In a country mansion, a newly-wed couple, John and Miriam, settle down in the hope of domestic bliss, until Miriam's mother moves in unexpectedly. Then a friendly ghost appears in John's study—and John decides to engage him to scare away his unwanted mother-in-law!
(See Page 11)

11.25 NEWS
Late-night news round-up

THE EPILOGUE
by the **Rev. Malcolm A. Beaton**, Geneva Road Baptist Church, Darlington

Close down

Young at Heart

'Young at Heart' was first broadcast on Wednesday, 4 May, 1960. It was one of Tyne Tees' first programmes aimed at the teenage audience. It was screened at 6:30pm and was hosted by Sir Jimmy Savile and Valerie Masters who was best known as a vocalist in the Ray Ellington Orchestra. Jimmy was relatively unknown in those days as it wasn't until 1964 that he made the 'big time' when he launched 'Top of the Pops' on BBC television. I remember Jimmy on Radio Luxembourg, however, when he presented the 'Teen and Twenty Disc Club'. He made quite an impact at TTT with his zany style and outrageous dress-sense. 'Young at Heart' ran for eight weeks and each week Jim appeared on the show with his hair a different colour (although black and white television would not have done justice to that). He wore long winkle-picker shoes which were shown on the opening camera shots as the cameraman panned from Jim's feet up to his face. Jim used to commute from his home in Leeds in one of the three cars he

owned, one of which was a white Rolls Royce having the licence plate JS954.

The show was themed on a coffee-bar with invited members of the public forming the studio-floor audience and, off-camera, were other audience members on theatre-style seating. I remember my mother taking me to see the show in 1960 when I was 13 years old. I was enthralled by the glamour of the whole production and decided I wanted to be a cameraman when I grew up.

One feature of the show was where the guest artiste would record a song live on a disc-cutting machine. The disc, which of course was the only one in the world, was used as a prize in a competition featured in The Viewer magazine. One of the supporting acts in the show was a young Scots vocalist called Ray Coussins who was also seen in the TTT programme 'Tyne Tees Top Tunes'.

'Young at Heart' was produced by Malcolm Morris who produced many programmes at Tyne Tees including the 'One O'Clock Show'. Some years later Malcolm was appointed

6.30 YOUNG AT HEART
A teenage programme with Mum-and-Dad appeal

Compere :
JIMMY SAVILE
featuring
VALERIE MASTERS
RAY COUSSINS
THE HILLCRESTERS
THE VISIONAIRES
Guest Star :
CRAIG DOUGLAS
Settings by ERIC BRIERS
Produced by MALCOLM MORRIS
A Tyne Tees Production

Sir Jimmy Savile and Valerie Masters with the disc-cutting machine which was used to make live recordings of guest vocalists.

rogramme Controller at Tyne Tees.

the musical accompaniment on 'Young at Heart' was provided by the musionaires seen here with Valerie Masters. The band proved to be as popular as the artistes and attracted a lot of fan mail. The Musical Director was Dennis Ringrowe and forming the line-up seen in the picture are Joe Ferris (vibes), Charlie Smith (guitar), Ken Wright (bass), George Hann (drums), Bobby Carr, Bill Sowerby, Harry Nicholson, Alf Joseph (trumpets), Les Hughes, and Syd Warren (sax's). Billy Hutchinson (not in camera) was on piano.

met Sir Jimmy Savile when he made his annual pilgrimage to Newcastle for the Great North Run. He has a lot of affection for Tyne Tees as 'Young at Heart' was his first television series. He just happened to be in George Black's office one day when the opportunity to host the show came up. George wasn't very impressed with Jimmy's act and didn't think he would go very far in the business. Jimmy was nearly sacked by Tyne Tees for continually saying, 'How's about that, then?' When the story hit the press, many viewers wrote to TTT saying, 'Leave him alone!' Sir Jimmy joked, 'Everyone says that now.' He remembers that everyone on the show was under pressure to make it work within the time slot as it went out live. It was a terrific strain as many of the people on the studio floor were very new to television.

Sir Jimmy is seen jiving to the music of The Hillcresters. At the bottom-right of the picture is guest star Ronnie Carroll who had a minor hit that year with a cover version of the Steve Lawrence hit 'Footsteps'. Two years later Ronnie Carroll sang the British entry in the Eurovision Song Contest. The song was 'Ring A Ding Girl' and it came fourth.

Bestest wishes from Sir Jimmy Savile

Larry Parker and Happy-Go-Lucky

The first edition of the children's programme 'Happy Go Lucky' was screened on Thursday 22 January 1959 at 5:25pm. Lucky the Clown made an appearance each week and many children wondered who he actually was. It was really Larry Parker... 'Oh you spoiled it'. Larry Parker had worked as a clown in theatre but Bill Lyon-Shaw knew him from his appearances in BBC's 'Crackerjack' and in Associated Rediffusion's 'Small Time'. Bill sent one of his producers, Bernice Dorskind to see Larry's act at a London theatre and soon afterwards Tyne Tees invited him to star in a new TTT children's show. Larry accepted the offer and asked Bill who would be writing the scripts.
'You are!' bellowed Bill in his 'loveable' style.

Larry used to write the scripts in London and commute to Newcastle each week for the show. There was always a logic behind the scripts and they weren't just 'silly' humour. The show appealed to adults as well as children and on the night train home, sometimes the guard would recognise Larry and tell him how much he'd enjoyed the show.

Gwenda Lea played the 'girl' in the first series and Syd Kirkness played the children's song requests on the piano. This proved to be one of the most popular items in the programme and the 'Top 5' most requested songs were
1. Little White Bull
2. Robin Hood
3. Davy Crockett
4. Seven Little Girls (Sitting in the Back Seat)
5. Fings Ain't Wot They Used to Be.

Jim Alder was the show's naturalist and used to talk about wildlife and the 'land'. At the end of Larry's 'Lucky the Clown' spot, he would open a suitcase and the camera would move in close and focus on a caption inside which read 'Popeye the Sailor Man' which was the cue for the cartoon.

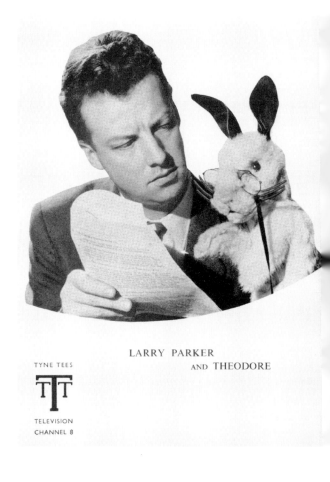

LARRY PARKER AND THEODORE

TYNE TEES

TTT

TELEVISION
CHANNEL 8

Larry wrote to me from his home in Sittingbourne, Kent: 'In the second series, the show had a coffee bar theme which made it easier for people to 'come and go' throughout the programme. Norma Evans was the 'girl' for a while but sh

Lucky the Clown : 'pensive in Penshaw'

Left to right: Colin 'Tiny' Prince, Wacky Jacky, and Larry Parker in an episode of the long-running 'Happy-Go-Lucky'.

was always a sound effect. Occasionally Wacky would come into camera wiping ink off his hands with a dirty rag. He spent most of his time, however, as the 'Chief' (and only) Reporter. The newspaper theme of the show allowed us to roam around gathering stories. One day we tracked down a black pudding that had gone 'berserk' in the Highlands. This must have been during the period that the programme was networked to Grampian Television. On another occasion we masqueraded as a couple of medieval strolling minstrels called 'Pestle and Mortar'. In another episode, we rescued the 'last Camembert' in Paris, in a parody of the Scarlet Pimpernel. Wacky disguised himself as a 'sawn-off' Toulouse Lautrec. When you think about it, how many kids in Byker would have heard of Camembert cheese?

'Happy-Go-Lucky' was very unusual in one way - we never had a studio audience. This must have been almost unique for what was really a 'sitcom'. Personally, I preferred it and I think Jack did too. The comedy and timing was dedicated to the viewer, not a studio audience who could hardly have seen what was going on anyway, half the time.

Jack had a variety and touring revue background, unlike many people in television, he knew what actually made people laugh. I think in those early TV days we all learned very quickly. Jack developed a rapport with the 'camera' and there were times when he had to tell the director that the shot was wrong. A close-up wasn't funny when the viewer needed to see the reaction of the other person in the sketch.

...as replaced by Kate Beckley who stayed with the show till ...e end. Jack Haig didn't join until September 1959 when ...acky Jacky soon became a household name. Jack was ...metimes difficult to work with, but I ...ver fell out with him as we had a quiet ...spect for each other, both having ...me from similar backgrounds. In a ...etch one day, Jack was doing some ...Y. The gag was that Jack would ...mmer a nail in the wall and burst a ...pe, squirting water in his eye. The ...chnician behind the wall turned the ...ater hose on too strong a jet and the ...ater damaged Jack's eye. He had to ... rushed to hospital to receive ...eatment.

...he budget for 'Happy-Go-Lucky' was ... small that we always had to restrict ...e number of actors we used. The ...me applied to the sets, although most ... the time we included the offices of ...e 'Ambleford Gazette'. Jack was in ...arge of the actual printing although ... never saw the printing press and it

Part of the 'Happy-Go-Lucky' signature tune called 'Song of the Maggie'.

...ack Haig and Larry Parker as ...estern 'dudes' attempting to con ... tribe of indians in Happy-Go-...ucky.
...ne O'Clock Show' writer, Herbie ...utchert is the indian on the far left.

Some young directors glorified in complicated camera scripts. Others, quite rightly, went for simplicity. Unfortunately Jack was sometimes not the most tactful of advisers, but he was usually right.

Over five and a half years, 'Happy-Go-Lucky' evolved from a 'magazine' programme with 'funny bits' into a full situation comedy. It seems a pity that no videotape remains in Tyne Tees' archives, but I suppose that nobody thought we were doing anything more than producing a children's programme and making a living. The best 'lift' you could get in those days was to meet 'Mr George and Mr Alfred' (Black) in the canteen after transmission and they said, 'That worked well today.' '

Colin 'Tiny' Prince, who was bass player in Dennis Ringrowe's band, joined 'Happy-Go-Lucky' and used to sing the children's song requests as well as acting in the sketches. The request spot attracted hundreds of letters from the younger viewers.

The series lasted for over five years and in September 1964, the last edition was screened. On 1 October 1964 the programme 'Young World' with Joe and Heather Ging took over the Thursday spot.

Today, Larry Parker is performing as a comedy magician and was top of the bill when he appeared on the QE2 and at the German variety theatre 'GOP Variete' in Essen where he appeared with his new rabbit assistant called Hepplewhite.

Left to right: Colin 'Tiny' Prince, Wacky Jacky, and Larry Parker.

126

PROD. NO. 5721
AMPEX: 15.11.61
TRANS: 15.11.61
(STUDIO 1)

YNE TEES TELEVISION LIMITED
RESENTS
HAPPY GO LUCKY
ith
LARRY PARKER
THEODORE
JACKY JACKY

SCRIPT BY LARRY PARKER

Producer.....................George Adams
Production Assistant....Beryl Mitchell
Vision Mixer.................Anna Moore
Floor Manager............Bill Sykes
Designer.....................Jan Bruce

Complete S. & L.	08.00 - 08.45
Dry Run	08.45 - 09.00
Cameras	09.00 - 12.30
Lunch	12.30 - 13.30
L.U.	13.30 - 14.00
Ampex	14.00 - 14.35

PROGRAMME NO. 12 AMPEX & TRANSMISSION: 15th NOVEMBER, 1961
PRODUCTION NO: 5721

F/U
. CAM.1 TTT CAPTION   CAPTION: TTT PRESENTS
MIX
. CAM.2 HAPPY GO LUCKY ROLLER   ROLLER: "HAPPY GO LUCKY"

SHOT OF ALLEY OUTSIDE
GAZETTE OFFICE.
MIX TO LARRY SEATED AT HIS
DESK IN THE INNER OFFICE.
HE SWITCHES ON THE
INTERCOM
(THEO SPEAKS)

LARRY:

MIX
. CAM. 3 LARRY IN OFFICE

Theodore, put me through to Jacky in
The Dark Room, will you?
(THEO SPEAKS. F/X SWITCHES
AND BUZZING.
THEO SPEAKS AGAIN MUFFLED)

JACK: (O.O.V. WITH DISTORT.)
I'm sorry, Master Theodore. I can't be
disturbed at the moment. I'm busy.
(THEO SPEAKS.)
JACK:
Oh, all right.
(F/X SWITCHES ETC.)
JACK:
Photographic department. Wedding
groups, Boy Scout Troupes, and babies
on cushions, our specialities.
W. Jacky, Esq., speaking.
LARRY:
Jacky, stop playing around, have you
got those photographs ready yet?
JACK:
Just taking them out of the fixing tank
Mr Larry. Won't be a minute.
(F/X CLICK OF SWITCH)

LARRY:
Thank you Theodore.
(THEO SPEAKS AND SWITCHES OFF.)
LARRY:
Now then, if Jacky has a decent
photograph for the front page story - that
should leave enough room for the piece on
Fred Ugthorpe's pigeons to go beside it...
(JACK HEARD SINGING O.O.V.
JACK ENTERS TO LARRY
CARRYING SHEAF OF
PHOTOGRAPHS.)
JACK:
Here they are Mr Larry. Take your pick.
Each one a photographic masterpiece.
Here is a picture of the Ambleford Football
Club, last Saturday.
LARRY:
But there's nobody on the field.
JACK:
They must have been playing away.
LARRY:
How can you be so idiotic?
JACK:
It isn't something you can pick up overnight
you know. It takes years of.. Yes. Ah now
you'll like this. This is Willie Woodford's
One Man Band. He plays the drums with his
feet, the harmonica with his mouth, the
tambourine with his knees, and the vibraphone
with his elbows.
LARRY:
What does he do with his hands?
JACK:
He holds them over his ears.
Here is a picture of the windmill on the
Ditchfield Road.
LARRY:
I thought Mr Snaith had two windmills there.
JACK:
Yes he had. But he took one of them down.
LARRY:
Why?
JACK:
Because there wasn't enough wind for two.
LARRY:
Is that what Mr. Snaith told you?
JACK:
Yes.
LARRY:
And you believed him?
JACK:
Naturally.
LARRY:
How old are you?
JACK:
I'm er - er - I don't know.
LARRY:
You must know your own age.
JACK:
I don't. It's very difficult to remember it.
LARRY:
Why?
JACK:
It keeps changing every year.
LARRY:
You are the most witless, obtuse, vacant
blockheaded numbskull I've ever met.
JACK:
Well nobody is perfect.

**By kind permission of Larry Parker, Theodore, and Tyne
Tees Television.**
Note: L.U. = Lights up.   S & L = Set & Lights.
F/X = sound effects. OOV = Out of vision. F/U = Fade up.
AMPEX = Video recording equipment.

Shirley Wilson

Shirley Wilson was 19 years old when she won the final of the Daily Sketch National Talent Contest. The prize was a two year contract with the Ted Heath Agency, a silver trophy and a recording contract with Columbia records. I met Shirley at her home in Leeds and she picked up the story from there.

'Winning the contest meant that I had to live and work in London which I wasn't too happy about. I was one of ten children, and we are a very close family. We've always lived in Middleton so I didn't like living in London one little bit. I lived there for three years and they were the unhappiest years of my life. I was very lonely but because my mum and dad were so proud of me, I didn't have the heart to pack it all in and come home. Ted Heath placed me with the Don Smith Orchestra who later came to the Oxford Galleries in Newcastle. I wasn't very happy with my singing and when Ted Heath sent me for professional lessons with Harold Miller, he discovered the reason. He told me that I was not a pop singer as I was a 'head' singer not a 'chest' singer and was more suited to classical soprano singing. Don arranged for me to sing light classical pieces as a cabaret spot on his shows. It went down really well but I was still homesick. I came home one Christmas to see my family and I met Harry Williams on Christmas Night. I'd known Harry for many years but I think our romance really started on that Christmas Night. We got engaged a month later and we were married in September 1957. I resigned from the danceband in June that same year. In about October 1958 I received a telegram out of the blue from George and Alfred Black asking me to go for a screen test for a new television station called Tyne Tees. I passed the test and joined the station as resident singer on 'The Boys Request' programme. I wasn't involved with the planning of the programme but I remember I was given a selection of songs to choose from each week. I preferred to sing songs from musical comedy shows such as 'The King and I'. One night Larry Mason and

I were singing 'Porgy, I's Your Woman Now' from 'Porgy an Bess' and I wasn't happy with the song at all. I got myse quite worked up about the number as we were singing liv Dennis Ringrowe played the introduction and I came in on whole octave higher than the pitch I should have sung. Yc should have seen Larry's face, his eyes were like marbles. thought, 'How am I going to get out of this?' Dennis wa glowering at me and Larry had that look of panic on his fac

Shirley Wilson was voted 'Fema Personality of the Year' in 195 and again in 1961 by readers 'The Viewer' magazine. Th photograph was taken in 1961 an shows Keith Beckett (second fron left) who was voted 'Producer the Year' and David Hamilto (right) 'Male Personality of th Year'. The awards were presente by Dame Vera Lynn. The othe people in the photograph ar readers of 'The Viewer' who wer invited to the studios on the nigh of the presentation of the award They are Elizabeth Way, Roge Arthur, and Mrs Alderson.

Dennis Ringrowe conducts the orchestra as Shirley Wilson dances with her husband Harry (seen in the foreground). Behind him is Heather Ging and Bill Slark jnr.

managed to 'slither' down one octave as if I was ad-libbing. I was expecting loads of letters complaining but I didn't receive a single one - no-one had noticed my mistake.

After a while, Tyne Tees offered me a seven year contract and I appeared regularly on the 'One O'Clock Show' as well as many other music productions. We had some fun on the 'One O'Clock Shows' and the audiences were wonderful. At the end of the show I could never get home for an hour or so because many of the children in the audience wanted to meet me and bring me flowers. The amount of flowers I received was amazing. I couldn't keep them all so many of the staff had flowers in their offices after each show.

Sometimes I used to act in the comedy sketches on the 'One O'Clock Show'. I remember one day Terry O'Neill and I were in a sketch with him as a door to door salesman and I was acting the part of a housewife. I have never smoked in my life but for the sketch I was dressed in a 'turban' style headscarf , a pinny over my dress, and I had to smoke a cigarette. A young stage hand called Vic Slark had to light the cigarette for me as I didn't even know how to do that. I was really apprehensive about the cigarette and it looked so funny. Some of the stage crew started to laugh which set me laughing too. I accidentally inhaled the smoke and couldn't say the lines for coughing and laughing. Terry had to say the lines for me. Ten minutes later I was scheduled to sing a song and I could hardly sing for coughing. It showed how sensitive my throat was.

When I was acting in sketches, there wasn't time to go to the dressing room to change, so we had to change costumes behind a partition at the side of the audience seating. There wasn't much privacy as the audience members who were sat right at the edge of the high seating could see down to where we were changing. The Wardrobe Mistress Irma May was quite bossy and would say,
'There's no time for modesty girl, as we've only got 30 seconds before your sketch.'
Irma was very good at her job as she had gained a lot of experience in the film industry. She would often come onto the studio floor to see what the set looked like. She would then choose a dress for me which blended well with the set. She knew what she was talking about and was very firm. I'd sometimes hint that I wasn't too keen on the

dress she'd chosen for me and she would say,
'It'll look very nice dear; you're going to wear it anyway.'
Sometimes Irma would take in the seams of the dress far too tight so I could hardly breathe. It made singing very difficult so I would often unpick some of the stitching just before I went into the studio. She always had a cigarette in her mouth which never moved when she talked because she'd wedge it in the gap between her front teeth.

The Make-up girls would give me a time at which I had to go to the department for my hair-do and face make-up. The make-up was much heavier than what you would wear outside but wasn't as heavy as stage make-up. Sometimes a guest artiste may be appearing and they would ask the Make-up girls if they could make themselves up. Heather Jackson would say, 'That's fine, as long as I stand by your side and guide you.' Many artistes would like to use dark, heavy lines around their eyes. Heather would point out that the lines would 'close' their eyes when they were on camera. Some artistes would ignore Heather with disastrous results when they appeared on camera.

We used to record two 'One O'Clock Shows' on Mondays as there wasn't a show broadcast that day. We'd do a live show on a Tuesday and record a second one later that day. It meant I was working three and a half days a week at Tyne Tees and had three and a half days a week at home. I was usually learning new songs when I was at home as well as having to do the housework. I remember doing the ironing with my music copies on the ironing board next to the clothes, and rehearsing while I was ironing. I had to learn about 12 songs a week but we were allowed to use 'cue boards' where we would write the words on large white cards using a marker pen. One day, the Producer David Croft asked me to sing the Ella Fitzgerald song 'By Straus' which I didn't like at all. I had to memorise the words because I had to walk through a series of arches while I was singing, so we couldn't use 'cue boards'. Rehearsals went fine, but when we came to do the show live, I caught the hem of my dress on some scenery. That put me right off and I completely forgot the words. I just sang anything,
'Shafamanadavazan mah mee. Walla walla deepadoo Som bom.' I couldn't stop - it was a live show. I wasn't even singing English. David was furious and told me off. 'What a mess,' he said. The audience thought it was great - they thought I was singing in French. I didn't receive a single complaint from the viewers. Who knows? they were probably too polite to complain. I couldn't do anything wrong in their eyes; the North-Easterners were wonderful to me.

We had some fabulous orchestras at Tyne Tees which was a new experience for me. I'd sung with bands but never with a full orchestra with a string section - it was wonderful but quite nerve-racking. During rehearsals I had to stand next to Dennis Ringrowe while the orchestra played the arrangement of my song. That would be the first time I heard the arrangement and sometimes I was overwhelmed by the magnificent sound of the orchestra.

I used to travel to Tyneside on Sunday and stay with r grandmother at North Lane in Washington ready for rehears on Monday mornings. I loved the work at Tyne Tees but was so tiring. I used to get a taxi from Tyne Tees to r grandmother's and most nights I was absolutely exhauste Granny Chicken was so proud of me and she would sometim invite friends and neighbours to her house and they would waiting to meet me when I arrived home after work. Afte hard day's work, the last thing I wanted was to socialise, b she just wanted to show me off. Sometimes I'd stay witl lovely couple called Dennis and Jean Grieves who worked the offices at Tyne Tees and lived in Chester-le-Street. I al lodged with Mr and Mrs Stobbart who had a guest house Newcastle, and it was like a home from home.

I stayed with Tyne Tees for over seven years and they were t happiest years in my whole working life. The atmosphere the studio was so happy and the letters from the viewers we wonderful. When my contract with Tyne Tees ended I work for Yorkshire Television for a while and also appeared in loc clubs. The clubs were wonderful but were always very smo which started to affect my throat very badly. My throat g worse and worse until I had to have an operation which I fe was due to 'passive smoking' in the clubs. I had to give singing but I wasn't devastated about leaving showbusine because I always treated it as a job and my family alwa came first.

Some time later I got a job as an usher at Leeds Magistra Court. It was a very interesting job and I met many peop during my duties there. Once in a while, someone from t North-East would be in court and might approach me a say,
'I must be mistaken, but you are the spitting image of Shirl Wilson who used to sing on Tyne Tees Television.'
I would smile and say,
'That's because I am Shirley Wilson who used to sing on Ty Tees Television.'

I worked at Leeds Magistrates Court for 17 years until I retir in 1997. '

Shirley Wilson in 1998

Request Time

as initially titled 'The Boys Request' and was presented by the singing commere, Sheila Mathews. Sheila would play tape-recordings of messages from soldiers stationed abroad in regiments such as the Durham Light Infantry, the Royal Northumberland Fusiliers, and the Green Howards. They would send greetings to their loved ones back home, and the resident singers and musicians on the show would then play the requested songs. It was probably the television version of the popular BBC radio show 'Two-Way Family Favourites'. The first 'Boys Request' was transmitted on Thursday 22 January, 1959 from 6:40pm until 7pm. It moved to the later slot of 10:15pm on 19 March 1959. Resident singers on the show included David Macbeth, Shirley Wilson, and the Barry Sisters. After a break in the summer of 1959, the show returned in September with the new title 'Request Time'. A new series, hosted by Norma Evans, started on 9 December 1959. It was screened on Wednesdays from 7pm until 7:30.

The last 'Request Time' was screened on Thursday, 23 March 1961 and gave the viewers a rare opportunity to enjoy all four Barry Sisters singing together.

> ### 7.0   REQUEST TIME
> introduced by
> **NORMA EVANS**
> and starring
> **THE BARRY SISTERS**
> **DAVID MACBETH**
> **SHIRLEY WILSON**
> and
> **DENNIS RINGROWE and his ORCHESTRA**
> Tonight's requests include *Mr. Blue* sung by David Macbeth, and a performance of the *High Spen Rapper* by students of King's College. The Anniversary Corner recalls song memories of the year 1935
> *Settings by* JOHN DINSDALE
> *and* MICHELLE
> *Produced by* PHILIP JONES
> **A Tyne Tees Production**

Sunshine Street

'Sunshine Street' was written and produced by David Croft and was first screened on Friday 31 July, 1959 at 7pm. It starred 'One O'Clock Show' host Terry O'Neill, Peter Hammond, Marion Williams, Graham Tennent and Tyneside's David North (McBeth). It was a half-hour show with music, dancing and light-hearted sketches. The Bel Canto Singers provided the harmony vocals and choreography was by Patricia Kirshner who often appeared in the Tyne Tees production 'Your Kind of Music'. 'Sunshine Street' ran until August 1959. A second series was produced in May 1960 which featured Rex Garner (who starred in 'Shadow Squad'), and comedienne Paddy Edwards who had starred in the Jack Jackson Show. David Croft and Tyne Tees Musical Director, Dennis Ringrowe wrote the signature tune:

Everything will turn out fine
When you're living on Sunshine Street
Ordinary water tastes like wine
On Sunshine Street
The people are free and easy
That's the way they feel
Everybody's pleased to meet you
You can tell by the way they greet you
Funny how the skies look blue
When you're living on Sunshine Street
Corny old dreams, it seems come true
How long it can last nobody knows
That's the way it always goes
On Sunshine Street.

David McBeth

'When I first started singing around the clubs, I was a salesman for Andrews Liver Salts. I entered the Carroll Levis Talent Show at the Sunderland Empire and came in first. In the audience was an agent called Eddie Arnold who was also a most wonderful impressionist and had appeared at many top theatres including the Palladium. He said that he would like to manage me but he didn't like my surname, McBeth. He said that it sounded too Scottish. As I came from the North, he decided to call me David North. I accepted his suggestion and when Tyne Tees came to town, I entered their talent show 'At the Golden Disc' as David North. I remember I sang the Shirley Bassey hit 'As I Love You'. I won several heats in the Show but Bill Lyon-Shaw asked me to withdraw from the competition as they wanted to give me a contract to become one of Tyne Tees' resident singers. The contract was for £50 a week which was a lot of money in those days. If you had a £20 a week job, you were thought of as successful, and there I was on £50. I couldn't believe it. I made a record called 'Mr Blue' which went to No8 in the charts locally and No18 nationwide. The record company didn't like the name David North and suggested Scott Weston. I thought it sounded like a biscuit company. The next day they rang me to say they weren't happy with Scott Weston either and asked me what my real name was. When I said 'McBeth' they thought it was great and that's the name I took from then on. That's why many people think my real name is 'North' when it's actually McBeth. The media, however, used the spelling 'Macbeth'. My mother and father were over the moon as it was the family name. The first programme I appeared in on TTT was 'The Boys Request' starring Sheila Mathews, Shirley Wilson and the Raindrops. The show featured tape-recorded requests from soldiers stationed abroad and we would sing the requested songs live. I remember that there were a lot of people at Tyne Tees who had never worked in television before and they were making it up as they went along. They would say, 'You are the guest artiste on the 'One O'Clock Show' next week.'
They didn't tell you what to do or how to even walk on set. It was my friend Dickie Valentine who taught me how to walk

David McBeth in romantic mood with Chris Langford

on stage and other techniques of presentation.
George and Alfred Black were wonderful. They gave me th[e] best advice I have ever received in my life. They told me [t]o get a good accountant so that I wouldn't get into deep wate[r] with income tax and the like. They suggested a particula[r] firm and I've been with the same accountant for 40 year[s]. Terry O'Neill was great to work with and would suggest gag[s] for me to use in my act. Jack Haig was a true profession[al] and I learnt a lot from him. I was a b[it] frightened of Bill Lyon-Shaw. He asked [to] see me one day and said that the music[al] introductions to my songs were too long. [I] got together with the lads in the band an[d] next time we saw Bill we let him hear o[ur] new arrangement of the song 'You Mak[e] Me Feel So Young'. It started with on[e] very quick chord from the band after whic[h] I came straight in with the first line. H[e] wasn't amused.

David McBeth (centre) with Jack Hai[g] (left), Terry O'Neill (right), and the Lor[d] Mayor of Darlington and his wife.

remember I compered a special show at Newcastle Civic
Centre one day. The guest of honour was Prince Charles and
I was very honoured to be chosen to be the MC. I was
walking down Northumberland Street a few days before the
show and two old ladies stopped me and said,

'We hear that you are going to compere the show that Prince
Charles is attending. Will you be speaking to him?'

I explained that I didn't know whether I would or not. The
women continued,

'Well, If you do speak to him tell him that Mrs Wilson of Blyth
Women's Institute thinks he's lovely, but,' she continued, 'I was
going past her house last week (Buckingham Palace) and I
wasn't impressed when I saw her windows. Will you tell
Charles to tell his mam that her nets are hacky.'

I told that story when I was on Terry O'Neill's television show
in Australia and the switchboard of the television station was
jammed with ex-patriot Geordies who were enthralled as they
hadn't heard the word 'hacky' for years and years.

I remember working with Larry Mason and Ronnie Hilton on
a Tyne Tees show. Larry used to get very nervous whereas I
was always calm. I don't know whether that was a good thing
or not. Ronnie was always playing tricks on stage and he
asked me how we could 'break the ice' for Larry. Larry's song
was 'Standing on the Corner' and he had to lean against a
'prop' lamp-post which had a lead weight on its base to stop it
falling over. The rehearsal was fine but just before the live
transmission, we removed the lead weight from the base of the
lamp-post. When Larry came to sing his song, he leant against
the lamp-post and it went flying with him after it. How on
earth he managed to keep on singing, I'll never know. Larry
said, 'I'll strangle that McBeth.' On another show Larry's song
was, 'That was a Real Nice Clambake' from 'Carousel'. I had
to come through Western style swinging doors just before
Larry burst into song. I got a cigar and squashed it so it
looked like the doors had smashed in my face. I came bursting

David McBeth (left) with Chris Langford, and Larry Mason
in 1967 appearing in the Tyne Tees production 'Memories
are Made of Hits'.

through the doors with the cigar in my mouth and said, 'The
Milky Bars are on me.' Larry took one look and couldn't sing
for laughing. The band had to play the introduction over and
over until Larry composed himself.

For me, television came too soon. I wish I'd gained some
stage experience first before TV. I think it was a case of
'ignorance is bliss'; I just didn't know what was going on. If
I did, I would have been a nervous wreck. For me, the best
Producer at Tyne Tees was a Canadian guy called Don Gollan.
He would just say to me, 'Sing your song and I'll 'shoot' around
you'. That made things so much easier for me as I could then
imagine I was singing to an audience at a cabaret. When all
the music shows at Tyne Tees came to an end, I decided to get
the experience in stage work that I lacked. In 1963 I did a 42
night tour with The Beatles, Gerry and the Pacemakers, and
Roy Orbison. It was a terrific experience. I worked in South
Africa, Australia, America and all around Europe. After a
while I started to get homesick and that's when I bought Greys
Club. I bought the club from Ladbrokes in 1982. I like to
take it easy these days and I have a manager who looks after
the club most of the time while I improve my golf handicap.'

**David McBeth in 1998, owner of Greys Club in
Newcastle upon Tyne**

Larry Mason

'In the 1950's I was working as a Rington's Tea salesman during the day but at night I came 'alive' when I sang with the 'big-bands'. I sang with a 14 piece band at the Queens Rink in Hartlepool for eight years and then I was with Al Flush's Band at the Black's Rink Sunderland.. It was my sister-in-law who wrote to the 'Golden Disc' talent show at Tyne Tees and put my name forward to enter the show. I received a letter asking me to attend an audition at a church hall just around the corner from the studios. Billy Hutchinson was on piano and when I started my audition I was enthralled with his playing. I had never heard anyone as wonderful a player as Billy and he boosted my confidence 200%. With Billy playing I could reach two notes higher than my normal range. I passed the audition and the next stage was to meet the producer Philip Jones. Philip was a lovely man and he was great to work with. I was very surprised when he asked me to sing on the show the very next week. I won my heats in the contest and went on to win the Grand Final on Friday 5 February 1960. During the Grand Final I was terrified waiting for my turn to sing, and couldn't remember what my song was. When my spot came up, the band played the introduction, and everything was fine. My song was 'Smoke Gets in Your Eyes'.

Soon after the final, work at Tyne Tees started to come my way. We didn't have a telephone at the time, so I would get a telegram asking me to appear on a show and I would return to the Rington's depot, hand in my cash bag, and dash off to City Road. After a while, the supervisor at Rington's got a bit fed up so I decided to go professional.

Tony Martell must have auditioned thousands of acts for the 'Golden Disc' show and he kept all their names and addresses. When the show finally finished, he opened his 'Television

Shirley Wilson and Larry Mason singing a duet from 'West Side Story' on Tyne Tees 'Request Time'

Academy' in Newcastle to offer training in television presentation techniques, modelling, social etiquette and dancing. He must have sent mail shots to all of the people who had auditioned for the show and many people subscribed to the Academy with perhaps a hope of getting work in a television studio.

When George Adams became a Producer, I worked for him from time to time on the 'One O'Clock Show' but my 'Big Break' came when I won a 13 week contract to sing on 'Request Time'. I worked with the Barry Sisters and the lovely girl singer Shirley Wilson. Of the thousands of letters we received for songs to be sung on 'Request Time', 80% were for Shirley and I to sing a duet. We used to blend together very nicely. Whenever a man and a woman have to key-set for a duet it can be very difficult, but Shirley and I always sang in the same key. On one particular show, Shirley and I were singing 'This is my Lovely Day' from the musical 'Bless the Bride'. Tyne Tees had hired a beautiful vintage car which Shirley had to sit in as we sang the song. I had to walk up to the car and step onto the running board. During rehearsals, when I stepped on, the car's springs squeaked loudly which was picked up by the microphone. It sounded really funny and it started us giggling. The camera crew joined in and before long we couldn't rehearse for laughing. We eventually composed ourselves and an hour later we started the dress rehearsal

TONIGHT AT 8.55

£350 ALL-WINNERS NIGHT
AT THE
GOLDEN DISC

introduced by

TONY MARTELL

The winner from last week's semi-final
joins :

THE GAMBLERS   HAROLD HALL
LARRY MASON

for prizes of £250 and £100

Star Judging Panel :

JACK PAYNE (Chairman)
MARION RYAN
JOE " MR. PIANO " HENDERSON
JIMMY HENNEY   ALAN FREEMAN
with
DENNIS RINGROWE and his
ORCHESTRA

'The Viewer' magazine listing for the Grand Final of the second series of 'At The Golden Disc' which was screened on Friday 5 Feb. 1960. Dorothy Townsend from West Hartlepool was also one of the finalists.

irley was dressed in a magnificent wedding gown with a
ain which must have been ten feet long. When she stepped
to the car, I had to lift her train and bundle it into the seat
side her. The train was starched and was very difficult to
ndle. When I eventually got the train into the car, Shirley
as submerged by a mass of white lace like candy floss which
me right up to her chin almost obscuring her face. It was so
nny and set us laughing again. The Director was furious as
ne is money in a television studio. Wardrobe had to trim
ve or six feet off the train so we could do the number.

appeared on the 'One O'Clock Show' one day singing a
afaring song. In the studio was a replica of the bows of a
ll ship and I had to stand at the bows and sing my song while
oking 'out to sea'. We must have rehearsed the song all day
id everyone was fed up. When I came to sing the song live,
went quite well but George Romaine thought the scene needed
me special effects, so right at the end he sneaked onto the
t, out of camera shot, and threw the entire contents of a
icket of water at me. The water was freezing and it was a
omplete surprise causing me to yell at the top of my voice.

n another edition of the 'One O'Clock Show' Jack Haig was
aying the part of a carpet salesman in a comedy sketch with
ie rest of the cast. The studio set was a row of house front
oors and Jack knocked on each door in turn trying to sell a
oll of carpet which he had tucked under his arm.
Vould you like some of this carpet in your lounge?' Jack
iquired as the first door opened. The door was quickly
ammed in his face.
ome of this lovely carpet for your dining room?' Jack pleaded
o the owner of the next house.
Jo I don't want any carpet!' was the annoyed reply.
it the third house door, Jack started straying from the script
s he often did.
Vould you like this carpet in your back passage?' Jack shouted.
'here was an embarrassed silence and the band was cued to
trike up with some music. There was hell on and Jack had to
eport to the Black Brothers and apologise.

iill Lyon-Shaw had a heart of gold but he used to put the fear
f God into us sometimes by bellowing out instructions during
ehearsals. Sometimes he'd shout at me,
What the hell are you doing with that song, Mason?'
Ie would pay nice compliments too. One day, as I was passing
is office, he asked me in and said,
You know the 'Desert Song'? well this is the show's star, John
Ianson.'
Ie introduced me to John and said,
This is Larry Mason, our station singer. There's only one
lifference between Larry's singing and your's John - you get
aid more money for it.'

was still singing with the Al Flush Band when the Black's
Rink Sunderland was taken over by Top Rank. Al was asked
o go to Top Rank's Head Office in London and I went with
im to share the driving. I'll never forget Al's ashen face when
ie came out of Top Rank's office. His band had been given
he sack as Top Rank were bringing their own band to the

dance hall. They'd offered Al the job of DJ playing records in
the interval. He was devastated. The Top Rank management
had also said,
'We would like Larry Mason to work for us with Ronnie
Carrol's band at the Majestic dance hall in Newcastle.'
I was sorry for Al but I needed the work so I reported for
'duty' at the Maj. To my horror, the bandleader didn't know
I'd been assigned to the Majestic and it was a very embarrassing
first booking with the Ronnie Carrol Band. It worked out fine
in the end however and my appearances at Tyne Tees helped
to promote the band.'
Larry was with Tyne Tees for six years after which he continued
his singing career at theatres and nightclubs throughout the
UK. Larry retired in 1984 but still sings occasionally for
charity functions.

Larry Mason in 1998

Jimmy James Show

Jimmy James was much liked and respected by Programme Controller, Bill Lyon-Shaw. Jimmy, of course had come to the rescue on the opening night of TTT when the star of the Big Show, Dickie Henderson fell ill. At first, Jimmy found it difficult to work on television as he had been used to theatre audiences, and although there was usually a studio audience, it was often remote from the performers who were surrounded by cameras and production staff who did not always react to Jimmy's patter. On the opening night, Jimmy turned up late and had to be quickly ushered through the public entrance and onto the studio floor via the audience. Consequently Jimmy got a reaction from the audience right from the start which put him at ease, and his act when down really well. Soon after Jimmy appeared in Tyne Tees' Birthday Show in January 1960, Bill Lyon-Shaw asked him if he would like to do a series of four shows. The first show was broadcast on Wednesday 6 April 1960 and among the supporting acts were local singers Larry Mason and Owen Brannigan. Larry had been 'discovered' on TTT's talent show 'At the Golden Disc' and Owen Brannigan was already established as a popular baritone. Assisting Jimmy were Bretton Woods alias Eli, and Dick Carlton. Norma Evans, daughter of comedian Norman Evans, gave the show a touch of glamour to offset Jimmy's zany comedy routines. It was quite common for Jimmy to stray from the script which threw the Producer into a panic, not to mention Jimmy's two partners who sometimes hadn't a clue what was coming next.

Jimmy was just as zany offstage and would often clown around in the most unlikely places. Chris Langford remembered a time when she travelled to London on the train with Jimmy and his company.

'The train was packed and we couldn't get seats together. One seat was free and Jimmy asked Eli to sit there while we stood in the aisle. Jimmy then launched into his patter with Eli.

'Now son, I don't want you to be sick again like you were in the station. Sit up straight lad and try not to throw up again. You know what you're like when you eat tripe. I told you not to eat it but you don't listen to me.'

This patter went on for about five minutes and I had to stop myself laughing out loud and giving the game away. Before we knew it, half the carriage was empty and we all had seats together for the whole journey.'

Jimmy James with Eve Boswell, guest star on the Jimmy James Show. Eve Boswell had a UK hit that same year with the song: 'Pickin' a Chicken'.

A scene from the Jimmy James Show in 1960. The lady on the left is Laura Cairns, wife of announcer Adrian Cairns

7.55 THE JIMMY JAMES SHOW
starring
JIMMY JAMES
and his friends
with guest artiste
OWEN BRANNIGAN
and
singing discovery
LARRY MASON
THE DENNIS RINGROWE ORCHESTRA
Settings by MICHELLE
Produced by PHILIP JONES
A Tyne Tees Production
(See Page 8)

eat The Band

ot the Tune was a popular networked programme produced
Granada Television. Tyne Tees' show was the opposite to
at; the contestants had to try and name a tune which Dennis
ingrowe and the band couldn't play. The show was the
ainchild of Harold Berens who had presented the show on
adio Luxembourg. Tyne Tees producer Philip Jones had
oduced the Luxembourg version. Occasionally the
ntestants on the show would name a tune which was not
ona-fide. The band simply made up a tune on the spot and
o-one ever complained that it wasn't correct. The band's
eds player, Rees Hughes is shown in the photograph below.
he photo to the right shows Harold Berens (with the checked
irt), George Black, (centre) and the show's Producer, Philip
nes on the right. The show had a fairly short run from
hursday 16 July until 10 September, 1959.

Left to right: Harold Berens, George Black, Philip Jones
Sound man, Jim Goldby is seen on the far left.

7.30 HAROLD BERENS

invites you to
another attempt
to

BEAT THE BAND

Can you think of a tune which will " Beat the
Band " ? Contestants and viewers can win
prizes in this new musical quiz
with
THE DENNIS RINGROWE QUARTET
and
CHRIS LANGFORD
Settings by JOHN DINSDALE
Produced by BERNICE DORSKIND
A Tyne Tees Production

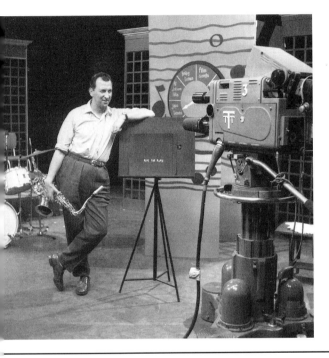

¬uess Who

¬uess Who' was a quiz programme where teams of
choolchildren would have to guess the names of famous people
ast and present. The programme was hosted by Mark Hughes
nd was screened on Tuesdays at 7pm. It ran from July until
¬eptember 1959. The show, which was produced by 'Lew'
¬ewenhak, sometimes featured TTT's personalities who
ressed up as famous historical characters. The panellists
ad to 'Guess Who'.

Who Knows?

Who Knows?' was an inter-schools quiz which was first
creened on Monday 18 March 1963. The Question-Master
vas McDonald Hobley and the programme was directed by
¬isle Willis.

Tyne Tees Top Tunes

Tyne Tees Top Tunes' was a 15 minute music programme
roduced by George Adams. It often featured singers George
Romaine and Chris Langford singing popular songs of the
lay.

Spotlight

On a more serious note, 'Spotlight' produced by H K Lewenhak
and investigated by Leslie Barrett, was a 'no holds barred'
discussion programme which tackled controversial subjects
of the day such as electoral reform, birth control, and
drunkenness. The programme was screened on Tuesdays at
10:15pm - the first edition was on 20 January 1959.

Answers to Advert Quiz on page 35

1. Cadbury's Milk Tray.
2. Brylcream.
3. Pepsodent.
4. Hovis.
5. Flash.
6. Medley.
7. Cadbury's Snack.
8. Heinz Beans.
9. Strand Cigarettes. (the tune was a hit but the fags weren't)

Bill Maynard

Bill Maynard was an established stage and radio comedian when Tyne Tees invited him to appear on the 'Big Show' on the opening night of the station. One of Bill's spots was to introduce the feature called 'Folks With Jokes'. This was where members of the public were invited to tell their favourite joke live on camera. Bill had created the routine when he worked for the BBC Television show 'Great Scott, it's Maynard'. One of the catch phrases on the show was 'When You're In' which led to a BBC radio show named after the catchphrase. Bill's Tyne Tees show was first screened on Monday 19 January 1959 from 8pm till 8:30pm. A few weeks later it moved to the 9:30pm till 10pm spot. I spoke with Bill on the telephone and he recalled his memories of Tyne Tees.

'Folks With Jokes' was featured on Tyne Tees' first ever variety show and soon after I was given my own series on Monday nights which also featured the 'Jokes' routine. We used to give away big prizes like washing machines and television sets. Children also used to send in jokes which I would read on the show. We would send the kids book tokens and things like that. Sacks and sacks of mail would arrive every week with letters from viewers who wanted to be on the show. One week, a chap was in the middle of his joke and he collapsed with a heart attack. The show was live of course and we had to stop and call an ambulance. The story hit the press the next day and some newspapers accused me of staging the whole thing as a stunt. It wasn't a stunt, the bloke really did have a heart attack.

I did three series of that show for Tyne Tees and I remember staying in Houghton-le-Spring with a friend who had a dentistry practice. I'll never forget - his surgery was above the Red Lion pub. I suppose his patients could get 'numbified' in the pub before venturing upstairs to his surgery.'

The last show was screened on Monday 9 March, 1959.

Bill Maynard in 1959 on Tyne Tees Television's 'Big Show inviting Bella Armstrong to tell her joke live on camera *Image transferred from Tyne Tees Television's archives Multicord Video, Dunston .*

The contestants were escorted to the hot-spot on camera by one of the show's two hostesses, Avis Crowther and Claire Dodds. On meeting Bill, the joke-tellers would say, 'I've got a story for you.' By today's standards, the jokes were a shade on the corny side. Here are some examples.

A man took a room in a down-town boarding house. He was prepared for beetles and mice, but didn't expect fish - the room was damp.

I knew a man who collected elephants and put them into jam jars, by looking at them through the wrong end of a telescope and using tweezers.

Why is an elf always fit? Because it takes full advantage of the National Elf Service.

A man found a cure for a greyhound that couldn't take a corner to the left - he put lead in its ear ... using a revolver.

Some years later Bill was seen on the ITV network playing the part of a musical agent called Micky Malone in 'Coronation Street'. Bill played Frank Riley in 'The Life of Riley', Stan the Fryer in 'Trinity Tales' and the accident-prone Selwyn Froggitt in 'Oh No! It's Selwyn Froggitt'. His performance in 1973 as a straight actor in 'Kisses at Fifty' was praised by the critics. More recently, he has been seen as the loveable character Claude Jeremiah Greengrass in Yorkshire Television's 'Heartbeat'.

Bill Maynard in 1998 playing Claude Jeremiah Greengrass in Yorkshire Television's 'Heartbeat'. Claude's dog is called Alfred.
Photograph is by kind permission of Yorkshire Television.

A typical Monday night's entertainment on TTT in March 1959. Ned's Shed was a 20 minute advertising magazine which was directed by David Croft who later joined the BBC and produced such classics as 'Dad's Army', 'Allo Allo', and 'Are you Being Served?'

Bill Maynard, now one of the stars of Yorkshire Television's 'Heartbeat', had his own show live from City Road.

I Love Lucy' has stood the test of time as it was still being shown in 1997 on Channel 4.

MONDAY
MAR 9
TT CHANNEL 8

.40 NED'S SHED
An Advertising Magazine
d .... Lisle Willis
ocker .... Dan Douglas
g .... Maud Foster
Script by Dan Douglas, Julia James and Lisle Willis
Set designed by John Dinsdale
Directed by David Croft
A Tyne Tees Production

.0 I LOVE LUCY
starring
LUCILLE BALL
DESI ARNAZ
in
LUCY WANTS NEW FURNITURE
with
William Frawley
Vivian Vance
nother hilarious episode the lives of the Ricardos

.30 SHADOW SQUAD
starring
TER WILLIAMS   GEORGE MOON
as Don Carter   as Ginger Smart
in
ONE WHITE LIE
Episode 1
Written by John Warwick
Designed by Paul Bernard
Directed by Claude Whatham
enry Adams tells a white lie and finds himself the shadow of a heavy prison sentence. Don arter is called in and is confronted with a ngle of evidence. Why are so many people pporting what he knows to be a lie?
A Granada Production

.0 THE LARKINS
starring
EGGY MOUNT and DAVID KOSSOFF
in
VERY IMPORTANT PARENT
A domestic situation comedy by Fred Robinson
with
RONAN O'CASEY
ALAN GIFFORD
An ATV Production

8.30 WAGON TRAIN
starring
AUDREY TOTTER   WAYNE MORRIS
WARD BOND   ROBERT HORTON
in
THE TENT CITY STORY
with
Slim Pickens   Dennis McCarthy
June Ellis   Bill Henry   Frank McGrath
Yvonne White   Peter Coe   Earl Hanson
Carol Henry
Written by Norman Jolley
Directed by Richard H. Bartlett
When one of the wagoners foolishly kills a buffalo. The Indians threaten to attack in revenge. And Major Adams' imprisonment of the man responsible so angers Flint that it seems the train will lose its ace-scout for ever

9.30 THE BILL MAYNARD SHOW
with
CHRIS LANGFORD
LEN MARTEN
THE DENT BROTHERS
THE DENNIS RINGROWE QUARTET
introducing
FOLKS WITH JOKES
Set designed by John Dinsdale
Produced by Adrian Brown
A Tyne Tees Production

10.0 NEWS
ITN spotlights world news

10.15 CAN PHOTOGRAPHY BE AN ART?
asks
SIR KENNETH CLARK
Can the photograph ever be considered a form of art? Sir Kenneth Clark will examine the path photography has taken since its early days and will talk of the possibilities, values and pleasures photography has to offer
Produced by Michael Redington
An ATV Production

10.45 ICE SKATING
THE NORTHERN AND MIDLAND ICE SKATING CHAMPIONSHIPS
O.B. Cameras visit Birmingham Ice Rink to televise the winners of the Championships
Commentator Leslie Dunn
Directed by Kit Plant
An ATV Production

THE EPILOGUE
by the Rev. Charles Tompkins, Rector of Handsworth, Birmingham
Close down

'The Viewer'

Most of the independent television companies around the country listed their schedules in a national magazine called TV Times. From as early as 1958, the directors of Tyne Tees decided to have their own listings magazine and it was to be called 'The Viewer'. It was thought that a dedicated magazine would provide a better outlet for local programme publicity. It was also in line with Tyne Tees' policy to be the most regional of all the independent television stations.

'The Viewer' was published by the News Chronicle which was a national daily paper of the time but 'The Viewer' had its own staff of journalists and artists who worked at an office on Forth Lane near Newcastle's Central Station. In 1963 the Dickens Press took over publication and the staff moved to the Tyne Tees offices at City Road. Bob Stoker's name appears time after time as author of articles in the magazine; his weekly feature was 'Tyne Tees Topics'. It is said that Bob used to 'prowl' around the studios and offices of Tyne Tees looking for stories and people had to be careful what they said when Bob was around as it could appear in the next week's Viewer.

As transmission first started on a Thursday, the first issue of 'The Viewer' covered ten days from 15 to 24 January 1959. Following issues ran from Sunday to Saturday, they were published every Thursday and cost 4d. (approximately 1.5p) 160,000 copies of the first edition were printed and were sold out before TTT even went on the air. A further 25,000 copies had to be quickly printed. The second issue was given a 200,000 print run and the magazine gradually increased in circulation. A year later it was the biggest selling magazine in the North-East with a staggering circulation of 300,000 per week. Some subscribers to 'The Viewer' didn't even have television sets. Newsagents reported that when some folks went on holiday, they cancelled the newspapers but still had 'The Viewer' delivered as they wanted to read up about the programmes when they returned.

Compared to the Radio Times, it was a much higher quality publication on good quality paper. The photographs were high definition and the schedules were well layed out; the text being fully justified or centred in columns. 'The Viewer' was printed by a company called Samuel Stephen Ltd who used what was the very latest gravure process. At Christmas a special edition was printed in colour. As a young lad I kept scrapbooks of cuttings from 'The Viewer'. As well as pictures of the stars, I cut out programme listings and made notes when the programmes were first transmitted. My favourite networked programme was '77 Sunset Strip' and I kept a separate scrap book for that programme.

The very first issue of 'The Viewer' dated 15 to 24 January 1959.

On 17 March 1962, the design of the front cover was changed slightly and the programme listings were re-designed. From time to time special editions were published. For example the front cover banner of the 1-7th May 1960 issue was printed in Royal purple to commemorate the wedding of Princess Margaret and Antony Armstrong-Jones. The first Viewer to be printed in full colour was the Christmas edition in 1959. By the end of 1965 the front cover was in full colour on a regular basis.

'The Viewer' was regularly advertised on Tyne Tees. The commercials, which were often presented by Douglas Arthur or David Hamilton, would end with a little jingle such as the shown below. (For those who don't read music, it's the last two bars of the tune 'The Blaydon Races'.)

The magazine was not without its problems. In the summer of 1959, a union dispute stopped the normal format of 'The

Be sure to get the Vie- wer

THE VIEWER, June 27th, 1959.

THE TYNE TEES ITV PROGRAMME JOURNAL

June 28 - July 4   **3d.**

IT'S SUMMER TIME ON CHANNEL 8!

CHANNEL EIGHT dresses in its seasonal best next week to bring you the tops in summer entertainment.

The fun starts on Sunday, when those two crazy people, Jewel and Warris present a new quiz show entitled **For Love or Money.**

Bernard Delfont's Sunday Night At The Prince of Wales has an all-star bill headed by singing star Eve Boswell.

Monday brings **Johnnie Ray Sings.** Johnnie, who is reputed to be better than ever these days, will be assisted by Shani Wallis and Jack Parnell and his Orchestra.

Another top American entertainer graces the small screen on Wednesday. Dusky blues singer

Dinah Washington stars in **The Variety Show.**

A new TTT series starts on Wednesday called **Star Parade.** Featuring clips from the top films, it's bound to be a sure-fire winner with movie fans.

Starting the same day is **The Verdict is Yours.** This programme brings you moving court drama, in which actors portray a trial and a studio jury brings in a verdict.

Thursday sees the start of **Skyport,** a new serial dealing with the bustle, adventure and fun at a huge international airport.

In yet another new quiz show, **Full House,** engaged couples will have the chance to win furniture and an all-electric kitchen.

On to Friday — and another new quiz show. Called **The Brighter Sex,** it's a fast-moving, hectic battle of the sexes.

Sally Ann Howes presents her own **Saturday Spectacular** show this week.

And last, but not least, here are the major time changes that will affect your regular favourites during the summer:

The Bobby Thompson Show, Monday 8.30; **Wagon Train,** Monday 9.0; **Dial 999,** Monday 11.0; **Emergency Ward 10,** Tuesday 8.0 and Friday 8.0; **Wyatt Earp,** Tuesday 10.30; **I Love Lucy,** Tuesday 11.0; **Gun Law,** Wednesday 7.0; **Crime Sheet,** Wednesday 8.0; **The Boys Request,** Friday 6.35; **Cheyenne,** Saturday 9.0; **Great Movies of Our Time,** Saturday 10.0

EMERGENCY EDITION

BECAUSE of the printing dispute, publication of our normal issue has had to be suspended.

Meanwhile, as a service to our regular readers, we are carrying on throughout the emergency with this reduced version of the paper.

You will still be able to plan your Channel 8 viewing from this sheet, which is the only publication to contain advance details of seven days' programmes.

We apologise for not being able to provide you with your normal "Viewer," and because of the reduction in our service the price of the paper has been reduced temporarily to 3d.

We hope we will be with you again very soon in our normal format.

---

iewer' from being printed. Nevertheless, an emergency edition ith limited articles and programme details was published. he emergency edition did not have the usual red banner but as black and white throughout with poorer quality notographs. The price was reduced to 3d and it wasn't until id-August 1959 that the normal Viewer returned.

yne Tees have every copy of 'The Viewer' going back to hen transmission started on Thursday 15 January, 1959; 498 litions in total. They also have every issue of the 'TV Times' ter that. They are beautifully bound in half-yearly volumes nd are in quite good condition. The earlier issues from 1959 the mid-sixties were printed on better quality paper and are better condition than copies of the 'TV Times' from the 970's. 'The Viewers' make fascinating reading and reflect e fashions, styles, and way of life of the region throughout te 1950's and 1960's. They have been an invaluable source f information during research for this book and many pages f programme schedules and front covers have been reproduced y kind permission of Tyne Tees Television and the Directors f the Dickens Press.

1968 the Independent Television Authority announced the ew ITV contracts and stipulated that all the independent television companies must publish their programme listings in ne national magazine which was to be the 'TV Times'.)vernight Tyne Tees' TV listings magazine lost its unique arochial style. The very last issue of 'The Viewer' was for ne week September 14 to 20, 1968.

The last issue of 'The Viewer' was published for the week 14 to 20 September 1968. It was issue No.498

Random Memories of Tyne Tees

One of the production staff remembered a night when nothing much was happening as there was a film on. One of the women announcers was on duty and although the lights were turned down in the studio while the film was on, you could still see the announcer on the monitor. She must have been shopping that day as she started to try on different blouses. It was totally male in the control room, in the engineering room and at the transmitter. The boys in the control room fed the picture down the line to the transmitter and before we knew it there was soft porn being relayed throughout the whole engineering fraternity. It was very risky; if anyone had accidentally pressed the wrong button, the pictures could have gone out on the air.

In 1958, before the station started transmitting, there was a lot of building work going on in the studios and offices with many tradesmen coming and going. One enterprising local hairdresser thought it would be a good idea to set up a salon in the Tyne Tees offices. Perhaps he tried to find someone in charge to ask permission, but because of all the building work, the management proved to be elusive. He found an empty office and set up shop. For many months the man carried out his trade at City Road and everyone assumed he was Tyne Tees' official hairdresser. The production staff were working very intense schedules in those days and nobody really had the time to go outside to find a hairdresser. Consequently this chap was doing a roaring trade. Each manager assumed that one of his colleagues had given the hairdresser permission to set up shop, when in fact, no-one had.

Connie Richardson was canteen manageress in 1960. The canteen served 650 cups of tea and 400 cups of coffee every day as well as 300 meals. She used to say that it didn't matter whether you were a star or a sweeper-up, if you wanted to use the canteen you had to stand in the queue. However, Bill Steel remembers that you could sometimes 'con' your way to the front of the queue by saying, 'I'm on air in ten minutes.'

One of the top executives at Tyne Tees was prosecuted f[or] not having a TV licence. He had been given a compliment[ary] TV by the company and assumed that the company wou[ld] also look after the licence. Well they hadn't and a TV licen[ce] official called at his home and asked to see his licence. The[re] were some red faces in the boardroom.

Tyne Tees engaged resident singers in the early years and o[ne] young lady had been awarded a contract to appear regula[rly] in the 'One O'Clock Show'. She had never been to Newcas[tle] before and when she arrived at the Central Station, she w[as] late for rehearsals and hadn't a clue where Tyne Tees w[as]. She asked a passer-by and was told to catch a trolley-bus [in] City Road. On a lamp-post near to the trolley-bus stop wa[s a] pull-handle with a notice saying, 'Pull for City Road' so wh[en] trolley buses came along she pulled it. She didn't realise [it] was the handle to operate the trolley-wire points and she w[as] sending most of the trolley-buses down the wrong route.

Mrs Rosa Kennedy, who was company nurse from 1962 [to] 1982, remembers treating members of staff, personalities [of] the time and even members of the audience who sometim[es] fell ill during live shows in the studios. She treated the 196[0s] singing star, Frank Ifield who was suffering from a sore thro[at] and confessed that she did not recognise him at first. M[rs] Kennedy remembers the company doctor was Roy Thor[ne] who was a plump jolly man and rather like a traditional fami[ly] doctor. He was superseded by Doctor Mike Fisher.

One summer, one of the outside broadcast units was coveri[ng] cricket from Jesmond. The OB vans were parked overnight [at] the ground and one of Tyne Tees' security guards was post[ed] to watch the vans throughout the night. The guard had broug[ht] a sleeping bag and decided to grab a few hours sleep in th[e] early hours while everything was quiet. The next morning, [to] the guard's horror, all of the vans had been daubed with 'N[o] Apartheid' slogans.

Recent Memories of Tyne Tees

Throughout the two years it took to compile this book, I made many visits to Tyne Tees at City Road to carry out research. During one visit I was invited to sit in the gallery of Studio 2 and view live transmission of 'North-East Tonight with Mike Neville'.
In the gallery is a huge array of television monitor screens which show the output of each camera, videotape machine, live 'feeds' from outside broadcast units, and 'off-air' signals from the Bilsdale and Pontop transmitters. There is a noticeable delay between the 'off-air' picture and the output of the studio. This is due to the time it takes for the television signal to reach the transmitter and back again to the studio. The Director, Production Assistant and the Producer sit at the control desk. A fourth production staff member operates the Autocue which displays the news stories' text to the presenters. In the centre of the monitor screen panel is a large analogue clock, which runs in perfect synchronism with a digital clock mounted underneath. The programme's running order, which is

displayed on a computer screen, informs the production sta[ff] of the time of each item to the second.
Five minutes to go and the studio is requested to rehearse th[e] introduction of the programme. One minute to go, Mike Nevil[le] cracks a joke and all the gallery staff break into laughter. Te[n] seconds to go and the PA counts the seconds out loud.
The opening titles run, Mike does a live voice-over as th[e] headline images appear, and the programme is underway. Th[e] Director calls the camera shots over the talk-bac[k] communication system and the PA gives a countdown to eac[h] new item. Pam Royle takes her place next to Mike while h[e] reads the headline story. Pam has trouble with her microphon[e] cable. A staff member's voice is heard over the talk-bac[k] giving a detailed account of another problem. The Direct[or] needs the talk-back urgently. 'I'm sorry, I'll have to kill her,' h[e] rules, and presses his override button. While Pam reads th[e] local news for viewers in the Pontop region (Northumberlan[d] Tyne & Wear and North Durham). Dawn Thewlis is sitting i[n]

studio in Billingham reading a different news bulletin to
[vie]wers tuned to Bilsdale (Teesside, South Durham, and North
[Yo]rkshire. The switch between transmitters is seamless.
[te]n seconds to commercials.'
[Ba]ck on air is due at 18:17:30.
[M]ike is heard (not on air) to mumble over the script of the
[ne]xt item. Wynn Lowes from the Print Room calls into the
[ga]llery with some last-minute changes. Back on air and
[ca]meraman Ian Westwater is heard over the talk-back as
[Bi]lsdale rejoins Pontop. A live feed comes in from Westminster
[an]d the gallery give their instructions to Gerry Foley.
[Pr]ogramme Editor Graeme Thompson announces, 'We're ten
[se]conds over time. We'll have to lose the last sentence.'
[Th]e Autocue operator stops the machine and the text slowly
[de]celerates without jerking. Sports Presenter Ian Payne takes
[hi]s seat next to Mike and is mic'ed up. The day's sports news
[is] presented and the second commercial break is scheduled for
[18]:42:00. Bob Johnson takes his seat and the PA counts down

to the third section of the programme. The titles roll and the
Director looks up at the 'off-air' monitor and shouts,
'We're not on air yet! Stop the tape.'
The wrong return time was given and the Transmission
Controller at Leeds had not switched back to Newcastle. A
mild panic ensues as the videotape of the titles is re-wound
just in time. Mike chats with Bob (not on-air) as an item on
videotape is presented. It's 18:47:00 and there's 40 seconds to
go to the weather report. Bob and Mike come into vision and
the Autocue simply reads,
'Bob and Mike: Ad-lib.'
18:50:30 and the closing titles roll.
The Director leans forward to the talk-back microphone,
'Thank you everyone.'
Graeme escorts me downstairs to Studio 2 to meet Mike.
'May I use some of the stories you told me today Mike?' I ask.
'Use what you like, baby,' replies Mike and hurries off.

Tyne Tees Trivia

[W]hen the station was in its infancy, the title 'North-East
[T]elevision was proposed but George Black was concerned that
[th]e initials NET may be extrapolated by some people to
[N]ETTIE. (Geordie slang for toilet.) 'Tyne, Wear, And Tees
[T]V' was also proposed.....

[T]yne Tees first ever outside broadcast was from Bill Lyon-
[S]haw's home in Wylam. It was a training exercise for the
[st]aff, however, and the pictures weren't transmitted to the
[p]ublic.

[H]ead of Cameras Ian Westwater was nicknamed 'Zebedee'
[(f]rom the Magic Roundabout) because he would suddenly
[ap]pear 'out of the blue'. If Tyne Tees cameramen were planning
[a] booze-up, they would tell their wives they would be late as
[th]ey were working on the Epilogue that night.

[T]yne Tees' Wardrobe Mistress Irma May, used to be Ava
[G]ardner's dresser.

Michael Miles with 'Take Your Pick' at TTT

Coronation Street, Double Your Money, This is Your Life,
and Take Your Pick , were all produced at Tyne Tees studios
on a few occasions when the studios where the programmes
were normally produced, were occupied. The photograph
below shows Michael Miles presenting the 'Yes/no interlude'
in the quiz programme 'Take Your Pick' which was produced
in Tyne Tees studios in April 1962. 'Coronation Street' was
produced at Tyne Tees in 1963.

'The Three Rivers Fantasy' overture which was played before
each transmission was a medley of the following Tyneside
tunes: Blaydon Races, Bobby Shaftoe, The Keel Row, Oh!
The Bonny Fisher Lad, Billy Boy, Sair Fyeld Hinnie, The
Colliers' Rant and The Waters of Tyne. It was arranged by
Arthur Wilkinson.

George Black, one of the station's original Programme
Directors, had a habit of rattling the loose change in his pocket
which became a signal to staff members that one of the bosses
was approaching. Bill Lyon-Shaw had a habit of flicking
cigarette ash over his shoulder, but it usually landed on his
suit giving the impression he had 'terminal dandruff'.

A regular reader of the Epilogues on Tyne Tees was the Rev
Cassidy. He presented so many Epilogues that the camera
crew used to nickname him 'Epilogue Cassidy'.

Dickens Press, the publisher who produced 'The Viewer'
magazine, also published a 'sister' magazine called 'Look
Westward' which was the programme listings magazine for
Westward Television in Plymouth. It was edited by Gordon
Laing who also edited 'The Viewer'.

On the 'Happy Go Lucky' programme, the voice of the puppet
Theodore was supplied by Heather Ging who worked at Tyne
Tees for many years before forming her own television
company called Chariot Productions. Adrian Cairns' wife
Laura also supplied Theodore's voice on several occasions.

Other books by Geoff Phillips

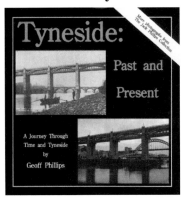

Tyneside: Past and Present

Over 100 photographs of Tyneside as it used to be alongside views of the present day. Intrigui facts and information about each photograph along with a descriptive journey around Tynesi which shows the reader the views in the order as they appear in the book.

Price: £6.95   ISBN 0 9522480 0 X

Tyneside Pubs: Past and Present

Tyneside Pubs: Past and Present is another book in the hugely successful Past and Present series. It presents the reader with a nostalgic pictorial pub-crawl through time and Tyneside. More photographs from the Jack Phillips Collection show pubs in Newcastle and its suburbs as they were in days gone by along with modern photographs showing how things have changed. A pub quiz is included to test the reader's knowledge of bygone boozers.

Price: £6.95   ISBN 0 9522480 2 6

Old Pubs of Newcastle

A collection of photographs of pubs from the past.
Why remember old pubs of Newcastle? For many Tynesiders the pub is their second hom a place to unwind, a place to hear a good story or joke, a venue for a dart's match, a foru for an impromptu discussion on any subject under the sun. The pub is part of the culture a town or suburb; a sociologist wanting to study a town's ethos might visit a pub for a instant picture of the townspeople's attitudes and way of life. Pubs also form part of t history of a city, its architectural heritage, its styles and fads.

Or maybe its just a place to enjoy a canny pint and a bit crack with your mates.

Price: £4.95   ISBN 0 9522480 4 2

Newcastle: Past and Present

Geoff Phillips has revised his best-selling book and arranged for a limited printing of this Special Edition. Some of the new views have changed since publication of the first edition and have therefore been photographed again for this edition. Some new past and present pairs of photographs have been added and the most interesting of the old views have been enlarged to reveal more detail. The text has been revised to include some interesting new facts.   112 pages, paperback. ISBN 0 9522480 1 8.

Price: £6.95   ISBN 0 9522480 1 8

Newcastle: Then and Now

Earlier books by Geoff Phillips have mainly featured photographs of Newcastle upon Tyne ar Tyneside as it was in the late 1800's and early 1900's. This book compares Newcastle upon Tyne today with a time that many people will remember; the 1950's and 1960's. As in earlier book there are nearly always links between the old and new photographs. Sometimes these links a very hard to find which adds to the enjoyment of the book.

Price: £6.95   ISBN 0 9522480 5 0

**Obtainable where you bought this book,
or by mail order from G P Electronic Services, 87 Willowtree Avenue, Durham City DH1 1DZ**